The Enigma of
Consciousness

The Enigma of Consciousness

A Philosophy of Profound Humanness and Religion

Gene W. Marshall

 iUniverse

The Enigma of Consciousness
A Philosophy of Profound Humanness and Religion

iUniverse books may be ordered through booksellers or by contacting:

iUniverse
1663 Liberty Drive
Bloomington, IN 47403
www.iuniverse.com
1-800-Authors (1-800-288-4677)

Because of the dynamic nature of the Internet, any web addresses or links contained in this book may have changed since publication and may no longer be valid. The views expressed in this work are solely those of the author and do not necessarily reflect the views of the publisher, and the publisher hereby disclaims any responsibility for them.

Old Testament quotations are from The New English Bible, first published in 1961, quoted from the second edition, copyright © 1970 by R .R. Donnelley & Sons.

New Testament quotations are from J.B. Phillips translation, first published in 1958, quoted from the, copyright © 1960 edition as published in America by The Macmillan Company in 1965.

ISBN: 978-1-4917-6969-0 (sc)
ISBN: 978-1-4917-6968-3 (e)

Library of Congress Control Number: 2015909083

Print information available on the last page.

iUniverse rev. date: 06/23/2015

Table of Contents

Acknowledgments vii

Introduction: The Meaning of Enigma ix

Part One: What Is Truth? 1

  1. Beyond Consilience 4

  2. The Scientific Approach to Truth 7

  3. Cause, Chance, and Choice 14

  4. The Contemplative Approach to Truth 21

  5. It, I, and We 29

  6. The "We" Approach to Truth 35

  7. Open and Closed Societies 40

Part Two: What *Is* Consciousness? 43

  8. Qualities of Consciousness 45

  9. A Sixth Force in the Structure of the Cosmos 53

  10. Consciousness and Evolution 56

  11. Five Layers of Consciousness 65

Part Three: Inescapable Wonder? 85

  12. The Thought, Feel, and Choice of Wonder 87

  13. Space/Time, the Eternal Now, and the Enigma of the "I Am" 97

  14. Describing Nine Aspects of the "I Am" 109

  15. Nine Habits of Escape from the "I Am" 126

  16. The Journey into Profound Humanness 137

Part Four: What Is Religion? 139

  17. The Death of Mythic Space and the Redefinition of Religion 141

  18. The Origin of Religion, A Speculative Story 151

  19. Religion as Practice 154

  20. Religion as Social Process 171

  21. The Vital Variety of Religious Practices 187

Part Five: Six Ways to Imagine the Unimaginable 191

22. Six Primal Metaphors for Religious Formation 193
23. The Primal Metaphor of Sub-Asia 196
24. The Primal Metaphor of Arabia 198
25. The Primal Metaphor of Europe 202
26. The Primal Metaphor of the Orient 207
27. The Primal Metaphor of Sub-Saharan Africa 213
28. The Primal Metaphor of Native America 217
29. Spirit Completeness Beyond all Metaphors 223

Part Six: The Ethics of Response-Ability 227

30. A Being Basis for Responsible Action 229
31. The Roots of Motivation 231
32. The Ethics of Radical Monotheism 238
33. Contextual Ethics and Responsible Action 247
34. The Universal League of Profound Humanness 255
35. The Battle with Dysfunctional Religion 258

A Short Reading List 263
About the Author 265

Acknowledgments

I am grateful to Joyce Marshall and Alan Richard for continuing help with this book. Also, members of the Symposium on Christian Resurgence and participants in the Storywarrior web site (http://www.storywarrior.net) have made many editorial and substantial contributions to this book. The authors whose insights have gone into this work are too numerous to mention, but prominent among them are: Adyashanti, A. H. Almaas, Wendell Berry, Rudolf Bultmann, Richard Feynman, Søren Kierkegaard, Susanne K. Langer, H. Richard Niebuhr, Joseph Mathews, Charlene Spretnak, Paul Tillich, and Ken Wilber.

GWM

Introduction
The Meaning of Enigma

E • nig • ma: [in-nig'-muh] *a puzzling or inexplicable occurrence or situation.*

We navigate a river of enigma in a land of mystery. That enigma is openness and freedom, noticing and intending, paying attention and taking initiative. That enigma is consciousness, a consciousness that is conscious of being conscious. We know we are conscious, yet we do not know what consciousness is. It is an enigma, a mystery, something to be curious about.

Curiosity is itself an aspect of consciousness. Curiosity is a desire to know what is not yet known. The human mind feeds on mystery. When we joke that "curiosity killed the cat" we may be overlooking the fact that curiosity also made the cat an unusually enduring species. And the human being is capable of a depth of curiosity that no cat can experience. The human being is curious about the origins of the cosmos, the true nature of life and of human life, the very process of thinking itself. Curiosity is an affirmation of enigma, and this affirmation of enigma is an affirmation of that overall "land of mystery" that is the actuality in which we dwell. Reality continually confronts the human mind with enigma.

This book is an exploration of several areas of enigma: truth, consciousness, wonder, religion, primal religious metaphors, and response-able action. The underlying focus of this book is this core enigma: "What is religion?" "What sort of consciousness within human nature makes religious practices a recurring aspect in human society?" "What makes for a healthy or healing religious practice and what makes for sick, depraved, illusory, destructive, or demonic religious practice?"

Such questions about religion presuppose a human means for exploring these questions. Indeed, what is truth? Or perhaps the better question is, "What are the 'valid' approaches to truth that are possible and appropriate for the human mind?" Is truth simply a matter of arbitrary opinion: is any viewpoint as valid as any other? Or does the quest for truth imply some sort of "other-than-me thereness" that challenges our lesser or partial truths and validates our more complete truths? And is our quest for truth such that we can arrive at a final resting place, or is our quest for truth an endless revolution in human understanding within a vast ocean of mystery that can never be fully mastered by the human mind? The enigma of truth will be our starting place in this book, a book that is primarily an exploration of the nature and validity of religion.

Part One

What
Is
Truth?

Table of Contents for
Part One: What Is Truth?

1. Beyond Consilience
2. The Scientific Approach to Truth
3. Cause, Chance, and Choice
4. The Contemplative Approach to Truth
5. It, I, and We
6. The "We" Approach to Truth
7. Open and Closed Societies

Introduction to Part One

My best friend in high school was a fan of President Harry Truman. He liked Truman because he talked bluntly and stuck with what he had to say no matter what others thought about it. Truman had a reputation for uttering hard sayings. During a 1948 presidential campaign speech a supporter yelled out "Give 'em hell, Harry!" Truman replied, "I don't give them hell. I just tell the truth about them and they think it's hell."[1]

I count this as a profound statement, applicable to the final Reality.[2] Contrary to a literal understanding of biblical stories, Reality is not wrathful or angry with us. Reality only "tells us the truth," and we think it is hell. A fuller truth than the one we hold is often a hell of an experience, because it challenges the lesser truth to which we are still clinging and using to organize some portion of our lives. Furthermore, there is the humiliating fact that we never know the full Truth. The Truth with a capital "T" is a mystery, an almighty unknown that is pushing against us, but is unknown by us and unknowable to us. This enigmatic nature of Truth is not just a religious idea: it is a secular fact. The Truth is this: the more we know about Reality, the more we know we don't know. The more we know, the more we know our limitations, including the limitations of our finite minds to comprehend the Truth. This is a hard saying that feels like hell to anyone who is clinging to what they currently think.

---

[1] Taken from Wikipedia. Even if Truman never said this, it seems to be the public memory that he did.

[2] Throughout this book I will be capitalizing "Reality" and "Truth" whenever these words are pointing the mysterious finality of Reality or Truth, rather than the realities and truths that are comprehensible to the human mind. Other words for "Reality" will also be capitalized.

Nevertheless, it is also true that there are approaches to Truth, and that in terms of these valid approaches to Truth, it is true that some statements about Realty are more true than other statements. Einsteinian physics is more true than Newtonian physics. And the philosophy of truth seeking that I am going to articulate is more true than what I used to believe, and it is more true than what many people still believe. So if you, my reader, hold to the notion that you already have the full Truth, or that Truth is such a distant topic that any statements you choose to hold are just as good as any other statements, prepare for a bumpy ride, yes "one hell of a trip" into the enigma of Truth.

Chapter 1
Beyond Consilience

Consilience: agreement between the approaches to a topic of different academic subjects, especially science and the humanities.

I came across the following quote as I was reading an article entitled "The Decider" by Tom Siegfried in the December 6, 2008 issue of Science News:

> "Perhaps" write neuroscientists Alireza Soltani and Xiao Jing Wang, "we are entering a new period of consilience between the science of the brain and the science of the mind."

The article is interesting in its news about the amount of new insight in brain research and how various parts of the brain relate to our inner mental experience. But the phrase "science of the mind" raises deep philosophical issues that are central to this book. Millions of smart people do not understand that there can be no such thing as a science of the mind. The word "mind" points to a subjective experience. Empirical science does not deal, and cannot deal with subjective experiences. There can be a science of the brain. There can be a science of human behavior, but the mind cannot be an object of scientific study. Why? Because the mind cannot be an object.

I will use the word "mind" to mean what we see with the inward "look" of consciousness concerning what we can notice to be the workings of our brain and nervous system viewed by the inward looking capacities of our consciousness. This inward looking is not science, so there cannot be a science of the mind. Scientists may look inwardly at their own mind's process of hypothesis creation, but the test for the truth of a scientific hypothesis is found only in outward experiences that a group of scientists can all observe. The inward look is not a group experience. It is a solitary experience: it is one consciousness looking at its own conscious processes.

This inward looking approach to truth can be intelligently done, and systematically related with an objective science of the brain and nervous system. And my inward looking can be compared with the inward looking of others and these conversations can result in a body of communal wisdom. Inward looking is an approach to truth. But the inward looking approach to truth needs to be clearly distinguished from empirical science. Let's call this approach to truth "contemplative inquiry." Contemplative inquiry is not empirical science. It is different from science, when we define science carefully. As I will explain in the following chapters, there can be no consilience between science and contemplation. Science and contemplation indicate two different approaches to truth. Both approaches to truth are approaching truth about the same overarching Reality; nevertheless, these two approaches to truth need to be distinguished from one another in order to maintain philosophical clarity about what we mean by "truth," and "Truth" as well as "consciousness," "wonder," "religion," "Reality," "realistic behavior," and more.

So what is scientific research and what is contemplative inquiry? And how are these two different approaches to truth related to one another? I will show that without clear answers to such questions, an adequate understanding of consciousness is not possible. And if an adequate understanding of consciousness is missing, then we are also without an adequate understanding of religion. In the following chapters I will explore all this in some detail.

Further, if we do not know what we mean by "consciousness," we do not know what we mean by "mind." And, if we do not know what we mean by "mind" we do not know what we mean by "scientific research" or "contemplative inquiry," for each of these approaches to truth is a function of the mind. Both of these two approaches to truth are actions that the mind is used by consciousness to perform. The mind is a tool of our consciousness. The mind never contains or reaches the fullness of truth, but it is a tool that can be used to approach the truth. And what is truth? This is an important question, a question that underlies many other key questions.

Consilience

I first met the word "consilience" reading a book by Edward O. Wilson entitled *Consilience: The Unity of Knowledge*.[3] I read this book because I highly respected Wilson's earlier book *The Diversity of Life*. But I found *Consilience* disquieting. I saw that Wilson was putting too much faith in the scientific approach to truth and manifesting too little awareness of the contemplative approach to truth. In his book he seeks a way of explaining in terms of the scientific approach to truth,

[3] Wilson, Edward O., *Consilience: The Unity of Knowledge* (Alfred A. Knopf, New York: 1998)

those experiences of truth commonly sought through the humanities, the arts, and religion. By "consilience" Wilson means a pulling together into one scheme of thinking this wide scope of human experience and thought.

Later, I read Wendell Berry's book *Life is a Miracle: An Essay Against Modern Superstition*.[4] The "superstition" Berry focused on was Edward O. Wilson's attempt at consilience. Berry encouraged me in my disquiet over Wilson's book. Berry satirized Wilson's effort to contain this broad scope of experiences within a single rational system. Berry maintains that Reality is a Mystery that is ultimately incomprehensible to any possible scientific overview. I join Berry in dismissing all hope for a Wilson-type consilience. And I am going to explore why this is so, why the scientific approach to truth is limited and why the contemplative approach to truth, which is also limited, is a necessary companion of the scientific approach. I will also explore how the contemplative approach to truth is limited, and why it cannot take the place of the scientific approach to truth. I am going to show that we need both approaches to truth, but that neither can provide a consilience that encompasses the other approach to truth.

Some will recognize this discussion as a new version of the old struggle between science and religion. And so it is. Many current forms of authoritarian religion have made conflict with science inevitable. And some forms of scientific philosophy have sidelined or dismissed religion entirely. I will explore how a full understanding of the scientific approach to truth and a full understanding of the contemplative approach to truth bring a fresh level of clarity to this old struggle. I will show that both science and religion are necessary parts of our life and how there need be no conflict between them. I will show that religion came into being to perform an essential function in human society, as essential as economics, politics, or education. There exists, of course, corrupt and obsolete religion, just as there is corrupt and obsolete economics, politics, and education. In Part Four of this six-part exploration, I will explore the proper function of religion and how that proper function can be illuminated by an exploration into the enigma of consciousness. These formidable tasks of clarification have long intrigued me. I hope they also intrigue you, and that you find the following efforts of clarification resonating with your own experience in these areas.

---

[4] Berry, Wendell E., *Life is a Miracle: An Essay Against Modern Superstition* (Counterpoint, Washington, DC: 2000)

Chapter 2
The Scientific Approach to Truth

The scientific approach to truth yields what we often call "objective knowledge." Here is a simple illustration of the scientific method. Let us say that a man has the hypothesis that he can fly by jumping off a building and flapping his arms. So he tests that hypothesis. If he crashes into the ground, that hypothesis is not true. If he soars through the air, it is true. That is how we arrive at objective knowledge. All scientific research is a sophisticated version of this way of approaching truth.

The Nobel-prize-winning physicist Richard Feynman is a philosopher of science that I deeply admire.[5] Here is my summary of his colorful description of the scientific approach to truth: (1) you guess a new "law" of nature; (2) you devise a test for that guess that can show to a community of observers in an outwardly observable fashion a "Yes" or a "No" to that guess; (3) if that test says "Yes," the law stands for now until some test says "No"; (4) if that test says "No," you guess again and continue this process. Furthermore, if there is no test that will test your guess, you are not doing science; you are doing speculation.

If we accept this definition of the scientific approach to truth, we find that scientific truth is both approximate and progressive. It is approximate, because scientific truth is never more than a human guess that works well for now. It is progressive, because once a "No" has been observed to a previous guess; there is no going back. For example, once the Einsteinian guesses were documented by the community of physicists, there was no going back to the Newtonian guesses as the normative postulates of physics. The science of physics went forward, guessing and testing new guesses on the foundations that the Einsteinian revolution had established.

As Feynman pointed out in his book *The Character of Physical Law*, the Einsteinian law of gravity was "discovered" in this way: Tests raised doubts about Newton's

---

[5] Feynman, Richard, *The Character of Physical Law* (first copyright 1965, 1994 Modern Library Edition)

formulation of the "law of gravity." Einstein guessed something else. Tests were conducted. Results were better. A new law of gravity became our tradition. Observations of the orbit of the planet Mercury provides an example of how such a new theory is tested. The Newtonian theory of gravity did not account for the seemingly odd nature of that orbit. But when Einsteinian theory spelled out how gravity is a change in the nature of space rather than a force operating at a distance, the orbit of the planet Mercury was accurately predicted. Even more dramatic, the Einsteinian prediction about the equivalence of mass and energy was made obvious to the entire public when that first nuclear bomb blew a small Pacific island to smithereens.

It may seem to some that something more obscure than these simple dynamics is happening when physicists set up a multi-mile diameter circle of machinery to accelerate protons to near the speed of light and them crash them into one another. But here is what they are doing: they are testing some guess about the elemental structure of the cosmos. It does not matter that these tiny subatomic particles are unimaginable to the human mind. For example, the electron is a picture in the human mind that no one has seen directly. Scientists have only seen signals on a screen and other observables. These observations tell us things about the elemental structure of the cosmos. Indeed, they tell us that this electron, this invisible "particle" also acts like a wave. Not only have we not seen the electron directly, *we must picture it in a manner that is contradictory to our common sense.*

Nevertheless, the scientific approach to truth is the same in the most complex arenas of scientific work: guess, test, and guess again. The fact that many of the elemental "objects" that physicists discuss can never be directly observed does not alter the essence of the scientific approach to truth. These "objects" are sense-validated bits of human imagination. Their test for truth may have to do with visible streaks on a screen or visible movements of a dial or some other sensory experience. The factuality of scientific truth has to do with sights, sounds, smells, tastes, and tactile feelings entering into a human psyche. Though the love of mental order pervades the scientific method, its tests for truth are not found in the mind, but in the human senses of outward experience. It is experience that tests theory. A scientific theory is in need of improvement or abandonment if it does not pass these sensory tests. Any departure from this elemental understanding results in a bogus theory of scientific truth.

The "objective" nature of scientific knowledge is objective because in this approach to truth, we attempt to set aside our subjectivity and simply observe the "things" around us as they impact us through our senses. Such conscious noticing of our environment includes the functioning of our minds. The "things" of science are mental abstractions; we use our minds to form recognizable pictures of chosen aspects of the flow of our ongoing outward perceptions. An infant does not see a breast or a woman: it only sees total multi-sensory experiences and reruns of those experiences not yet differentiated into breast and woman and so forth. The infant perceives and begins to order those perceptions in terms of genetically provided images that direct attention toward that nourishing nipple. But these genetically provided images are still human creations by the human organism. They are theories that need to be tested in sensory experience. Scientific research is not required for testing at this infant level of living. All that is required is the image-using intelligence that the infant has in common with all animal life. The infant will find that nipple without the aid of sophisticated science. But the pattern is similar.

Sophisticated science requires the use of our abstraction-inventing minds to create clarified mental entities that point to and stand for differentiated aspects of our surroundings. Categories such as "cat," "tree," "woman," "man," "child," are all creations of the human mind. Each of these words identifies rational forms that we associate with recognizable aspects of our ongoing flow of perceptions. Though we can meaningfully say that there are cats in our experience, the symbol "cats" is a rational form that we have created. Depending on how we have constructed this rational form, "cats" may or may not include "hyenas." Are hyenas dogs or cats or neither? We have to define our rational forms more carefully in order to answer that question. Our minds can discriminate the common features of cats and dogs and then see which of these apply to hyenas. It is clear that some of each apply, so perhaps we decide that hyenas are neither cats nor dogs, but something else. We can also notice that all three are what we call "mammals." Again, we have created the symbol or rational form "mammals." We have other symbols like "reptiles." We notice that there are creatures in the archeological record that might be dubbed transition animals between reptiles and mammals. We may not know which they are. We have to decide or create a new category. We accomplish this by further defining the rational forms with which we are giving order to our ongoing perceptions.

Science works with objective reality, but it also works with these rational forms that humans have created in order to point to the "reality" of our outward experience more usefully—that is, more related to what we already know or think we know. These rational forms have made an "it" out of that actuality of which they are rational forms. Science deals only with "its." In the scientific method of truth, subjectivity is assumed as the "I" who is observing these "its," but the reality of the "I" is not observed scientifically. The "I" is not an "it," and therefore the "I" cannot be observed in the sense that science "observes." The scientist is an "I" observing "its." But the scientist as scientist is focused on the "its" not the "I." This is true even though the scientist may spend considerable time in the subjective mind formulating theories to be tested. But the truth that the scientific approach is testing is not the truth of the subjective "I," but the truth of the environment of the "I", an environment that the "I" has mentally formulated into objective "its."

What I have just described is a severe limitation that characterizes the scientific approach to truth. Science can construct objective knowledge about any topic, but such objective knowledge is only a partial view of that topic. The entire truth cannot be apprehended through the scientific approach alone. In a later chapter I will look in detail at the contemplative approach to truth that does deal directly with the "I."

Let us examine further what we mean by a scientific fact. Science deals with facts, but a fact is a creation of the human mind that has a credible level of correspondence with the ongoing flow of perceptions as those perceptions are currently formed into thinkable "its." Facts are indeed tested with these objective perceptions, but even these objective perceptions are carefully defined and humanly crafted mini-experiments. A perception is not simply there. Perceptions are also intellectual creations pointing to what we who are the community of scientists agree is there. Sensory signals are indeed coming into our brains; but when we mentally perceive those signals, we have created that perception. We have ordered it into a mind item. Facts are assemblies of such perceptions. Our facts change as our perceptions change, and our perceptions can change as we observe more carefully or in some way view more clearly our incoming signals.

The definition of a "fact" is further illuminated by distinguishing *historical facts* from the *facts* used in *natural science*. An historical fact is assumed to happen only once. Did Booth shoot Lincoln? Such a fact is not repeatable. It did or did not happen. And if it did happen, it happened at a particular place and time only once. But the facts used in the natural sciences are repeatable. We can run experiments over and over to see if we get the same results. This awareness that there are two types of facts warns us that facts are created by the human mind to fit within frames of reference known by that mind. Though this is clearly true, this does not mean that the human mind is the sole creator of a fact. The factuality of a fact is based entirely upon the sensory inputs coming into the mind. Though the mind creates the forms of factuality, the scientific mind defines factuality as a validity determined by sensory inputs from an "objective" world.

Good science includes a willingness to look beyond the inherited current theories and factual definitions. Good science is open to other facts that do not fit into the current consensus of objective knowledge. Indeed, the facts that do not fit are the most interesting facts of all, for they challenge the scientist to create a better theory that includes those new facts as well as the facts already included in an older theory. This is the great gift of science: it does not allow factually ungrounded superstitions to reign in the common mind of society. Science can and often does challenge every commonly held tenet to the test of factual verification. This does not mean that scientists cannot turn some of their discoveries into new dogmas and even new superstitions. For example, the clockwork or mechanical view of the cosmos turned out to be a superstition, not a factual truth. The mechanical quality of nature is only one small part of what nature factually is.

Science is a progressive movement toward ever-greater knowledge of the objective surroundings. There is no final scientific knowledge. There is always the possibility that more will be learned that will transform current scientific conclusions. Scientific knowledge is always approximate and tentative, never ultimate or final. But this does not mean that scientific truth is arbitrary. Rather it is an ongoing dialogue with what is factual, and this dialogue has a progressive nature. Once an objective truth is clearly seen, we cannot un-see it. We can improve it, but we cannot undo the advance. For example, once Darwin's theory of evolution has gained traction through the work of many documenting scientists, we cannot reject evolutionary theory because we don't like its implications for some of our cherished convictions. In other fields of study this is even more obvious. When we fill our prescription for antibiotics at the doctor's advice, we are assuming a germ theory in biology that took the place of previous theories that we now easily dismiss even though there was some truth in them, but the whole truth applicable to our cure of an infection has been expanded. Scientific knowledge is continually expanding its comprehension, but that does not mean that we can take lightly the new vision it continually brings. There is no justification for the views of the antiscientific dogmatists who want to live in a world unformed by a Darwin or an Einstein or some other key scientist in the ongoing progression of scientific knowledge.

The truth that scientific knowledge is progressive is also the truth that it is approximate. No current theory is an end-of-the-road truth. Current theory is vulnerable to change though the assault of new facts. Yet, the past theories that have been so transformed were not wholly wrong. They too were approximate truth. These past theories may even hold fragments of truth better than the newer and more powerful theories that have replaced them. The best scientists know this and continue to mine past theories for clues for better theories to be tested for future knowledge.

Approximate and *progressive* can be seen as serious limitations on the veracity of scientific truth. Yet within those limits, the truth quality of the scientific approach to truth remains. The scientific method is not illusory or wrong because its results are constantly proven wrong. Empirical science is a life method that is built into the nature of being human. Science is a sophisticated version of one of the natural and normal aspects of human thinking. The roots of science preceded the human species and the human symbol-using form of intelligence. A dog is a sort of scientist in its trial and error learning. The dog can venture assumptions, try them, and if they fail, try something else, until some "theory" actually works for its intended purpose. Both dogs and humans simply do not live their lives without this trial and error process of learning. In order to live better, we need truth; and trial-and-error science is one of the ways we seek truth.

But when we choose to view science as the all-inclusive pathway to truth, then we are living in an illusion. I will examine in a subsequent chapter how the "I" approach to truth (which I will also call "contemplative inquiry") is another approach to truth, an approach that is distinctly different from the scientific approach to truth. Nevertheless, I will show how and why the contemplative approach to truth is equally valid as the scientific approach to truth, and equally necessary for living our lives.

In order to see that both scientific research and contemplative inquiry are equally valid approaches to truth, we have to give up the notion that Reality is rationally understandable by the human mind. The word "Reality" with a capital "R" will be used in this book to indicate that Reality is a mind-assaulting Mystery that becomes ever more mysterious the more we know about it. As many good scientists have asserted in one form or another, "The more we know about nature, the more we know we don't know." If we resonate with such a statement, we are recognizing the Mystery (the yet unknown and finally unknowable) that surrounds and penetrates all our knowing. If we dream of someday discovering a scientific theory that explains everything, then we do not accurately understand science or Reality. We have entered into an illusion, an illusion about the capabilities of the human mind and the unfathomable quality of Reality.

In summary, empirical science is an approach to truth that yields a body of knowledge. The current body of knowledge is vulnerable to change. To conduct the approach to truth called "empirical science," the scientist creates overviews or theories to be tested by facts that have been humanly formulated from the flow of sensory experience. It is the sensory experience (sights, sounds, tastes, smells, feels) that gives facts their factuality. The human mind does not contribute factuality, it relates sensory factuality to the rest of what the human mind already knows, or thinks it knows. The scientific approach to truth yields an objectivity about our surroundings that is true and yet approximate and progressive. The truth of science is approximate because it can be improved. It is progressive because once a new era of scientific research has been entered, you cannot go back to the previous era. Once we have a well-documented germ theory, we cannot go back to "demons" or "humors" as if bacteria and viruses are not real. Since Einstein's theory of gravity has now been documented by the physics community of scientists, we cannot go back to the Newtonian theory, even though the Newtonian theory can still be used in special cases. Yet in spite of this progressive nature of scientific knowledge, no final scientific knowledge is possible or expected by a totally lucid scientist or philosopher. Each new documented theory is still vulnerable to transformation as further sensory experience enters the scientific discussion. Part of the meaning of "objective" when applied to scientific knowledge refers to the communal nature of science. A factual formulation is viewed as objective if the community of scientists, who are versed in this topic, can independently test the formulation and come to the same conclusions. In the following chapters, I will dig deeper into the limitations of the scientific approach to truth, but these limitations do not mean that empirical science is not an approach to truth. Indeed, the process of empirical science defines part of what we mean by the word "truth."

Chapter 3
Cause, Chance, and Choice

Cause, chance, and choice are three ways of interpreting our experience of Reality. In our ordinary living all of us use all three modes of interpretation. All three modes of interpretation appear in playing a game of cards. We explain the hand we are dealt with the story of *chance*. We explain the various plays that we make with the story of *choice*. And we use the story of *cause* to explain the movement of our hand that pulls a card and places it on the table. Notice that I am simply describing what we do. I am not making an argument on the basis of some philosophical system. Nevertheless, these three modes of interpretation, once we notice them, do indicate deep insight into the philosophy of truth.

First of all, the word "truth" presupposes that there is something to be discovered that is beyond the current content of the mind. Indeed, the mind does not contain the truth somewhere in its internal recesses. The mind is simply a tool we can and do use for approaching the truth. Cause, chance, and choice are three mental games we use to approach the truth. We assume that cause, chance, and choice are qualities to be found in Reality. But we need to check that out. We need to notice if the correspondences between our mental pictures and Reality are true to our experience. Cause, chance, and choice are processes of the mind, and all processes of the mind are creations of our species or perhaps creations of the evolution of our species. At any rate, it is not obvious that any of these mental contents correspond with Reality. To discern whether a mental process corresponds with the operations of Reality, we have to look and see. So let us look first of all into the discipline of physics and its attempts to approach the truth, the truth we seek through the sensory inputs from our environment.

Cause

Newton's laws of motion use the story of cause. First of all, he used the story of local cause—one billiard ball bumping into another. In his theory of gravity, Newton also used the story of cause from a distance—the sun of great mass attracting the planets. Einstein also favored the story of cause, but he rejected cause from a distance. All cause is local in Einstein's special and general theories of relativity. In his view of gravity, the sun does not attract the planets; the sun's great mass alters the character of space around the sun. The motion of the planets is "caused" by their interaction with the space they are touching. Einstein sought to extend the story of *cause* to explain the phenomena of quantum mechanics, but he never succeeded. No one has ever succeeded. It appears that the story of *chance* has proved necessary for our human minds to account for the activities of a photon of energy or any sub-atomic-sized particle of matter.

We might say that Einstein sought a consilience within physics and sought it in terms of the mental imagery of causal relations. He rejected probability or chance as an ultimate explanation of the physical realm. As he once put it, "I cannot believe that God plays dice with the universe."

Chance

Other physicists have been more sanguine with the probability mode of thought, but we amateur and professional philosophers of science may still be amazed that these two conflicting modes of thinking still reign in the discipline of physics. What are we to make of this? If we simply notice and accept that both cause and chance are no more than models of thinking located in the human mind, we find some illumination of our puzzlement.

When we play a game of pool, we are using the model of cause to judge what will happen as balls strike one another, bounce off rails, and enter pockets. Reality in this limited sphere seems to agree totally with our causal thinking. We may use the probability story to explain the errors in our stroking of the cue ball, but we do not expect any uncaused options to happen among balls and rails. This is true in many, if not most, areas of our lives. We typically assume that every change has a cause that happened before that change happened. When we say, "Why did so and so happen?" we are assuming "causes" as the answer to that question. To speak of uncaused changes that are due to chance is a departure from our customary causal mode of thinking.

Probability thinking is also deterministic thinking: that is some probability number determines the outcome of the happenings we are talking about, but in this case the outcome is viewed as an array of options each of which is an uncaused occurrence. When we throw a dice we assume that each of its six sides is equally likely to turn upward. When we play a card game we assume that each of 52 cards is equally likely to be drawn. This notion of randomness is clearly in our minds, and we use the story of chance to predict outcomes. In the real world, one particular dice may not be perfectly cubical, and thus its faces may not be equally likely to turn upward. Similarly, the cards in a particular deck may not be equally slick or sticky. So the probability or likelihood that our mind assumes for the real world are in most instances approximate—that is, probable. When we figure poker hands, we assume that three of a kind is less likely than four of kind, and we can put a number to this probability or likelihood.

The probability mode of thinking has been developed into a complex mathematics we call "statistics." We answer many of our questions with estimates of probability. We drop our causality thinking and simply assume a randomness in reality that is loaded one direction or another, which "loading" we assume can be approximately measured with a probability number. Take the example of a poll taken on some political issue. The pollsters use a carefully selected sample of the population that has a high probability of matching the whole population with a predictable margin of error. But even this margin of error is probable. And even though the margin of error is highly probable, the specific truth about the whole population is not being predicted with an exactitude similar to balls and rails on a pool table. Chance is a different interpretive story than cause.

I am using simple illustrations to call our attention to the ordinary and well-known truth that both cause and chance are well-practiced modes of human thinking. Their correspondences with Reality are actual and useful to us, but we simply do not know whether Reality as a Whole is finally causal or finally random or neither or both. And the plot thickens still further with the introduction of a third interpretive story I am calling "choice."

Choice

Neither cause nor chance can explain the existence and the functioning of that enigmatic something we are calling "consciousness." The reality of consciousness presupposes a mode of explanation that we typically call "choice." ("Freedom" and "free will" are other terms we typically use to describe this aspect of our experience.) "Choice" is a mode of human explanation that we use to interpret those aspects of our lives that appear not to be handled with explanations of cause or chance. When we rise to go the bathroom, we say that we choose to do this. There are causal factors involved. Our bladder is stretched by the presence of an accumulation of fluid. The coffee we drank earlier is being processed by causal factors in our biology. Nevertheless, we choose to go to the bathroom. We could pee on the living room floor, but we choose the bathroom instead. We explain these alternatives of future outcome with the story of choice. Choice is one of our useful explanations of real world happenings.

So what is choice? Choice is an action of consciousness that is not determined by any cause. Choice is an uncaused happening. Also, choice not a random event—that is, a choice is not the result of some chance, measurable and predictable by some probability number. Rather, you or I, the conscious being, choose something based on a raw freedom that exists alongside of all the causes and probabilities. We choose with an infinite degree of arbitrariness. If this arbitrariness is not there, choice is not there. If there is any cause that totally explains an outcome, then choice was not operative. If so-call "choices" are caused, they are not choices. Choices are chosen. Also, choices are not outcomes that can be explained with the story of chance. No probability explains my choice to play my ace of hearts rather than my queen of hearts. I choose that. No probability explains my cat's jump upon the table. This cat chooses that. This cat might have chosen differently. And my cat has "learned" that the alternative choice is the one that is approved by me. We might use probability thinking to talk about the likelihood of the cat jumping on the table or the likelihood of my peeing on the living room floor, but we do not really believe that chance rather than choice is operating in these instances. We commonly expect cats and humans to make choices that are not based on any probability number. We intuit that conscious beings operate differently than photons, electrons, and other subatomic entities. These tiny foundational aspects of our physical being operate in a manner that is accurately predictable with probability numbers. We may not know what a particular subatomic particle is going to do, but its range of options is highly predictable. Statistically, though not causally, we know how these entities behave. We could know more, of course.

Biology, the study of living beings, uses (indeed needs to use) the explanations of cause, chance, and choice to cover the scope of our experience of these beings. We see causal relations in the mechanics and chemistry of the physical bodies of living beings. When we explain the survival of a specific species within its environment, we employ both cause and chance. When we explain the fertilization of an egg by a particular spermatozoa, we typically employ chance. When we explain mutations in the genes of a species, we typically employ chance. It might be that some mutations are caused. It might even be that some mutations are chosen. We don't know. But most biologists prefer to assume that mutations are chance happenings. Many biologists also assume that there are happenings in the behaviors of conscious beings, especially humans, that are chosen.

Choice is most obvious in our own human lives, but it is also quite obvious in the lives of the more complex multi-celled animals. Our cats and dogs clearly make choices. We demean their existence if we assume that all of their behaviors can be explained by cause or chance. Living beings are not machines—that is, not machines only. To some degree each living being is conscious. Living beings make choices that are not "caused." And they make choices that are not "random."

Some might say that humans make choices, but animals do not. But even simple microbes appear to make choices. When we watch amoebas under a microscope, we can notice that they take in signals from the environment concerning food or danger and make appropriate responses. Somewhere inside that amoeba's skin, a determination is made about the "meaning" of the incoming information, and a "response" is initiated by that organism. We can try to explain those observations with our mental story of cause, for there are causal relations among the chemicals and electrical signals as well as in accord with genetic patterns created in the past. But these amoebas are not rocks, and they do not operate like rocks. Nor are they dice or electrons with fixed sets of probabilities determining their actions. An amoeba can make mistakes, do unpredictable things, learn from experience, or so it seems to those of us who watch them carefully. To we human observers the amoeba appears to be alive in ways that are analogous to our own inwardly experienced aliveness. So for purposes of this discussion, let us simply assume that being alive includes choice as an aspect of being alive.

And let us notice within our own experience that choice is not the same as cause or chance. Choices are not caused; choices are uncaused selections by an enigmatic something that we will call "consciousness." And this choosing aspect within the fabric of the universe is not explainable with the story of chance or probability. A choice is not probable; rather a choice is a guess, a risk, a try that may or may not produce the expected result.

I am concluding that the capacity to choose is part of the basic meaning of the term "consciousness." A conscious being makes choices. A conscious being is attentive to its environment. A conscious being is sensitive and responsive. A conscious being is both gifted with attentionality and intentionality. A conscious being pays attention, and a conscious being takes initiative or intends responses. This does not mean that all human actions are chosen. Even though we humans have a highly developed form of consciousness, we do most of our actions unconsciously. For example, our childhood conditioning may, in many situations, "determine" our behavior rather than our paying attention and taking initiative through conscious choice. But we also have the potential to pay attention and take initiative, and we sometimes do. If we insist on reducing choice to cause or chance we are violating our own experience of being a conscious being. We are playing a mental game with our experience that does not fit our experience. If someone tells you that every happening to totally explained by its causes, that person is selling you a theory that is contradicted by your and my experience. If someone tells you that probability is the final and most basic of all explanations, that person is substituting the useful mental game of probability for our whole experience of Reality. Upon a close inspection of what is actually going on in the process of Reality, we can see validity in all three of these interpretations: chance, cause, and choice. The test of truth with regard to these interpretations is not found within our minds, but within our experience of Reality.

Most important for the content of this book is our view of consciousness. Consciousness is not all that is going on within a living being. There are causal processes within our organism and its behaviors. There are also chance processes. But in addition to cause and chance there is consciousness. And consciousness makes choices. Choice is part of the description we need to make about living beings in order to have an adequate understanding of them.

Nevertheless, we will encounter some scientific-minded philosophers who will insist that both chance and choice are merely ideas in the human mind, but not ultimate factors in Reality itself. Probabilities, they will say, are only a convenience of the mind for use with complex systems: the ultimate explanation of which is still causal. A dice turns up as it does through a complex series of tiny causes. These strict determinists also say, that we only seem to make choices, the ultimate explanation is causal. Those causes, they say, are deeply hidden from consciousness; our seeming choices are merely the result of our genetic make up, our social conditioning, our personal history, or something else. But let us each ask our own consciousness if these assertions are actually so. Is it actually so that cause is the ultimate explanation for the living operation of our lives? Indeed, is it not more likely that cause, like chance and choice, is merely one of three mental modes of explanation invented by the human mind? It is not more likely that Reality is so vast that all three modes of explanation (cause, chance, and choice) have their relevance? Why do we prefer that there be one mode of explanation that is the ultimate mode? Can we not simply conclude that we do not have (nor need to have) an ultimate explanation of the operation of Reality? Is it not more realistic to admit that cause, chance, and choice are all three modes of explanation in the human mind that assist us to relate to a Reality that is beyond all three explanations? It may be that our mind or ego prefers simple answers, and there is a value for simple explanations over excessive elaborations where the simple will do, but there is also such a thing as "oversimplification." We commonly indulge in oversimplification in order to escape from disagreeable portions of our real experience.

If we choose to simply give up our unsubstantiated "need" to possess an ultimate rational consistency for Reality, we can say all three of these things: (1) Our beings are caused. (2) Our beings are an accident. And (3) our beings are chosen. All three modes of explanation are valid. We need not insist that one of these modes of explanation must cover our entire experience of Reality. Indeed, when we insist on the ultimate consistency of causality, we are choosing this mode of explanation! And we are probably choosing it in order to believe that the human mind has a capacity for a full correspondence with reality that it does not actually have. So let us choose the more "obvious" truth that the human mind is a finite development and that Reality is only fragmentarily understandable by this amazing and yet puny human capability we call "mind." Our mind uses cause, chance, and choice because all three of these modes of explanation help us perceive and predict our sense of reality, our sense of past and future, our sense of present living, and the choices we might make today and tomorrow.

In the final analysis the human mind confronts Mystery (a Finally Unknowable Mystery). The human mind is only a tool of a consciousness that is also mysterious, unknown in its fullness, unknowable except in that direct sense of knowing we experience when we consciously contemplate our own consciousness. And though Reality and consciousness remain mysterious, we are still curious; we seek to know with our minds what can be known in order to live our lives more consciously and fully. Part of what we can know with certainty is that our minds are only a meager tool in the quest for truth. With the use of our minds, our consciousness seeks a more useful hold on Reality (Reality with a capital "R" means the all encompassing Thereness that is forever beyond our full comprehension).

Chapter 4
The Contemplative Approach to Truth

Scientific research entails an objectification of our perceptions into impersonal "facts" that are then ordered into ongoing knowledge. In addition to science, there is another approach to truth that focuses our consciousness on the processes of consciousness itself as experienced in our interior being. Ken Wilber calls this the "I" approach to truth and distinguishes it from the scientific approach which he calls the "It" approach.[6] In this reference "It" is a symbol for the outward, impersonal, and rational formulation of the scientist's objective facts.

Clear scientific thinking need not dismiss the "I" approach to truth. By being objective in its approach, science is intentionally *silent* about interior truth. This vow of silence about the subjectivity of the scientist reveals the presence of and the need for another approach to truth. Ken Wilber called this approach the "I" approach to truth. I like that, and I will also use the phrase "the contemplative approach to truth." The term "contemplative inquiry" is also useful.

The psychologist A. H. Almaas has given considerable clarity to the term "inquiry." "Contemplative inquiry" can be defined as consciousness viewing the dynamics of consciousness itself. If we define "mind" as what consciousness experiences of the brain's workings from the inside, then contemplative inquiry means consciousness using the symbol-using mind to point beyond those symbols to the process of consciousness itself.

The field of psychology illustrates the presence of both the scientific and contemplative approaches to truth. In a strictly scientific approach to the human psyche only human behavior and human reports of interior experience are studied. There is no way to objectively look "inside" at the consciousness of another human being. When we think we see another's consciousness, we are actually looking inside our own consciousness and making comparisons with what we observe about

---

[6] Ken Wilber; *Sex, Ecology, Spirituality* (Boston: Shambhala, 1995). I am not following Wilber's models exactly, but I credit him with inspiring me in constructing the models I will use.

another person's behaviors and that person's reports about their inner experience. Psychology is a field of study that straddles the scientific approach to truth and the contemplative approach to truth. The "It" aspects of psychology are glorified in the behavioral schools of psychology, and the "I" aspects of psychology are glorified in the depth psychology schools. But all schools of psychology use both approaches to truth. If they did not, they would have no way to study the human psyche.

When we read psychology, we find it meaningful to the extent that it illuminates our own interior experience. Art is another aspect of human culture that came into being to illuminate our interior experience. Unlike psychology, art does not need to even pretend to be scientific. Indeed, art needs to be liberated from objectified reason. Artists need to feel free to use wildly expressive forms of symbolism—myth, ritual, icon, dance, drama, story, song, poem, painting, sculpture, and architectural design. The truth of artistic expression is not the truth of science. It is part of an approach to truth I am calling "contemplative inquiry" or the "I" approach to truth.

Outer and Inner Time

In the contemplative approach to truth, the essence of time is experienced differently than the way we experience time in the scientific approach. In the scientific (or "It") approach to truth, time is pictured as a line representing past, present, and future. This line is divided up into years, hours, seconds, milliseconds, and other measurable "lengths" of time. Time is viewed as a dimension of reality in the same sense that there are three dimensions of space. The scientist can locate events as occurring at some space/time coordinate. The most mysterious aspect of time from the scientific point of view is the present. The past can be ordered into plausible stories. The future can be predicted in terms of more plausible or less plausible, likely or unlikely outcomes. But the present is viewed as a point on a line that divides past from future—an infinitesimal nothingness that is neither past nor future.

But in our contemplative approach to truth, we do not experience the present as nothing. Indeed, from the contemplative perspective, the present is the only time there is. The past is only a memory—a memory experienced in the present. And the future is only anticipation—an anticipation experienced in the present. In the contemplative approach to truth, the time is always Now. (I will capitalize Now in order to symbolize the felt lastingness of our conscious experience of time.) Our contemplative inquiry is inquiry into the Now of consciously being conscious of the contents of consciousness. This does not mean that there is no time. Rather, time is experienced as a flow, as a ceaseless changing of content. This flowing content is coming into being and going out of being in each moment of experience. This flow can include the relative continuation of some aspects of our experience while other aspects of our experience begin or end with relative abruptness. Consciousness is a flow. And our consciousness of consciousness is a flow. And this flow is taking place through an enduring stillness we call "Now."

Further, consciousness is not merely a passive attentiveness to the flow of the Now. Consciousness can interrupt or redirect this flow. Consciousness is a capacity for taking initiative, a capacity for intentionality, a capacity for choosing aspects of reality to focus upon. We choose memories of the past to interpret. We choose anticipations of the future to embrace or avoid. Consciousness includes making decisions in the present to move the flow of Reality in chosen directions through employing the powers of consciousness, intelligence, body movements, as well as our social accumulation of historical power that is currently allotted to the subject doing the contemplating. All this attention and intention takes place in the Now of consciousness. The future Now is being affected by conscious choices, and also that future is going to be a surprise beyond the control of consciousness.

When we are using the scientific approach to truth, we view time objectively as a line extending backward into the past and forward into the future. Strange as this may seem, we do not have to choose between our scientific knowledge of time and our personal experience of time. Both are valid in their own way. We confront a seeming contradiction between these two approaches to truth because the finite human mind is attempting to describe a truth that is beyond the mind's capacity. Neither of these two approaches is wrong; nor is either all-inclusive in the sense that it can dismiss the validity of the other approach. Perhaps this situation is similar to how contemporary physics views light as both waves and particles. We have these contradictory images of light because the actuality of light is more than what can be contained in either picture. Similarly, the actuality of time is more than what can be pictured by the human mind in one consistent picture.

Outer and Inner Space

Our three-dimensional picture of outer space works well for our navigation in the world, but here again we have a different awareness when we focus on the contents of contemplative inquiry. In contemplative inquiry we do not have a subject viewing an object that is external to the viewer. The "subject" doing the inquiry is also the "object" of the inquiry. Some philosopher might argue that the "subject" is seeing his or her consciousness as an "object" that existed in the past, but this view is inadequate, for memory and anticipation are parts of what is happening Now to the "I" of consciousness. This means that when we have opted for the process of contemplative inquiry the dualism of subject and object has been replaced. A subject ("I") is inquiring into the contents of an inner space known only to that "I." Further, that inner space is present only Now. There is no "objective experience" in the scientific sense. Inner space is a construction of the "I" in the here and now.

The scientist, using the scientific approach to truth, can realize the he or she is a subjective "I" that observes objective inputs that are not the subjective person doing the observing. But this scientific observer keeps a distance from the things observed. That is part of what it means to call science "the 'It' approach." Science does not study the conscious "I," even though the scientist is clearly a conscious "I" studying some specific realm of "Its." Science can correlate the reports and behaviors of conscious beings with the brain functions that can be studied in an objective laboratory. Scientific theories can be formulated to say which functioning entities of the human brain correspond with which reports from a sample of brain owners who are reporting their feelings of fear or joy or whatever. Note that such scientific work does not entail a direct experience of consciousness. Only the brain owners looking into their own inner experience have a direct experience of consciousness.

In the "I" approach to truth there is no inquiry into the brain as an outwardly experienced entity, and there is no "need" for correlating inward reports with brain functions. Rather, the "I" approach focuses on the solitary person's experience of his or her own consciousness. If the word "brain" is used in the contemplative context, it means inwardly noticing very subtle feelings in the head area. The word "mind" is the word most used for our inward experience of brain functioning.

In the "I" approach to truth we can notice the operation of something we call "mind" handling images and symbols. We can notice how mind correlates these elements of thought with sensory inputs that are directly impressed upon the inner being as contents of consciousness. "Sensory inputs" is a scientific metaphor. When we use the term "sensory inputs" as contents within the field of consciousness, we are pointing to an inner experience of specific sounds, sights, smells, tastes, and touches. These sensations are movements within the field of consciousness. Thoughts are also movements within the field of consciousness. Emotional feelings are likewise movements within this field of consciousness. Everything in inner space is part of a flow though the ever-present Now.

As we attempt to describe how different the "I" approach is from the "it" approach, a confusion also arises about the meaning of the word "objects." Neither scientific research nor contemplative inquiry observes objects. Scientists observe sensory inputs. Objects are mental creations that give meaning to these sensory inputs. No one has actually seen an electron or a proton or an atom. These are all inventions of the human mind to hold some very carefully gathered sensory inputs.

We could say the same for the object "cat." We have created "cat" to hold in our minds our experiences of a certain set of moving, jumping, meowing sensations. Similarly, when the contemplative approach is observing our interior subjectivity, we have only our conscious noticings. We are inventing with our minds whatever interior "objects" we say we notice. For example, states of feelings or patterns of thought are just a set of noticings to which we have given defining names. This is a surprising insight only because our mind is always at work to help us with our inputs and noticings. We have to slow our mind down to a very slow walk to notice how much of what we assume to exist has been created by our busy minds. Obviously, we intend for our mental creations to have helpful correspondence with what we actually experience, but we can notice that we create this correspondence and recreate it again and again. Unless we pay attention to this dynamic, we will drift into some humanly invented unreality from which perspective we then flee from or fight with what is Real.

The Limitations of the Contemplative Approach to Truth

An experienced contemplative inquirer, Rupert Spira, inadvertently helped me see more clearly the limitations of the contemplative approach to Truth. Focusing on our experience (by which he meant "inner experience") Spira noted how we cannot discern where a line is located within the experience of conscious knowing between what is known and its knower. Conscious knowing includes consciousness, mind, body, and the beyond body inputs as one functioning whole within our inner "space." Where does the knower leave off and the known entity begin? Spira concludes that our experience reveals something strange to our widely accepted idea that there is a subjective knower and an objective something that is known. Our experience reveals, according to Spiria, that there is no such separation. That is, there is no separate self that knows and there is no separate object that is known. The knowing and the known are all one process of reality. Spira applies this to the whole of Reality. Our conscious knowing of the Mystery of it all does not imply a separate self that is knowing the Final Reality. Therefore, who we Are and what Reality Is is one unity. Self and Reality are one cloth. "Separate self" is just an idea in our minds that we have devised, but which idea has no real reference in our experience.

I can see that Spira is consistent in his reflections, provided that we restrain ourselves to our inner experience—that is, to what I have called the contemplative approach to truth. My critique of his conclusions boils down to this question: Why restrain our approaches to truth to the contemplative approach? There is in human history another well-developed approach to truth that concludes that even a cat has a separate self, that a worm has a separate self, and that a human certainly has a separate self. Do we actually need to or want to dismiss this approach to truth? However weird it may seem to have two contradictory approaches to truth, let us look at how we, as scientists, do find it useful to begin with the basic understanding that I as a human being am a subjectivity that can be objective about inputs to my organism. This approach to truth is also limited as we have seen, but let us be open to the notion that it is no more limited than the contemplative approach to truth. Seeing myself as a distinguishable organism with an interior subjectivity that is viewing other distinguishable realities reflects an experience of some sort. Also, reflective of some sort of experience is intuiting a Final Mysterious Reality that encounters my organism as a Wholly Other that audits all my subjectively arrived at fragile conclusions. In other words, this separate-self model of thought contains some sort of connection with Reality that the contemplative approach to truth omits.

I think one reason some contemplatives prefer excluding the scientific approach to truth (or at least limiting it to a somewhat useful mind-game) is that the separate self-imagery implies the finitude of our consciousness. That is, it implies that our consciousness dies dead along with our body and its mental functioning. Even to the honest scientist, it may seem true that consciousness is a mysterious force in the cosmos (something that we do not understand), but that need not mean that human consciousness is, in any way, immortal, or in some way "One essence" with the Final Reality.

I find it plausible to conclude from my experiences that consciousness is finite—that when consciousness confronts Final Reality, the encounter is like hitting a stone wall or a total blackness that the light of consciousness cannot penetrate. Furthermore, I can imagine that the very existence of my consciousness is dependent upon that Final Reality for each moment of its existence. It is not an immortal soul or a monad due for further incarnations, but is more likely a dependent something that will require a resurrection of the body, mind, and consciousness if it is to enjoy a post-death existence. Yes, it seem most likely to me that immortality, reincarnation, and resurrection are all three myths of the mind that each witness in their own way to the truth that the human does have a conscious relation with the Eternal, that consciousness is indeed a stretch between experience of the Eternal and experience of the temporal. And that such a consciousness is a like a "third term" neither exclusively Eternal nor exclusively temporal but a mysterious something that is conscious of its itself as conscious of both the Eternal and the temporal. More on this paradox later.

Living with Contradictory Approaches to Truth

While the scientific and contemplative approaches to truth are quite different and contradictory in many ways, yet each of them includes a view of the other approach. When we opt for the "I" approach, we view the scientific approach to truth as one of the useful processes conducted by the interior mind. Within the contemplative approach we see that the scientific line of past and future, divided by an infinitesimal point called the "present," is merely a concept in the mind. This line of time can be viewed as a useful concept for organizing memory and anticipation, but this organization of memory and anticipation takes place in the living Now. The "It" approach to truth is seen as a sophisticated mental tool for evaluating memories, assessing anticipations, and making decisions. From the contemplative view, the whole of science is seen as an activity in the Now conducted by consciousness using the facilities of the mind.

When we use the "It" approach to truth to view the "I" approach to truth, we see contemplative inquiry as a means of providing reports that can be objectively evaluated. These reports can be viewed as "Its" for scientific theorizing. For the scientist, these reports about states of consciousness are "Its"—objectively conceived states that exist in living animals. A clear scientific philosophy will assert that science cannot say anything about consciousness directly, for science has no direct access to consciousness. Science can only observe the behaviors and reports of conscious beings. Within such an understanding, good science is respectfully silent about consciousness and waits for consciousness to make its reports. Some scientists and philosophers of science have presumed to tell us how consciousness emerges from the material body or how consciousness is able to initiate the actions of the physical body. But such topics are beyond the competence of science, for consciousness is an "I" not an "It," and only "Its" exist in the realm of research for which science is competent.

If a scientist attempts to minimize or dismiss altogether the contemplative approach to truth (as some philosophers of science tend to do), the actual scientific person faces an enigma. As a human person the scientist is a subjective being, but in the *dedication* to be objective, the scientist must be *silent* about his or her own subjectivity. This intentional silence is a witness to the existence of subjectivity and to the need for an approach to truth that deals with it. This "other-than-scientific" approach to truth is what I am pointing to with the term "contemplative inquiry."

On the other hand, if a dedicated contemplative inquirer attempts to minimize or dismiss altogether the scientific approach to truth (as some mystical philosophers tend to do), this contemplating person faces this enigma: his or her memory and anticipation would be without content if the objective (scientific) approach to truth were not also operative. The contemplative inquirer commonly accepts patterns of objectivity about past memories and about future anticipations. For example, notions about a Big Bang beginning or about galaxies, stars, planets, species of life, evolution, or human history could not have entered consciousness without the operation of the scientific approach to truth. I am using the phrase "scientific approach" very broadly. Humanity has always been "scientific" in the elemental sense of ordering sensory inputs. Contemporary science is a sophisticated version of a truth-seeking process that is essential to human mental functioning. Other species also do trial-and-error learning with what I will call "images" rather than words and mathematical symbols.

Humans also use their image-using mind in trial-and-error learning. Let us use the illustration of attempting to bat a baseball. Our image-using mind turns the sensory inputs of the approaching ball into a sequence of memories—into an imagined path that is curving or not curving and is heading toward some anticipated location as it passes me, the batter. This elemental experience of the mind's working is a primitive aspect of the human mind's evolution, an aspect of mind functioning that we share with the dog catching a Frisbee. The conceptual complexity of contemporary scientific research is a sophisticated enhancement of the experience of that dog, or of that batter watching a ball approach the batter's box. Using symbols, science is a sophisticated operation of this more primitive mental process present in both dogs and humans. From a memory of sensory inputs, science fashions theories about the behavior of reality and thereby anticipates the future in meaningful ways.

There is no escape from the scientific approach to truth. The most accomplished and dedicated mystic of contemplative excellence is still participating in the scientific approach to truth. Each human being is both scientist and contemplator. These two approaches to truth are unavoidable—even though many humans persist in a foolish attempt to make one of them their whole quest for truth.

Chapter 5
It, I, and We

The distinction between the "It" and the "I" approaches to truth has been thoroughly explored for many decades,[7] but the concept of "We" needs much more attention. The reality of "We" is something more than can be explored with contemplative inquiry. And the reality of "We" is something more than a complicated object that is understandable through scientific examination. A "We" is at least two "I"s, which makes it more than an object. And because "We" is at least two, it is more than an "I" inquiring into that person's own inner "I."

Intimacy

Let us start by examining an intimate relationship between two persons, two conscious "I"s. Neither of those "I"s can see into the inner being of the other. Each needs the reports from the other and the behaviors of the other to intuit what is taking place within the inner life of the other. The guesses or "intuitions" about the life of the other are based on the inner knowing of one's own inner being. Sensing the inner life of another is based on the resonance that I experience through knowing my own self. Of course, we can be mistaken about another person. Such mistakes are usually rooted in blocks we have to paying close attention to the other person or in mistakes about our own person that we are projecting upon the other. Mistakes can also be based on the primal fact that we never understand any aspect of Reality fully. Nevertheless, we do often intuit (or guess) quite well elements of truth about the lives of others. Sometimes we are closer to knowing the truth about

---

[7] I am thinking of the work of Martin Buber in *I and Thou* as well as the work of Lewis Mumford in *The Myth of the Machine*. These older writers have been followed by a raft of contemporary psychologists, religious teachers, and philosophers of consciousness. Among those I most treasure for exploring this difference between the "It" and "I" approaches to truth are A. H. Almaas and Ken Wilber.

these persons than these persons are of knowing their own being. This limited, but real, knowing of one another is the foundation of intimacy.

Much more could be said about the nature of intimacy, but my concern in this chapter is simply to call attention to the fact that an interpersonal relationship between two persons cannot be understood through contemplative inquiry alone. The wisdom derived from contemplative inquiry helps, but is not sufficient. Wisdom about interpersonal relations comes from experiences with interpersonal relationships. And this learning is something different from contemplative inquiry. We are observing our own responses to the other, and we are observing the other's responses to us. There is a scientific element in such observing, but interpersonal learning is also something different from scientific learning. Interpersonal learning requires interior sensibility as well as outward observation. As we reflect deeply on the nature of intimacy we learn that we have a "We" approach to truth going on that needs to be distinguished from both the "It" approach and "I" approach.

Martin Buber helped us with this topic in his discussion of "I-Thou" relations. The "I-it" relation that we have with a hammer is different than the I-Thou relationship we have with another human being. In the latter we are aware or can be aware that there is another "I" looking back. Even though we do not experience the other "I" directly, we are somehow aware that the human other is not a hammer or any other inanimate object. In the I-Thou relationship there is a conscious being who has a perspective on my conscious being. Unlike a hammer another person possesses a sense of reality that agrees and/or disagrees with my sense of reality. This constitutes a boundary to my being that a hammer does not provide. And there is a potential inspiration and benefit provided to me that a hammer cannot provide. The interpersonal relation can assist me to know my own being better. A hammer cannot do that. I do not seek out a hammer for counseling.

We know that it is a reduction of what is real to treat our "I-Thou" relations as if they were 'I-It' relations. Very few other persons tolerate being treated as a mere thing in some other person's perception of the world. Also, we experience something uncanny about looking into another person's eyes for a sustained period. We realize somehow that there is another "I" looking back. In such an experience, we can experience a disquieting contradiction to any belief we may harbor that we are the only consciousness in the cosmos.

While we can understand Sartre's remark that "hell" is other people. We also know that when we surrender any need we may have for being the one and only person, other persons are clearly a huge blessing to us. We would not exist with out them. We would not talk and think without them. Even when another person challenges my illusions, such pain is, nevertheless, a blessing in terms of enabling my more truthful living. We have also experienced partnerships in which two perspectives on Reality were experienced as better than one. Like seeing with two eyes, two people can often see more clearly than one.

Also, encountering another "I" can inspire me to contemplate further the enigma of being the "I" that I am. While I must view my own "I" with my own solitary eyes of consciousness, the behaviors and reports of another "I" can call my own inner reality to my attention and can correct some of my misunderstandings about myself and others. Indeed, intimacy with others is not something established by me. When I awoke to being an "I," other "I"s were already there offering intimacy to me.

Intimacy is an enormous topic that it would require a whole library of books to fully describe. My purpose here is call attention to how exploring the nature of intimacy between two "I"s requires something more than exploring the "I" we explore in the contemplative approach to truth. It is also something more than what we explore in the "It" approach of scientific research. Furthermore, this approach to "We" realities is not simply a combination of the "I" and "It" approaches. We are viewing a third approach to the wholeness of Reality: the "We" approach to truth.

Commonality

In addition to intimacy, commonality is another aspect of the "We" approach to truth. Every relationship between two people or among many people includes something we can call "commonality." The language we use to speak to one another is an example of commonality. We also have common modes of association, common customs and moralities, common styles of living, common methods of doing things, common educational systems, common inherited wisdom, and let us not omit common religious symbols and practices. We also have common political and economic systems within which we live. We may be critical of much of this commonality, but we would not be human without some sort of commonality. It is seldom true that anyone would want to discard all inherited commonality. Most of the time we simply want to repair part of the commonality in which we live. Even a radical movement for social change will use much of the inherited commonality to make their desired changes. In a word, we conduct all our intimate relationships and all of our participation in social change within some aggregate of common social designs.

The "We" approach to truth includes attention to cultural, political, and economic commonality, and to actively support or change all those social processes. Such attention is aided by both scientific research and contemplative inquiry, but neither of these approaches to truth is enough to fully understand the experience of social commonality. For this we need the "We" approach to truth.

The Consensus Process

So how does commonality arise and change? Commonalty comes into being through the consensus of a group of human beings. We are born into, but also choose to function within a given social commonality. Many artists, inventors, organizers, teachers, writers, activists, leaders contribute to the advent and development of this commonality. Intentionally or willy-nilly, each group of people chooses to operate within inventions of commonality. It may be that our particular commonality was chosen by a small, powerful group that more or less forced it upon the rest of us. Perhaps persuasion was used rather than violence or the threat of violence. Perhaps we were just born into this commonality and were compassionately indoctrinated into it by parents who were mostly concerned to prepare us for living in the real social world that we have on our hands. No matter how our participation in a given social commonality came about, we joined it—to some extent willingly. We may also be rebellious or critical of elements of this commonalty. We may be dedicated to improving it or changing it or perhaps leaving it and finding another, better commonality. However that may be, what we need to understand is that every commonality came into being and comes into being through the establishment on an operating consensus among those participating in it.

So what is consensus? Properly understood, consensus does not mean everyone in a group totally agreeing. Nor is consensus some ideal like-mindedness that never entirely exists among any set of unique human beings. Consensus simply indicates a willingness of a group of humans to go along with some common mode of living together. Disagreements can still exist about what this means, or how important this is, or when and how it needs to be changed.

Consensus can also mean the willingness of a group of humans to join together in a movement for changing the common mode of living with which they started. Humans who devote themselves to a project of economic, political, or cultural change must consense upon some sort of vision, strategy, and group commonality in order to carry out their change project. Perhaps it is a troupe of actors putting on a play. Perhaps it is a group of protesters shutting down a coal-fired power plant. Perhaps it is a group of disciples following a particular teacher. Perhaps it is a group of devotees practicing together some religious ritual or discipline. In whatever human beings willingly do together, the dynamic of consensus is operating.

Again, it must be clarified that a group can embrace consensus in spite of having serious disagreements. Those disagreements are simply part of the consensus within which that group consents to continue functioning. As an extreme example, the peasants of a dictatorship may have serious disagreements with the policies of their king but, nevertheless, consense to be part of this kingdom rather than some other kingdom or trying to build a society on their own. Two political parties may disagree vigorously about many things, but nevertheless consense to operate within the same political system. Among practitioners of a religious organization there may be disagreements that are simply part of the ongoing consensus to be members of that religious organization. Even the smallest groups of consensus builders have disagreements. Sometimes people do what the Quakers called "stand aside" from supporting certain directions of consensus taken by the group. Standing aside means that one disagrees with the direction chosen, but nevertheless consents to remain part of the group and thus allow the undesired direction. If a group values the active participation of everyone, they will take dissenting persons seriously and make every effort to include their dissenting insights as much as possible. If a person truly believes that the entire worth of the group will be harmed or destroyed if a proposed consensus is taken, that person may insist on "blocking" that proposed consensus rather than standing aside. Such a choice forces the group to reconsider their proposal or go ahead with it even if that means splitting the group into opposing factions. At this point honest consensus building weighs up the value of staying together in tension with the value of the given directions being discussed.

I will not discuss the details of good methods for facilitating consensus-building discussions. I am only trying to define "consensus" in a general way in order to point to something universal within the conduct of building, being, and rebuilding social commonality.

When consensus does not exist to any degree whatsoever, a group typically breaks up into two or more opposing groups. That may be two or more religions, two or more political parties, two or more nations, even two or more warring factions. Where there are two or more classes within one society, the most powerful class may be enslaving the other classes (or races or cultures or genders). Even where serious oppression exists, a weak consensus may exist across those harsh boundaries, but such a society is vulnerable to revolution or fragmentation. In order for conflicts among opposing factions of a group to be overcome, a fresh statement of practical truth can often be found that will be more workable for all. The strength of a society ultimately depends upon the fullness of the consensus with which it is operating. The search for such a practical, workable truth by which to socially exist is the process I am calling "the 'We' approach to truth" with regard to social commonality.

Voting and the principle of majority rule provide only a rough approximation to finding consensus. Democracies that count on majority rule often realize that the majority's options need to be limited by a constitution-based legal system that protects the human rights of minorities from the majority. A thoroughgoing consensus process of decision making provides the minorities with more influence, and it more adequately honors the fact that fresh truth for human wellbeing is almost always a minority discovery.

Workability Verification

The "We" approach to truth is verified in part by the factual empiricism of scientific research. It is also verified in part by contemplative wisdom from the "I" approach to truth. Yet additional verification is needed to complete the "We" approach to truth. "Workability" is a word for that something more. We are employing the "We" approach to truth whenever we are asking this core question: "What actually works as a truth for directing this social group at this time in history in directions that this group choses to go to meet its challenges?" Such truth is not a rigid ideology or a directive from some supposedly divine source. It is the result of hard work by intensely thoughtful persons who are respecting one another and struggling with one another for a truth to live by that deals with an appropriate social response to existing natural and social challenges. The employment of some sort of consensus process to find a workable truth for a common social life together is a truth quest that is intrinsic to the social life of humanity. It is a third approach to truth. Both the reality of intimacy and the reality of commonality in human life make possible and necessary this "We" approach to truth.

Chapter 6
The "We" Approach to Truth

In this chapter I will examine further what constitutes truth in the "We" approach to truth. "Truth" can mean: (1) the Unknown Unknown that humans face, and (2) a knowledge that humans possess in their minds. The phrase "The 'We' approach to truth" implies both meanings. A capitalized "Truth" can indicate the still Unknown Objectivity, distinguishing this meaning of "Truth" from the "truth" of a specific group consensus. As spelled out in the last chapter, a group "consensus" is not some sort of absolute certainty. It does not even mean an articulation with which everyone in the group agrees. Consensus means an articulation with which a group is willing to operate for the time being. A consensus can be said to be "true" to the extent that it "works" as a pattern of operation that carries out the values of the group in response to the Truth being encountered in history,

Let us examine more closely the test for truth that I am calling "workability." Some social designs just do not work in relation to promoting the sanity, survivability, and other values and purposes of the members of the consensing group. Other social designs are without the minimum beauty for nurturing the human spirit. Still other social designs are without the minimum justice for holding the group together as a cooperating body. We have social designs that destroy the environment on which human groups depend. Clearly, there are social designs just do not work for a complex of reasons. In social affairs the pragmatic value of workability is important: it is the very essence of the social or "We" approach to truth. As the above illustrations imply, there is a degree of arbitrariness in our workability tests for truth. Any given society has numerous roads to workability. Nevertheless, this is the aim of a reality-affirming consensus process: to design guidelines for operation that are workable for this group's members and for the impact of this group upon the whole human species and upon the planet on which all groups and societies must live.

I have already noted the communal aspect of scientific research and the communal aspect of contemplative inquiry. The "We" approach to truth is something more than the communal components of these other two approaches to truth. It has to do with pulling together into an overarching social consensus the scientific findings and the contemplative discoveries currently operating within that particular society. All systematic philosophers—Plato, Aristotle, Plotinus, Augustine, Aquinas, Kant, Hegel, Kierkegaard, many others, including you and me—do this kind of pulling together in dialogue with others. Such systematic thinking is a "We" approach to truth. This book is a "We" approach to truth in the sense that I, in dialogue with others, am seeking to make a contribution to the overall social consensus about what is workable for human life on Earth at this time.

The "We" approach to truth is also present in the mundane aspects of our lives. Here is a simple illustration. Let us say that we have learned by empirical testing that throwing a wingless body off a high place results is a rapid descent to the ground below—that is scientific knowledge. Science cannot determine whether or not I love my cat—that requires contemplative inquiry. I have to look inside my own life and see what I mean by "my cat" and by "love" and then discern whether I really do love this particular cat. Perhaps I only tolerate this cat. Something is true, but this truth is not attainable through the path of scientific knowledge. Let us suppose that I discover that I do love my cat. Then, the "We" approach to truth might be illustrated as a pull together of these two bits of awareness. A useful overview of truth would be: "If I love my cat, I would not be wise to throw him out of a tenth-story window."

Human culture is made out of millions of such bits of pull-together of what we have found to be scientifically true, contemplatively true, and workable. Human culture is a We-construction. No one person creates it. We create culture through our capacities to share with each other our awareness about what is so and what patterns of wisdom and association enable us to live together in the most lively fashion.

This process of culture creation is very old. It reaches back hundreds of thousands of years. It probably preceded the evolution of our species. It is probably true that our enlarged brain evolved in order to do the ever more complex culture building that our sequence of species in the hominid line were doing. Surely many of those primitive experiments in culture building failed: perhaps their design did not maintain sanity, inspire motivation, deal with economic realities, handle crisis, or whatever. Some societies were simply unlucky. But only those societies that maintained *workable* sanity and survival skills were able to pass on to following generations their communal wisdom. This process continues today. The inherited traditions of past cultures are valuable to the extent that they have indeed maintained sanity, survivability, and other critical values. I am not implying here that survival implies that a society is good. Perhaps a surviving society is exceedingly mean in its patterns of injustice. Social workability includes surviving, but it also includes remaining sane enough to operate humanely, and patterns of justice that are workable enough to hold a body of human beings together.

Fresh challenges to sanity, survivability and other workability values arise with each change in social circumstances. Fresh scientific knowledge enters the discussion. Fresh contemplative wisdom enters the discussion. Fresh pull-togethers are assembled, taught, and used with the hope of fostering further sanity, continued survival, and quality living. This is the "We" approach to truth—the consensus-building approach to pulling together ever-fresh articulations of truth that promise to be socially workable.

Works of art, philosophy, sociology, history, etc. pull together our fragments of truth. Each of these disciplines of thought can illustrate the "We" approach to truth. Socrates was a breakthrough thinker, a contemplative innovator. Plato and Aristotle were his systematizers, writing for the "We" of their culture and the future of their culture. Archimedes, Copernicus, Galileo, Newton, Darwin, Einstein were breakthrough innovators in scientific research. They were followed by their cultural systematizers. The Buddha was a contemplative innovator followed by his systematizers. Jesus was a contemplative innovator. Paul and the Gospel writers were the initial systematizers of this breakthrough in contemplative awareness. Augustine was the grand champion of a long series of systematizers of Greek and Biblical heritage. Whatever obsolescences, omissions, and flaws we find today in Augustine's overview, we can still honor him for the power of his work, a work that laid cultural foundations that lasted eight hundred years before meeting major overhaul.

Thomas Aquinas was another systematizer, discerning the gaps in the then-existing overviews and constructing a new overview that both incorporated the more objective, scientific, Aristotelian heritage being recovered at that time and preserving the juice he found in his inherited Christendom. Recent science and contemplative thought have moved us well beyond the Thomistic synthesis. For example, Thomas' physics has been revolutionized by Newton and then again by Einstein and others. Biology and psychology have also undergone far-reaching transformations. Contemplative thought today is taking place in a whole array of new ways. We cannot go back to the Thomistic synthesis; nevertheless, we can honor Thomas as a hero of his era and take inspiration from him for facing our challenges to serve the sanity, survivability, and other crucial values that enter the consensus building of our existing and future human cultures. Indeed, we face enormous challenges to pull together the many partial truths of our era into workable guidelines for sanity, survival, beauty, equity, democracy, and other values of general well-being for this generation and its deeply altered planet. This is the "We" approach to truth. This is the consensus-building approach to the truth of workability.

While the "We" approach is dependent upon the breakthroughs of scientific research ("It" approach) and contemplative inquiry ("I" approach), it is a third approach to truth ("We" approach). It adds something to the human truth quest not handled by the other two. Perhaps the following chart can help hold this awareness in our minds:

Approach to Truth		Focus	Test for Truth
It	Scientific Research	impersonal objectivity	correspondence with factual formula-tions of sensory inputs
I	Contemplative Inquiry	personal subjectivity	resonance with descriptions of directly known experiences of consciousness
We	Societal Consensus	cultural integration	workability for the sanity, survival, & other values within a specific culture

A workable consensus will include: (1) the truth of scientific research and (2) the truth of contemplative inquiry. Workability is not a substitute for factuality or contemplative wisdom; workability is an additional test for truth (realism). If a societal consensus is not factual, neither is it workable. The factual truth will at some point reveal that the consensus is unworkable. A similar statement can be made with regard to contemplative wisdom. A societal consensus will at some point prove unworkable if the truth about human consciousness is ignored. But a societal consensus can be honoring of both factuality and contemplative wisdom and still be unworkable. The truth of workability is a test for truth that applies to a specific pull together for a specific group of the first two modes of truth as they apply to this group's circumstances in historical time. This amounts to an third test for truth—that is, does this pull together of insight and guidelines apply to these circumstances for this group at this time? Any social consensus that does not honor all three approaches to truth is less wise than one that does.

Having three approaches to truth rather than one may evoke distress in some persons—persons who wish to achieve the type of rational consilience described in Chapter 1. But such hope in the rational potential of the human mind is illusory, a "modern superstition" as Wendell Berry calls it. Why is it illusory? The human mind is a finite biological process confronting the Infinite scope of Reality. I am continuing to use capitalization to symbolize this disjunction between the Fullness of Reality and the processes and possessions of finite knowledge of which the human mind is capable.

We need to hold on to the awareness that the human mind is capable of assembling relative truth for effective living. The amazing capabilities of the human mind evolved because these abilities aided the human species to survive and thrive. Human consciousness is in need of realism in order to orchestrate survival and well-being. Nevertheless, the truth available to the minds of human beings is always approximate, partial, becoming obsolete or inapplicable to new circumstances and new experiences of Reality. Truth, for the human being, has a finite quality: known truth never becomes Final Truth. In ultimate terms, the human species will always remain ignorant. No matter how much we come to understand, there is always more. We are on a journey, a cultural journey, a "We" journey into an ever more preposterous Mystery.

Nevertheless, our knowledge is progressive in this way: once we have become relatively aware of some fresh aspect of Reality, we cannot go back to our previous stage of ignorance, even though many try to do so. What happens is that we inflict upon ourselves the psychological pain of knowing that we are denying what we know. But even when we are fully open to a new level of wisdom, we still remain ignorant. Further, we may even focus on some new wisdom to the degree that we, as humanity, forget things that we once knew. For example, most of us know little about flint chipping, even though many stone-age persons were good at it. More importantly, many of us have so focused on the wisdom of living in urban settings that we have forgotten much that humanity once knew about living in the natural world.

Our many forms of ignorance need not lead us to hopelessness or despair. This ignorance is simply our human condition, and this condition can be received as glorious and appropriate rather than as an offense to our unrealistic hope for some absolute certainty and security. Our best-case scenario is to humbly admit this ignorance. Indeed, let us rename such authentic facing of ignorance as "openness to and curiosity about more Reality." Such openness might even be called "wisdom."

Chapter 7
Open and Closed Societies

It might be argued that authoritative tradition is a fourth approach to truth. But I insist that the so-called authoritative tradition has truth-value only in so far it is in accord with the three approaches to truth outlined so far.

It is true, however, that the notion of authoritarian truth has played a large role in history. For example, Martin Luther's conflict with the Roman Catholic Church of his time was outwardly staged as a conflict between the authority of the Bible and the authority of the Church. In other words, it was a conflict within one overall system of authority: Biblical authority versus recent Church authority. But, within Luther's choice of the Bible as his authority, we can discern a deeper emphasis upon the autonomy of the individual person of faith. Such positioning of the solitary person over against the massive authority of the core institution of that society can be interpreted as a contribution from the pole of contemplative inquiry. Luther loved the Bible because he found in the Bible support for his sense of truth found in his own solitary depths. But quite soon in the history of Protestantism, the authenticity of the solitary person was neglected in favor of new systems of authority. One example of this is the rigid claim for the propositional veracity of the verses of the Bible (with selected verses having greater authority than others).

The authoritarian view of truth plays a role not only in religious communities but in scientific communities as well. Once Sir Isaac Newton's grand pull-together of basic physics had become "authoritative" for the conduct of "normal" science, there was strong resistance within the community of physicists to the revolutionary innovations being initiated by Albert Einstein and others. While the very essence of the scientific method includes an openness to further truth, scientists can feel quite secure within the older formulations and be defensive concerning those older theories, which they take to be authoritative. Once Einstein's system of physics was spelled out and mostly validated, Einstein himself became engaged in defending his new system from certain developments in quantum mechanics that he never accepted.

Such a conflict between authority and innovation goes on in every arena of culture. As an example, I will sketch how authority and innovation operated in pre-civilization tribal societies. Such societies were very slow to change. Their cultural norms and systems of wisdom had been accumulated over centuries of trial and error and were seen to be well-tested truth about which little innovation was needed. Indeed, these societies were slow to adopt innovation. This carefulness had justification, for new things did not have the lived experience and verification of the grandfathers and grandmothers of their society. They realized that human societies are fragile and that new things can have destructive as well as enriching potential. They were aware that nature is a stern Mother who does not put up with innovations that ignore her. The role of the shaman was to live on the edge of society in close contact with nature and nature's mysteries, and from that place of lookout protect individual persons and society as a whole from straying too far from nature's disciplines. In spite of this deeply conservative attitude, these early human communities could change rapidly if their most treasured values could be kept. A new stone tool, a new animal to use, a ritual that healed someone: these innovations could be quickly integrated into the whole. In some measure, ancient tribal societies were open societies, and they had been for thousands of years.

The dawn of civilization was both a radical innovation and a new sort of authoritarianism. It was radically innovative in terms of pulling together many small parochial, conservative tribal groups into a unified whole of greater numbers, greater scope of consciousness, and brand new patterns of social structure. This closer proximity of formerly separated groups forced dialogue on hither-to-ignored topics. This expanded dialogue fostered elements of openness and fresh innovation of cultural, political, and economic designs. The economic innovations of these hierarchically organized civilizations freed part of the population for an increased scope of creativity in art, architecture, religion, science, technology, and more. At the same time, civilizations were authoritarian arrangements in which a small part of the population was creating these "newer" traditions and forcing them upon the vast majority who had little opportunity for shared creativity or for protest against wrong directions and injustices.

In the context of this hierarchical structuring of human society, innovative pull-togethers often became oppressive "truths" that were actually a class-interested shaping of "truth" into partial-truths and lies that were used to support the empowerment, enrichment, and illusions of the ruling classes. This familiar development has given authoritative truth a bad press among many people today. Indeed, many people have come to fear any useful integration of a cultural consensus to be a threat to scientific research and contemplative discovery (not to mention a threat to people's own authoritarian dogmas).

This conundrum can find a degree of resolution only if we realize that *authority* in and of itself is not a test for truth. The inherited traditions of culture are useful to the extent that they are integrations of wisdom fully supported by scientific objectivity, contemplative authenticity, and consensual workability. These are the only tests for truth. Since every society is part of the ever-moving drama of history, we always need fresh reconstruction of the overall social consensus. There is no royal authority, no divine authority, no depth of historical tradition that cannot be changed. The creations of the past are useful studies, not because they were authoritative, but because they were pull-togethers by an earlier culture of people who were facing their own challenges and dealing with them well or poorly. We can learn from the past. We have our memory of the past as a great treasure. But in our present, we have only three approaches for seeking truth to live by: scientific research, contemplative inquiry, and the societal consensus building of workable forms for living within our particular moment of history.

The above thoughts can be summarized by defining what we mean by open and closed societies. A closed society is a society that is locked into past formulations and their current rationalizations. An open society is one in which detachment from the past and openness to fresh futures is present in a numerous and effective portion of the population. An open society need not hate the past or reject every aspect of it. Rather, the past is viewed as a valuable paint palette for painting a significantly new picture. The living Now is always both a departure and an opportunity. We can depart the patterns of the past when we see clearly our everlasting ignorance as well as the specific foolishness of the currently obsolete teachings that have been handed down to us.

* * * * * * * *

I am ending Part One of this six-part exploration by pointing out that a truly open society must be open to explore all three of these valid approaches to truth. Until we can form a working consensus on the topic of truth, we will not be able to form a workable consensus about the overwhelming challenges we confront. One of those challenges is the reconstruction of our understanding and practice of religion. In Part Four I will begin exploring how we can usefully discuss religion and see why religion is important. But before doing that, I will explore in Part Two the elemental topic of consciousness, and I will explore in Part Three "Inescapable Wonder," a foundational understanding for the discussion of religion.

Part Two

What
Is
Consciousness?

Table of Contents for
Part Two: What Is Consciousness?

8. Qualities of Consciousness
9. A Sixth Force in the Structure of the Cosmos
10. Consciousness and Evolution
11. Five Layers of Consciousness

Introduction to Part Two

When we get out of bed in the morning we may say to ourselves, "I'm awake." That is, we may notice that we are conscious. Perhaps we dreamed and remember dreaming, but at the time we dreamed we were not *there* in the way that we are now *here* remembering being *there* in the dream. Yes, it was I that was dreaming, and this "I" was recording in my memory banks the dream being dreamed by me, but "I," the conscious "I" who is now conscious of my consciousness of having dreamed was not exactly *there* during the dreaming. Some sort of consciousness was doing that dreaming, but my consciousness of that consciousness was not *there* at the time.

So what is consciousness? And what is consciousness of consciousness? Who am I as a conscious being? These are surprisingly deep questions, for which easy answers are not forthcoming. Our neuroscientists tell us interesting things about how our behaviors and brain waves correlate with our inner experience, but these discoveries do not answer the question "What is consciousness?" Indeed, these busy scientists do not always admit that the only direct experience of consciousness that any of us have is from a quite unscientific contemplation of our own interior world of being conscious. These inner noticings are not the same as the objective observations that are the bread and butter of our communities of empirical scientists. We inner noticers can compare notes on our noticings and propose theories that we test with further noticing. But this group thinking is not science. These noticings by solitary noticers who are noticing their own noticing do not qualify as *facts* in a well-defined empirical science.

Consciousness and the consciousness of consciousness are deep enigmas. In the following Part Two of this book, I am going to share my noticings for your comparison with your own noticings. I am going to employ the contemplative approach to truth and do my theorizing about what I "see." I am going to do some poetizing and philosophizing that may or may not enlighten your own noticing, but I am hopeful that we may agree that we are all very similar members of a magnificently evolved enigma.

Chapter 8
Qualities of Consciousness

Consciousness (kon' shas • nis): The state of being aware of one's own existence, sensations, thoughts, surroundings, etc.

The word "consciousness" is customarily used in a rather narrow sense, applicable only to beings who are conscious of being conscious. "Conscious" usually means being alert rather than spaced out, awake rather than asleep. But even spaced out is a state of consciousness, and sleep can also be viewed as a state of consciousness. It is conscious beings who sleep, not rocks. In this and following chapters, I will distinguish between consciousness as a general state within living beings, and the consciousness of consciousness, which is a state of consciousness that occurs within humans and perhaps a few other species.

The nature of consciousness can be explored with all three of the approaches to truth outlined in Part One, but only the contemplative approach (the "I" approach) can inquire directly into the nature of consciousness. The scientific approach (the "It" approach) can correlate the reports and behaviors of conscious beings with objectively examined brain functioning. This is important work that calls our attention to the biological foundations of consciousness and explores how our inner experiences are biologically supported. I will be referring to these findings occasionally, but my main focus will be on what we can learn from our own contemplative inquiry within our own being.

The "We" approach to truth can also tell us things about the nature of consciousness. The social interactions of humans provide us wisdom about the enigma of consciousness not accessible with only the "It" or "I" approaches to truth. The dynamics of an intimate relationship and/or the dynamics of building a common society together can reveal things to us that neither the "I" approach or the "It" approach can show us.

Without denying the importance of the "We' and "It" approaches to the truth of consciousness, I will be focusing in this and following chapters on the "I" approach—on contemplative inquiry into our own inner experience of consciousness. Each of us can experience ourselves as a human subject that is observing that very subjectivity within ourselves. We can even say that contemplative inquiry does not have an object of observation, because that object is the subject doing the observing. Nevertheless, when "I" am viewing the subjectivity of my own inner being, "I" am viewing something more vast than "me-the-observer" can ever finish observing. When observing our own consciousness, each of us faces an infinite well of mystery. Part of that mystery is the rather astonishing truth that human consciousness includes the capacity to be a noticer of our own consciousness. Herein is one of the profound mysteries of our lives: *we can be conscious of our own consciousness.* So let us notice within our own consciousness some of the qualities we observe about that consciousness:

1. As we are already noticing, a first truth that a contemplative inquirer can notice is this capacity to be conscious of our own consciousness, a capacity that makes contemplative inquiry possible. I, the inquirer, can be conscious of my own consciousness and of my own capacity to inquire into the nature of that consciousness. Though this may seem an obvious thing to say, it is an important truth.

2. A second truth the contemplative inquirer can notice is that he or she cannot be directly conscious of the consciousness that is within another conscious being. We can observe the behaviors of our dogs or cats or human companions, but we cannot directly experience the inner consciousness of those beings. With other human beings we can observe their behaviors and hear their reports about their inner consciousness, but we cannot be directly conscious of that other human's consciousness. Contemplative inquiry is a solitary enterprise. We can compare our findings with each other, but we must each find our verifications for these findings within our own solitary lives. We can make guesses, even very good guesses about what is going on in another person's consciousness, but the verifications for those guesses can only be found in that person's consciousness of his or her own consciousness. Furthermore, the guesses we make about another person's consciousness are based on our own experience of our own consciousness. The very language we use to make those guesses is defined (or needs to be defined) in terms of our own inward experiences.

3. A third truth that the contemplative inquirer can notice is that an accumulated wisdom about consciousness is possible. Indeed, such wisdom is about half of

all that each human culture counts as its common wisdom. All of a culture's artistic collections are expressions of our contemplative accumulation of wisdom. By "artistic collections" I mean paintings, sculptures, music, dance, story, song, poetry, dramas, and more. Architecture is also an artistic form as well as a design of functional dwellings. Further, all of a culture's religious collections are the result of contemplative inquiry. Those who claim that their formulated religious wisdom dropped down from a supernatural realm are simply making up a story to fill a gap in their understanding of these deep matters. Religious wisdom is acquired through contemplative inquiry. Consciousness views its own inner life and then these conscious experiences of consciousness are expressed in analogies, myths, cryptic sayings, diagrams, parables, dogmas, creeds, rituals, icons, and the like. The truth test for a culture's artistic and religious wisdom is found, and only found, in the type of verifications that can be acquired by singular persons consciously inquiring into their own consciousness.

4. A fourth truth that the contemplative inquirer can notice is that consciousness is both passive and active. It is both paying attention and taking initiative. It is both attentionality and intentionality. For example, we can pay attention to water spilled on the kitchen cabinet, and we can take initiative in wiping it up before it drains down and injures the woodwork. Consciousness is both taking in various qualities of our surroundings and putting out responses within those surroundings. Consciousness is a reception of sensory inputs (sights, sounds, smells, tastes, touches) as well as bodily pains, pleasures, and emotions. And consciousness is also an active relationship to those inputs, and the initiation of bodily mobilization for movement, including speech, and including the inner movements that we call "thinking."

5. A fifth truth that the contemplative inquirer can notice is close to point 4, but slightly different. Consciousness is a co-creative force along with other forces in the outcomes of history. There are other forces—aspects of my own body about which I am not conscious as well as the vast forces of the cosmos. Consciousness does not create the whole of reality, but along with these other forces consciousness does co-create the course of events. Take the very simple example of raising your arm. All sorts of electrical, chemical, and mechanical functions are involved, but consciousness can initiate this string of functions. I am not simply watching my arm move. I am an arm mover; I am putting into play all these other forces of arm moving. Similarly, if I am batting a baseball, I am batting. The concentration of my consciousness makes me a better batter than if I am half asleep at the plate.

How do we know that this co-creation of events is true? We know because we simultaneously notice the inner initiation and the simultaneous motion of our limbs. We are guessing a very plausible correlation between what our consciousness intends and what our outward body does. I am saying "guessing" because we do not scientifically or contemplatively "view" how conscious intending and bodily movements are related. Nevertheless, it is plausible to assume that when we are consciously initiating responses, our consciousness is making a difference in what our bodies do. We do not absolutely control the difference conscious intending makes, but we can assume that some difference results from what our consciousness intents.

So let us look at the co-creative power of consciousness more closely. When we guess that there is a correlation between our inner intentions and our outward movements, we are using both the sensory-scientific approach to truth and the inner-contemplative approach to truth. And we are assuming that the two truths are part of the same overall Reality and that the simultaneous nature of these two verities is not just a coincidence, but a linkage. It seems that we have no ability to prove this linkage, but a lack of linkage seems to us to be farfetched. How inner intentions are linked to outward movements cannot be investigated by either the scientific approach to truth or the contemplative approach to truth. Why? Because the scientific approach to truth cannot directly view consciousness and the contemplative approach to truth cannot view anything outside the realm of consciousness. So neither approach is capable of viewing the link between the two. Yet we tend to be quite sure that there is a link even though that link is one of the most enigmatic aspects of both scientific research and contemplative inquiry. We can easily opt to be quite sure that both approaches to truth are approaches to the same Reality, and we can come to realize that our mental make-up is such that our reason is not capable of a rational understanding of how our inner intentions are linked with our outer movements. Consciousness and its linkages with the overall sensory-discovered world are enigmatic to human thinking.

6. A sixth truth that the contemplative inquirer can notice is that consciousness has a fragile or passing finite quality. We can go to sleep and be mostly unconscious. Even in our waking life we can be more conscious or less conscious. Something infinite would not be subject to the categories "more" and "less." Consciousness is a finite process, for it can be spoken of as more conscious or less conscious. Also, we can notice that consciousness requires physical modes of energy to maintain it. Being conscious is hard work. We need to eat food to sustain it. We need to rest up after being

intensely conscious in order to be conscious again with full attention and intention. Consciousness is a finite process within our temporal lives and this is especially true of our consciousness of our consciousness. Much of our living is done without the participation of our conscious presence as a conscious intender. Our memory of the past has gaps in it where we were not consciously present. Our life went on without us, so to speak. Sometimes a person can have a night of drunkenness that he does not remember at all. Other people can report to the drunk that he had a good time, but the drunk can be so drunk that he or she apparently missed experiencing that good time. Seeing a movie for the second time can be surprising in a similar way, revealing that we were not vividly present for a great deal of that movie the first time through. Consciousness of consciousness is a fragile, temporal thing that is not always present or fully present.

7. A seventh truth that the contemplative inquirer can notice is that consciousness is only present in living beings. A rock is not conscious. It does not pay attention or take initiative. A mountain is not conscious. We sometimes ascribe consciousness to mountains and other "inanimate" objects, but when we do that we are defining "consciousness" in a way that makes the entire concept meaningless. We need to maintain our clarity. Calling a mountain "conscious" is an analogy or a projection created by a conscious human being. We also project the human quality of consciousness upon the quite different consciousness within our animal friends. We recognize them as conscious because their behaviors signal to us something familiar in our own consciousness, but we err to assume that their consciousness is everything that our own consciousness is. Our consciousness of consciousness, including the contemplative inquiry I am describing in this chapter, does not happen in our animal friends. Dogs, cats, horses, chimpanzees, porpoises, whales, etc. are clearly conscious beings, but humans enjoy (or are inflicted with) a mode of consciousness that I am calling "the consciousness of consciousness." Later, I will discuss in depth this human mode of consciousness and how it differs from the consciousness of other living beings.

Are All Living Beings Conscious?

This question pushes us to define "consciousness" more carefully and fully. Clearly, not all living beings are conscious of their consciousness as we human beings are, or at least can be. All mammalian life is certainly conscious if we define "consciousness" as using an inward intelligence to select appropriate behaviors. Whether or not dogs and cats and other mammals are conscious of being conscious we do not know directly.

We have to speculate about that on the basis of their behaviors. Do our other than human mammal friends have feelings? Again, watching their behaviors leads us to say, "Yes, they do." Clearly, pet dogs act lonely when their masters are missing. Cats require snuggle time. Horses, elephants and porpoises surprise us with their capacities for empathy with humans as well as their own species. All mammals, especially the females, create strong bonds with their young. Relative to reptiles, mammals are found to have large middle brains that correlate with these emotional capacities.

Are reptiles conscious? Apparently so, though they do not appear to possess the emotional sensitivities we intuit in mammals. Are reptiles conscious of their consciousness? Answering "No" to this question seems easier than answering "No" for mammals. Are single cell amoebas conscious? They seem to take in touch and taste sensations. They seem to have some way of filtering and finding "meanings" in those sensations. They design appropriate movements toward food, away from dangers, and other behaviors. Surely, this is some sort of consciousness. A rock does not pay attention or take initiative. Amoebas do. Are amoebas conscious of being conscious? The probability of this seems miniscule.

In whatever way we answer these questions about the other species of animal life, our observations of living animals supports the statement that at some point in the evolution of animal life, consciousness became conscious of being conscious. This mode of consciousness is clearly present in the human species. Or it can be. Perhaps some humans have fled this potential and become little more than complicated rocks or a machine-liked set of psychological habits that automatically play themselves out unconsciously. But however unconscious some humans may be, the species is clearly capable of being conscious of consciousness. And humans may not be the only species that has this capacity. There is evidence that consciousness of consciousness may have been present in the Neanderthal species and perhaps in still earlier big-brained, upright-walking primates. The Neanderthals buried their dead, apparently conducting some sort of funeral. This witnesses to a consciousness of consciousness. It is a plausible speculation that big-brained primates evolved these bigger brains to handle the consciousness of consciousness that was increasing in these species. Among currently living non-human mammalian species, it is doubtful that consciousness of consciousness is present. or at least not to the degree that humans experience. Some chimpanzees may be capable of such a human-type of awakenment, though perhaps not without extensive effort from human beings. And I have doubts that even the most accomplished of these amazing animals, are, in the human sense, conscious of being conscious. In a later section, I will explore why I believe it is possible for a non-human mammalian animal to be highly conscious and highly intelligent without being conscious of being conscious in the way that we humans can experience.

Is a tree conscious? Many plants can turn their leaves to face the sun and other adaptive behaviors. If consciousness is defined as sensitivity to environment and creative responses, then some form of consciousness can be attributed even to plants. But this form of consciousness need not to be assumed to include every aspect of the consciousness found in animal life.

Is a single-celled animal conscious? As we have already noted, our microscopic companions give meaning to their sensory inputs and initiate relevant responses. If such a capacity is our definition of consciousness, then at least some single-celled creatures are to some extent conscious. Are viruses conscious? Perhaps viruses are only biological scraps that require living cells for their replication. Perhaps they are simply products of the life processes of living cells rather than a form of aliveness that preceded cells in the evolutionary process of life. If so, viruses may not be conscious beings but only complex materials constructed by living cells.

In conclusion, it appears to my conscious reflections based on my empathies with other species that there is consciousness within other-than-human species of life. We need to note that this view is not derived from direct experience; it is a guess derived from our observations of these living beings. It also seems highly probable to me that among existing species only humans have the ability to be conscious of consciousness, and can thus inquire into the nature of consciousness as we (author and reader) are doing right now. It seems to me that our experiences of living with our animal companions support the conclusion that many of the aspects of the consciousness that I experience within myself also exists in these other-than-human living beings.

It seems plausible if not obvious to me that as living forms become more complex, a more intense consciousness can be supported. I am guessing (theorizing) that consciousness is a basic process of nature that seeks to become more conscious. If so, then consciousness is one of the driving forces of evolution. Perhaps consciousness works to develop more complex organisms in order that an increased consciousness can be physically supported and sustained.

Our biological life is clearly dependent upon mineral foundations, and our consciousness is clearly dependent upon biological foundations. But if we assume, as many do, that biological processes cause consciousness, we are assuming something far more complex than a pool-table-cause-and-effect process. Indeed, we know very little about how consciousness is related to its biological supports. We can make certain associations between brain processes and inner experiences, but the why and the how that pertains to these associations seem unfathomable.

Let us consider the following assumption (not yet refuted) about the relationship between biology and consciousness. Let us assume that consciousness is one of the cosmic forces that condition the coming into being of the biological supports for that consciousness. Let us assume that it is inadequate to suppose that the biological supports are the only causal factor. It remains true that certain conditions of temperature, chemical availability, and so on must be present for consciousness to do its creations. Let us hold in our minds the possibility that the first living cell on planet Earth did not come into being simply because some accident of physics came to pass. Let us guess instead that the first living cell came into being when consciousness as a force in the cosmos found on this Earth conditions favorable for its operation.

This assumption makes "consciousness" and "aliveness" companion concepts. Joining the concepts of "consciousness" and "aliveness" redefines both concepts. The concept of "consciousness" is expanded downward to the simplest cells. And the concept of "aliveness" is further distinguished from the chemical, atomic, and subatomic processes of the "physical" cosmos. The other elemental processes of the cosmos can be defined as unconscious or "physical" or "inanimate."

Subatomic "particles" are very different from the solid billiard balls of hard substance, but their dynamic energy exchanges and transformations do not qualify them as living or conscious. To say that an electron makes choices is a stretch. The behavior of a single subatomic entity is unpredictable in a strictly mechanical way. Indeed, contemporary physicists are reporting that the behaviors of these tiny entities require an explanation of chance or probability rather then cause. But chance is not choice. The behavior of these tiny entities has been named "quantum mechanics" rather than "quantum aliveness." Their behaviors do not require choice as an explanation; their behaviors can be accurately predicted with probability numbers. The behaviors of a living cell cannot be so predicted.

So aliveness remains a quality that has not been and cannot be analyzed by the discipline of physics. Physics can examine the behaviors of biological molecules and living bodies insofar as these entities are viewed in their pre-living or post-living aspects. But physics does not deal with consciousness or with life in its essence. And when biology is functioning as an empirical science, it also fails to deal with the essence of life. Aliveness is only known through the inner gaze of an alive being. To explore aliveness or consciousness we must employ contemplative inquiry. Empirical biology only studies the behaviors and the reports of living beings. The biologist assumes aliveness, and this alive biologist uses his or her own experience of aliveness to theorize about alive beings, but biology, as an empirical science, does not study aliveness directly. I repeat, scientific biology only studies the behaviors and the reports of alive beings.

Life and consciousness remain total enigmas within the scope of the scientific approach to truth. Yet this enigma of life/consciousness is clearly part of the cosmos. What part? I will explore this question further with a closer look at the physical world and the evolution of life.

Chapter 9
A Sixth Force in the Structure of the Cosmos

Students of modern physics have been made aware of the force field of gravity. In Einsteinian theory, gravity is not a force pulling from a distance but a force field created by the presence of mass. Gravity is a very weak force field. Each of my 160 pounds changes the shape of space around me, but this change is very, very small. On the other hand, the great mass of the Earth changes space considerably. It alters space in such a way that objects accelerate toward the center of that mass at approximately 32 feet-per-second-per-second (This is not a typo; acceleration can be measured in feet-per-second-per-second). What we all know, is that if we drop a pencil, it falls to the floor. Gravity is one of the primary force fields of the cosmos.

Electromagnetism is another. If you place a magnet under a piece of paper covered with iron filings, you see the filings line up with the fields of force created by the magnet. Electromagnetic fields operate in what we call "electricity." We also use the notion of electromagnetic fields to describe waves of light, ultraviolet rays, X-rays, radio waves, and more. Electromagnetism is another basic force field that characterizes the cosmos.

Within the interior processes of the atom, modern physics has discerned two more fields of force, typically called the strong force and the weak force.

Most physicists have claimed that these four basic forces are sufficient to explain the physical behavior of the cosmos. Other physicists have claimed that none of these force fields explain the phenomena of inertia. Why does an object set in motion continue in motion unless acted upon by another force? A fifth force field has been proposed, Higg's field.[8]

These four or five fields of force provide an amazing array of wisdom about the manner in which our cosmos functions, but none of these fields explains life. None of them explains the presence of consciousness and of choice in the structure of the cosmos. Biologists have attempted to explain how physical processes can become

---

[8] For more on Higg's field see Greene, Brian; *The Fabric of the Cosmos* (Vintage Books 2005) page 257

living processes, but none of these explanations are convincing. From the laws of physics we cannot explain how the soil, air, and fluids of planet Earth sprouted living beings. How and why those enclosures of sensitivity and response came into being remains an unexplained mystery.

So let us assume a proposition that few biologists and still fewer physicists are willing to even consider: *life/consciousness is a sixth force field in the structure of the cosmos.* Let us assume that whenever conditions are favorable, this force field kicks into action; consciousness begins making its choices, initiating its specific journeys of trial and error toward the goal of becoming more conscious and more practically effective in the environments in which it lives. Can we say that such a dynamic in the cosmos is less likely than the existence of gravity? The reason such an assumption seems outlandish to most physicists and biologists is that consciousness must then be viewed as not accessible to the physical or biological sciences. Consciousness can only be viewed inwardly by consciousness itself. Therefore, the strict empiricist is excluded from exploring consciousness and life directly.

When we creatures with human consciousness view gravity, we are doing something different than when we view consciousness. Gravity can only be viewed when consciousness "looks" outside the body in which this consciousness is living. Consciousness can only be viewed when consciousness "looks" inside the body in which this consciousness is living. We cannot see consciousness with the external view. Externally, we can see brains and nerves and genes and behaviors of living beings, but we cannot see consciousness. We only view consciousness when we look within our own now presently living consciousness. Externally, we can each see or hear reports from conscious beings through the motions and noises that these living beings make, but we do not experience their consciousness as they only can experience it. We base our assumption of the existence of consciousness in other living beings upon our experience of consciousness within our own living beings. This truth about consciousness is an offense to the usual assumptions of the physicists and biologists that consciousness will someday be explained by reducing it to one or more of the physical forces of physics.

If a direct experience of consciousness can only be had by our inward looking consciousness itself, we are stating an absolute limitation upon the scope of empirical science. This limitation on observation is not the case when we observe the array of factors we call "gravity," "electromagnetism," etc. All these forces are discerned by looking outward, by giving rational form to our outward experiences—experiences we have formulated into specific facts and have tested and retested in publicly repeatable experiences that a whole community of observers can observe.

Consciousness, however, must be explored within the singular person by the consciousness of that singular person. A community of persons can then compare notes on what they have discovered within their own beings. These inner experiences are not objective facts of scientific, empirical construction; they are interior noticings by human noticers. In terms of a strict definition of empirical science, interior noticing is not "scientific." Nevertheless, consciousness is something "objective" in this sense: *consciousness is there to be noticed.* Consciousness is not simply an abstract idea that has no reference in experience. Consciousness is an actuality about which ideas have been formed and can be formed. Consciousness is part of the structure of the cosmos. However different from empirical science our approach to this mysterious verity needs to be, consciousness is no less real than gravity.

If consciousness is a field of force in the cosmos, it is a field of force that is invisible to the scientific approach to truth. Its consequences are visible, but its "thereness" is not. We have to employ the contemplative approach to truth in order to notice consciousness. When we employ the "We" approach of truth, we can meld into our cultural overviews the outer truth approached by science, the inner truth approached by conscious contemplation, with the working hypothesis that consciousness is (or may be) another force field in the structure of the cosmos.

The assumption that consciousness is a sixth force field in the structure of the cosmos does not make necessary the assumption of a second universe alongside the universe described by physics. Consciousness is just another enigmatic force in the same universe as gravity. Nor does the assumption that consciousness is a sixth force justify belief in a supreme being alongside this one reality we experience inwardly and outwardly. Nor need we assume that consciousness is a mighty force that causes everything else. Consciousness is a history-creating force along with other history-creating forces, but this need not mean that consciousness has some sort of infinite standing. Seeking these and other truths about consciousness is simply a matter of noticing its functioning within our own lives.

In the chapters that follow, I am going to report on my noticings about this assumed sixth force of the cosmos. This can become a discussion and a joint project of understanding only if you, the reader, "look" into your own inner world of consciousness to see if my reports correspond with your experiences. Indeed, I have clarified my own noticing by hearing the reports of many other explorers of that inner realm to which each of us has access. This nonscientific contemplative exploration is in its own way "objective," for consciousness and the phenomena of consciousness are indeed real—real dynamics that challenge us to use our thinking minds to invent ever more profound clarity about these there-existing dynamics. Consciousness is an enigmatic reality in which we all dwell. So for the time being, let us just assume that consciousness is a sixth force field in the structure of the cosmos.

Chapter 10
Consciousness and Evolution

If being alive is being conscious, then our study of the evolution of life must include the story of consciousness. In this chapter, I will suggest that consciousness is an impetus that is seeking to remain conscious and become more conscious. Sometimes consciousness may choose to become less conscious. But in either case, if life is conscious and consciousness makes choices, evolution is surely affected by those choices. So, how do we tell the story of evolution with this in mind?

The classical theories of evolution describe evolution in terms of the causal factors of surviving in the specific environments in which species survive. Classical theories also describe evolution in terms of the chance factors of mutation within the genes of the evolving species of life. Less attention has been paid to the role that conscious choices play in the process of evolution. The facts of evolution can, in very large measure, be explained by causal factors and chance factors, but if consciousness has always been present in living beings, consciousness is also surely part of the explanation of evolution.

We need, therefore, to stretch our imaginations beyond the explanations of causality and chance when we tell the story of evolution. It is a bit too much to say that consciousness, through its evolutionary journey, chooses to develop eyes and ears and a sense of smell in order to be more attentive to its environment. It is bit too much to say that consciousness, through its evolutionary journey, chose to developed legs and arms and fingers in order to be more responsive to its environment. Yet these statements contain a fragment of truth. We need not assume that the whole of evolutionary development was an accident, though much of it certainly was. We need not assume that the whole of evolutionary development was environmentally caused, though much of it certainly was. So, let us assume that some aspects of evolutionary development can be and needs to be explained by choices, by conscious animal beings making choices. How can we train our minds to see this more clearly?

Here is a simple illustration. Let us say that some adult birds chose to move to a different environment. This move was not caused, and it was not accidental. It was chosen. Another environment might have been chosen. Then, this choice had consequences. The descendants that survived and flourished were those that were best adapted to that chosen environment, eating its food, escaping its enemies. At the end of this process we see birds, let us say, with a particular shape of beak. It is too simplistic to say that this species of bird chose their shape of beak. Nevertheless, it is true to say that the choices that adult birds made were part of the explanation for why that particular beak came into being.

Thomas Berry in one of his speeches made this basic point with respect to why we have both horses and bison. Both types of large grass-eating mammals came into being in very similar environments starting with gene pools that were also similar. Why then did some of this gene pool become horses and some of it become bison? Horses became horses, says Berry, for the love of galloping. The bison branch chose butting instead. Both choices worked well for the survival and flourishing of these two branches of life. Of course these statements of Berry's are a sort of poetry. It was surely true that the pre-horse and the pre-bison did not know how this basic direction was going to work out. They did not plan it. But choices were made. In the emergence of the horse clan perhaps the females just liked gallopers better than butters. In other words, consciousness does not plan or control its future evolution. Consciousness simply tries experiments in living. Some experiments survive and some do not. But consciousness trying things is choice, not chance or cause. Choices matter. Alongside chance happenings and environmental causes, choices also influence results.

We may also theorize about how much influence the adult experience has on the mutation of genes. Does the trial and error process within adult consciousness have some influence on the probabilities of changes in that animal's genetic structures? This process may look like random chance, but with consciousness being a factor, perhaps useful change has the capacity to be faster than a process of complete randomness. And this is what we often see in the archeological record—rather sudden rapid changes taking place that stretch the theory of random mutations to its breaking point.

Also, it is helpful to point out that "randomness" is just a concept in the human mind. Perfect randomness is not found in the real world. As chaos theory shows us, chaotic processes are never perfectly random but possess a measure of order operating within the apparent chaos. And nowhere in the real world is the factor of chance altogether absent. Perfect determinism, like perfect randomness, is not how our cosmos works. Cause and chance mingle together as modes of explanation of real world process. In the real world of living beings, consciousness also enters the mingle. Uncaused choices do take place, choices that are not causal- or probability-determined outcomes. To what extent choice is a factor in evolution remains open for further investigation.

Whatever such investigation shows, three things are true: Our living beings are caused. Our living beings are an accident. And our living beings are chosen. If consciousness is indeed what makes living alive, then choice must play some part in the explanation for how the evolution of life has worked out and how it is still working out. All three modes of explanation are valid. We need not say that having three modes of explanation is inconsistent. We need not insist that one of these modes of explanation must cover our entire view of evolution. When we insist on having the consistency of a single explanation, we are arbitrarily choosing that guess. We are probably choosing it in order to believe that the human mind has a capacity for correspondences with Reality that it does not have. So, let us be more humble. Let us accept the rather obvious truth that the human mind is a finite development and that Reality is only fragmentarily understandable by this amazing and yet puny human capability we call "mind." Our mind uses cause, chance, and choice because all three of these modes of explanation help us construct our sense of reality and predict outcomes well enough to enhance our survival and well-being. It is not necessary for our well-being to have one consistent explanation that covers everything. And any claim that our biology is wired to seek a completely rational explanation for everything is just one more human guess, for which certainty is lacking.

In what we call "human history," choice clearly plays a major part in that "story." We choose to remember our past in a specific manner. We choose to anticipate our future in a specific manner. These chosen memories and chosen anticipations guide our choices in the living now, choices we make toward those future "Now(s)" that we hope to experience. The evolution of pre-human life took place without this human quality of consciousness (this aware history-making intentionality), nevertheless choices were constantly being made by all living beings, and those choices surely affected evolution.

In considering the evolution of life, the human mind confronts mystery, enigma, and uncertainty. Life is an enigma. Consciousness is an enigma, unknown in its fullness, inexhaustible in its mysteriousness. Choice is not reasonable; choice is uncaused, and nonrandom. Choice is arbitrary in a way that no probability numbers can predict. "Choice" is a word for consciousness in action. Consciousness manifests its presence through choices.

The Origin of Life on Earth

Our scientific community has explored this planet's history deeply enough to have a fairly accurate picture of when life began on this planet. About three and a half billion years ago, single-celled life forms appeared. These simple cells had no nucleus or any other organelles within their membrane. These single-celled life forms are called "prokaryotes."

Over a billion years later, some of these simple cells formed the more complex cells that are called "eukaryotes." Eukaryotes amount to communities of simple cells (prokaryotes-type organelles) within the single membrane enclosure of the eukaryotes. One of these interior structures, the "nucleus" contains the chromosomes and genes. The familiar amoeba is an illustration of this development. The life of the amoeba has evolved since its first appearance and is still evolving, but as a form of life it is very primitive. If we look at it closely we get some clues as to what life is and how it arose on this planet.

We see its nucleus swimming in a fluid with millions of other simple life forms, each of which now depend for their survival and thriving upon the whole cell. They make their contribution to and they receive their needs from this overall complex organization. At some point in the deep past the ancestry of these many life forms *chose* to cooperate together rather than live separately. Yes, there were chance factors. Yes, there were causal factors. And we can also visualize that each of these organelles of life within the complex nucleated cells has its own sensitivity and response-ability. Further, this sensitivity and response-ability played some role in the coming into being of this complex nucleated cell type.

Biologists have attempted to explain the functioning of such cells in a mechanical manner. They imagine that the genes in the nucleus control the life of the cell like a computer program. Or to use another analogy, we commonly view the genes as the brain of the cell, an unconscious mechanical brain that determines causally all the parts and functions of the cell. But upon more careful observation we find that these genes are turned on or off by a very large number of switch-like entities. The study of these entities is being called "epigenetics." "Epi" means "over." These overlords or "switches" are manyfold larger in number than the genes. Now, this question arises: Who tells these overlords what to do? Who turns these switches on or off? It turns out that the skin or enclosure of the cell contains the sensors and responders of the cell. The skin or membrane of the cell turns out to be the brain-like feature of the cell. This skin takes in the environment and chooses what responses the whole cell needs to make to escape danger and select food. This skin also makes choices about the internal organization of the cell. The evolution of this single celled life form is in part conditioned by the choices made by its skin. And this includes changes made in its genes. So the evolution of the cell is not simply a matter of accidents of gene mutation. Rather the possibilities for gene change are in part selected by the skin's "consciousness" of what is needed for survival and thriving. The skin of the amoeba is alive with choices being made for the entire organism. And each of the tiny sub-cells or organelles that comprise the millions of subparts of this organism is also alive in a similar way. Each has its skin. The life of the amoeba is at least this complex. Indeed, the complexities are difficult even to imagine.

Nevertheless, let us imagine further. About a billion years after the first eukaryotes (amoeba-like beings) came to be, these complex cells began working together in multicellular organisms. Our human body is an example of that development. The human body has whole cells that specialize in being our skin. Those skin cells communicate our sense of touch to our nervous system and brain. We might say that our brain and nervous system is an evolutionary development of the function played by the skin or membrane of the amoeba. Our skin is part of our brain. Our eyes and ears are part of our brain. The amoeba was blind and deaf; it got by with a sense of touch, and perhaps taste and smell. Clearly the senses of the amoeba were fewer in number than own. We possess a much-expanded capacity for sensing the environment. With this expansion has come an expansion of our consciousness. Or we might say that consciousness in our evolutionary story participated in making choices that made for an increase in consciousness. We can meaningfully theorize that consciousness has the propensity to not only survive and thrive, but to expand the intensity of its consciousness.

When the first simple cells joined to make complex nucleated cells, they expanded the intensity of consciousness. When nucleated cells combined to form multicellular organisms, they expanded the intensity of consciousness. The evolution of our species demonstrates not only an expansion of relative brain size, but also an expansion in the intensity of our consciousness. We might even speculate that it was the expanding consciousness that kept opting for an expanded brain capacity to handle the thrust of that expanding consciousness. We need to assume that the story of life is at least this complex.

All this means that life forms are not the complete victim of their genes. Rather, to some extent the genes are developed to pass along the experiences of conscious living. Genes are not the brains or the consciousness of a cell. Genes are the gonads of the cell. And the evolution of the gonads is in part a product of the choices made by that skin of consciousness. And consciousness is the essence of being alive. Without consciousness an organism or a cell is just a rotting collection of complex compounds.

So how did that very first simple cell come into being? All our attempts to tell this story in a mechanical way do not succeed. All our efforts to create life from unlife have failed and in all likelihood will continue to fail. Some of the complex molecules appearing in living cells might come into being through physical processes, but how can we be content with the explanation that the appearance of an enclosure of such compounds within a skin that is sensitive and responsive was somehow caused by unliving causes? Indeed, we must at least consider that if we are only working with the axioms of physics, we have locked our minds into a box of reasoning that can never build a meaningful scenario for the appearance of a living enclosure—a skin that can take in what it needs to produce the ever-more-complex compounds it needs to survive, thrive, reproduce, and evolve. It is not beyond the bounds of plausibility to assume that these complex happenings of living forms required "choice."

So, we arrive again in the presence of the enigma of consciousness. Even if we cling to the story that a select number of the solids, gases, and fluids on this planet possessed the capacity for springing into life, we are asserting that these materials are strange indeed: they are more strange than the concepts of physics can express. We can just as easily suggest that consciousness is some sort of sixth force in the structure of cosmos, waiting to happen when conditions are right. Gravity and electromagnetism are also strange forces. Einstein's explanation of the nature of gravity is still quite baffling to most people. And electromagnetism, of which light is one aspect, is even more baffling. Is light propagated as waves through some kind of medium, or is light a stream of specifically sized energy packets? We have sophisticated mathematical elaborations for both pictures. So what is light really? The scientific approach to truth cannot come up with one image for light. Light is unimaginable in terms of one consistence picture. Life may be equally unimaginable within the bounds of any rational system that human minds have or can ever create.

Not only is consciousness enigmatic to the human mind, but also the scientific approach to truth cannot even observe consciousness directly. Science is restricted to observe only behaviors of and reports from conscious beings. In order to see consciousness in operation, we have to use the contemplative approach to truth. That is, we have to look within our own conscious being and report what we observe in our own inward experience. This is contrary to the objective and public nature of the scientific approach. Contemplative wisdom can be objective in the sense of being honest reporting, but such objectivity is not the same as public facts that can be tested scientifically. The behaviors and report of consciousness can be public facts, but not consciousness itself. Consciousness has to be inquired into contemplatively by consciousness. At the same time the scientific approach to truth does assume the consciousness of the scientist about whose consciousness the scientist, as scientist, is responsibly silent. And the scientific approach does encounter in the functions and evolution of biological life that unapproachable enigma of consciousness. The scientific knowledge we have about biological life can provoke us conscious beings to imagine an enigmatic presence of a reality we call "consciousness" or "aliveness"—the same consciousness and aliveness that we can contemplate within.

Finally, it is important to say that our having to use both the scientific approach and the contemplative approach to elaborate the presence of consciousness does not mean that Reality has two realms, the material and the spiritual. No, we can quite easily assume that there is only one realm—that we are merely looking at this one realm in two different ways. The material/spiritual duality of realms is a picture in the human mind—a picture that has become exceedingly doubtful in its application to what is Real. This picture has had some meaningful uses in the past, but it has worn out its usefulness in the actual living of millions of people today. Indeed, the very words ("material" and "spiritual") have become misleading to us. The good news is that the war between the material and the spiritual is over—because there never needed to be a conflict between the truth held in each of this two concepts. Humanity had always been experiencing not two realms but two approaches to the same unity. We cannot interpret our so-called spiritual insights as something material, as some materialists have attempted to do. And we cannot interpret our so-called material experiences as something spiritual, as some spiritualists have attempted to do. That old discussion has reached an absolute dead end. In the words "material" and "spiritual" we have two companion illusions fighting each other in an endless and futile battle. From now on we will be creating some confusion whenever we use the words "material" or "spiritual." We need to assign these words to the shelf of history as parts of an interesting, but now obsolete pattern of thinking.

The Confusion of Intelligent Design

Including consciousness and choice in our theories of evolution does not justify the theories of intelligent design that are being promoted by persons who oppose classical evolutionary thought because it conflicts with a literal interpretation of the two-story metaphorical writing of the biblical heritage. Intelligent-design thinkers have asked us to notice the complexity of the design of biological organisms and therefore to conclude that this complexity is proof that such designs could not have come about by chance occurrences. Such intelligent designs, we are asked to believe, imply the existence of a Final Designer occupying that assumed upper realm. These thinkers are not using the scientific method of thought; they are simply assuming the existence of a Final Designer from their acceptance of some authoritative source.

Let us examine more closely the thinking that is going on in this intelligent-design discussion. First of all, the word "intelligent" is rooted for its meaning in our experience of our own minds or perhaps also the minds of other animals. When we use the word "intelligent" to refer to Reality as a whole, we are using an analogy from our finite experience to speak of something that has infinite scope. All we have in the way of a direct experience of Reality-as-a-Whole (or Reality with a capital "R") is the experience of sheer Mystery. So when we suggest that Reality has an intelligent design we are extrapolating from our puny concepts of "intelligence" and "design" to a realm that can never be tested scientifically or contemplatively. To say that the Infinite Mystery is a Design is a myth. It is story made up by humans. The story may say something, but it is a story and, therefore, must not be taken literally.

Over seven centuries ago Thomas Aquinas used the term "Eternal Law" in virtually the same way that "intelligent design" is being used today.[9] But Thomas admitted that his "Eternal Law" is not accessible to the mind of humanity. He saw that Eternal Law was an analogy applied to an Absolute Mystery. Here is a paraphrase of Thomas' thinking: "Let us suppose that there is an Eternal King who promulgates an Eternal Law." This "supposing" is analogical thinking. The only lawfulness or design we have ever grasped with our minds has been a lawfulness or design invented by human beings. Such lawfulness or intelligent design is finite, a finite creation by finite minds. Thomas Aquinas called such finite designs "natural law"—that part of Eternal Law that the human mind can possess. Thomas also spoke of "human laws" as designs invented by humans to render social life workable. Final Reality, the "Eternal Law," is unknown to us. Final Reality is Sheer Mystery to us. All our experiences of design are partial, finite, limited, and changing. Furthermore "Eternal Will" is as good or perhaps a better metaphor than "Eternal Law."

We are speaking with analogies whenever we speak about Final Reality with such terms as law, will, mind, intelligent design, spontaneous generation, random madness, or anything else. Reality with a capital "R" is sheer Mystery relative to our human experience. Reality is infinitely beyond the capacities of our human minds to grasp. We can talk about Reality in stories or myths, but if we do not notice that we are creating myths, we veer into illusion—the illusion of literalism.

If we admit that we are doing analogical thinking, then such thinking is at least honest. And such honesty includes the admission that we are creating a sort of poetry about a Mystery of which we know nothing, rationally speaking. If we

---

[9] *Summa Theologica* "On the Laws."

speak of knowing God, we have to be pointing to how consciousness bumps up against Sheer Mystery. In such a way, our poetry may be expressing some inner realizations of our relations to Sheer Mystery. But our poetry is not science. Our poetry may be a witness to some inner truth, or our poetry may be an expression of some superstition. In either case our poetry is not science; that is, it is not literal truth.

As I will maintain throughout this book, religion has no quarrel with science when science is understood to be the creation of theoretical summations of what can be observed through the human senses by a community of observers. With these "outward" observations the scientist can widen his or her experience of that Final Mysteriousness about which scientific work creates a partial knowledge. But anyone claiming a "discovery" of intelligent design for the whole of Reality is not doing science. Such thinking is "pseudo-science," that is, it is actually an authoritarian religion seeking justification for itself through the practice of an incompetent view of science.

Consciousness and the Complexity of Life Forms

The complexity of life forms does, however, make implausible the claim that life emerged exclusively by chance mutations. The quickness with which new species have arrived suggests probabilities that are so low that it becomes a stretch to make chance our only means of explanation. Seeing consciousness as a third factor (in addition to cause and chance) in the story of evolution opens our minds to far more plausible explanations of what happened and is still happening in the evolution of living forms.

Life has been and is conscious. It makes choices. And these choices speed the emergence of survivable species. Like chance happenings, choices can create organisms that turn out to be mistakes in terms of survivability. But choice can do better than chance because it is a determination made on the basis of inputs from the environment sorted out in the lived consciousness of adult members of a species.

But however all this may be, my brief journey into evolutionary theory has been taken merely to open our imagination to the rather astonishing implications of seeing consciousness and choice as the very essence of aliveness. We move on now to observe consciousness more closely with the inner eye of contemplation.

Chapter 11
Five Layers of Consciousness

The consciousness that characterizes human beings contains at least five layers of evolutionary development: (1) the cell-based consciousness that humans share with single-celled creatures, (2) the image-using consciousness that humans share with animal life, (3) the emotion-based consciousness that humans share with the other mammals, (4) the symbol-using consciousness that is unique to humans among existing species, and (5) the consciousness of wonder that is foundational for understanding human religious practices. This fifth layer of consciousness is variously referred to with terms like "aware presence," "awakement," "enlightenment," "true nature," "essence," "holiness," "the numinous," "awe," "the nonconceptual" or simply "wonder."

Earlier primate species, such as Homo erectus or the Neanderthals, may have been gifted with: (4) the symbol-using type of intelligence and (5) the consciousness of wonder. But whether the dawning of these last two layers of consciousness took place before our species, with the dawning of our species, or after our species had evolved, it is probable that we now live on a planet on which only humans manifest the 4 and 5 layers of consciousness.

In the following discussion, I will refer to these five layers of consciousness as: (1) cell-based consciousness, (2) image-using consciousness, (3) emotion-based consciousness, (4) symbol-using consciousness, and (5) wonder-based consciousness.

(1) Cell-based Consciousness

As suggested in earlier chapters, I am assuming that all cells, including the cells of our own human bodies, are characterized by an elementary level of consciousness. A rock does not pay attention to its environment nor take initiatives toward its environment. An amoeba takes in signals from its environment and initiates responses. We can watch that under a microscope. Similarly, each cell in our body takes in signals from its environment and initiates responses. Strict materialists have tended to assume that a living cell is machine/like, similar to a very complex human-made robot. Such materialists tend to claim that a cell is understandable with cause and effect relations, and therefore devoid of self-initiated behaviors. Such a view does not look carefully enough at the enigma of life. A cell is a living being.

I do not believe that the cells of our bodies are conscious of being conscious. And I realize that I, though conscious of my consciousness, am unconscious (or only vaguely conscious) of the consciousness in my body's cells. My heart beats without any need for assistance from my self-conscious awareness. It may be true that my self-conscious stress may increase my heartbeat. It may be true that my consciousness, intensely applied, can affect my heartbeats to a limited degree. But basically, I am unconscious of the work of my heart cells and glad that they do their job without assistance from the conscious me. My limbs grow and repair without any input from my conscious awareness. Billions of life functions go on without my being conscious of them. Nevertheless, we can define these amazing cellular functions as conscious. We can define "consciousness" in a wide enough way to take in these cellular functions. In defining "consciousness" in this manner, we make clear that consciousness is aliveness, and that aliveness is consciousness. What distinguishes a tree from a rock is cellular consciousness. A tree is alive because a cosmic force field called "consciousness" is functioning in the tree. Being alive and being conscious are corresponding concepts. The implications of this perspective are vast.

(2) Image-using Consciousness

By image-using consciousness I mean a capacity for multi-sensory reruns that we humans call "memory." This layer of consciousness is present in all animal life. Snakes, lizards, dogs, cats and other animals appear to function with memory reruns. They learn from their experiences. I believe that the amazing intelligence of some of these animals is nothing less nor more than high levels of skill in associating and projecting the meanings of these vivid memory reruns. To do this, animal life uses what I am calling an "image-using intelligence."

Here is an illustration of how this image-using intelligence works. A dog, genetically driven to be curious, chases down a porcupine and painfully injures his nose on one of its quills. This multi-sensory experience is recorded in the dog's brain and reruns as a memory when another porcupine is encountered. Image-using intelligence uses this and other such memory reruns to create projections of possible future outcomes that inform the dog to construct a next response to porcupines that is less painful than the last one. This process does not require what humans call "thinking;" it only requires a form of image-using consciousness that need not be conscious of being conscious. This image-using process is a type of consciousness, however. Evaluations are made. Projections are made. Decisions are made. Image-using consciousness is not a billiard-ball-bouncing process or a probabilistic process. Image-using consciousness is creative, experimental, trial-and-error learning.

This mental process of using images (multi-sensory reruns of past experiences) is also an important process within human functioning. Because we, like all animals, are equipped with this image-using consciousness, we can identify with our dogs, cats, horses, frogs, snakes, and other animals. A key issue for defining "image-using based consciousness" is distinguishing it from "symbol-using based consciousness." Our dog or cat does not use words, numbers, or other mathematical and linguistic symbols. We humans do. Our languages, our arts, our mathematics allow us to build grand cultural memory banks that greatly improve our capacity to survive, to know ourselves, to know our world, and to create alternations in the course of events. This capacity for symbol-using is a significantly different capacity than the capacity of using images or multi-sensory reruns. Nevertheless, we humans are also dependent upon our image-using consciousness, just as we are also dependent upon our cell-based consciousness.

For example, imagine yourself swinging a bat at a pitched baseball. Your eyes pick up a flow of images of that arriving baseball. That flow of images becomes a flow of memories or reruns that your consciousness observes. Your consciousness uses those memories to predict where that ball is going to go next and how it will be curving or not curving as it passes you. At some point in your awareness about that ball you begin swinging the bat in the hope of meeting that ball where you "anticipate" it is going. All this is accomplished with images. You don't need your linguistic thinking process to bat this ball. You may use such thinking ahead of time to calculate what to expect from this pitcher. But in the act of batting itself, as Yogi Berra once remarked, "You don't think; you just bat." Image-using intelligence is operating in a vast portion of our lives. We would not be able to function as we do without this type of consciousness. We could not walk up a flight of stairs without image-using based consciousness. Without it, a dog would not be able to catch a Frisbee in midair. Without it, a cat would not be able to remember where its cat bowl was located. We would not be effective animals without these mental images that rerun in our "minds." The specific sights, sounds, smells, tastes, and touches we have keenly noticed in the past are recorded in our brains or nervous systems and these recordings of past multi-sensory experiences automatically associate with our currently happening experiences. This is only a rough sketch of this powerful mode of conscious intelligence.

(3) Emotion-based Consciousness

In mammalian life, sensory inputs have been augmented with the input of highly sensitive emotional feelings. Emotional feelings are a mode of sensitivity that allows for the bonding relations and charged responses not yet fully developed in a snake or frog. Emotions require a new layer of brain very minimally developed in reptiles. This mid-brain is highly developed in mammals. Emotions provide us with hot interpretations of the sensory inputs. These interpretations are hot in the sense that our present beliefs or taken-for-granted images of reality are involved. The quality of our emotions is not determined by sensory inputs alone. Our beliefs play a big role in determining the quality of an emotion. Emotions are indeed enacted by inputs, especially those that pertain to our individual survival, comfort, drives, projects, communal relations, and more. But the same emotions can happen when we incorrectly believe that the sensory inputs pertain to our survival, comfort, etc. Our body produces emotions in keeping with what our brains tell our bodies is happening. If our stories and beliefs are realistic, then our emotional responses are also realistic. But if our stories and beliefs are illusory, then our emotional signals are also illusory.

Here is a second key fact to take in about emotions. Emotions are a capacity in our biology that precedes the evolution of the human quality of consciousness. Emotions are clearly present in all forms of mammalian life. Emotions are one of the foundations upon which human consciousness has developed. This is not a critique of our emotional life. The emotional repertoire of mammalian consciousness is an essential component of human functioning. Without it we would be severely handicapped. Since all mammals appear to have emotions, it is obvious that emotional life can function without the presence of our uniquely human symbol-using consciousness. Emotional life is pre-human. It uses images not symbols. Emotional life becomes further enriched and more complex as symbol-using consciousness evolves.

Emotions are part of all mammalian life. Your dog has emotional feelings; including deep grief over your extended absence. Your cat may discharge anger by an all too vigorous scratching on the rug or other strange behaviors. Your pet snake has the drive for survival, pleasure seeking, pain avoidance, sensual sensitivities, and sexual urges, but its emotional life is paltry compared to a member of a mammalian species. A snake's capacities for bonding with you or with its own young are minimal compared with that of your dog or horse.

Emotion-using intelligence is one of the developments that distinguish the mammals from the reptiles and birds. In mammalian life, emotional inputs are added to the more primitive sensory inputs and image-using capacities. The remembering and anticipating process in mammals is enriched by the memory and anticipation of emotions. Mammals remember emotionally, anticipate emotionally, and choose their responses emotionally. Like humans, they apparently feel affection, loneliness, sadness, joy, fear, anger, and many other feelings. This highly developed emotional form of consciousness existed in mammalian life forms before that leap into the uniquely human quality of consciousness was taken—a leap that I am calling "symbol-using consciousness."

(4) Symbol-using Consciousness

Symbols are not the same as images. Symbols are not multi-sensory-reruns, not vivid memory recordings. "Symbols" is my term for mental entities that form complex generalizations from the more practical, vivid, and perhaps emotional charged image-formed memory reruns. For example, the symbol "four" applies to four cats, four dogs, four tables, four days, four years, four miles, etc. The mental entity "four" is not a sensory image, but an abstracted quality found in many images. Symbols can associate a large number of images into what we human treasure as abstract thought. Image-using alone, without any use of symbols, creates a high level of intelligence in many animals. A cat or dog does not require symbols to live its life. It is my belief that even when we humans have taught a very smart dog, horse, chimpanzee or bird to count, these animals still do this trick using their image-using consciousness. A human child of two years old, if raised in a human society, is skilled with symbols in a way that no other species can remotely match. As adults we use words, numbers, art constructions, and other abstractions with a facility that is truly amazing. With ease we compose large generalizations about life and ever more elaborate designs for living. Intelligent animals do something different. Their communication with one another does not use language and art, but "signs." A bow, a bark, a growl, a posture, and many other subtle acts are signs that indicate something to other members of their species, as well as to other species. Humans can communicate with other species using visible movements and oral sounds that operate as signs that communicate with the image-using intelligence of these companions. Humans communicate with one another in the image-using manner as well as with language, mathematics, and art. But words, language, music, painting, dancing, rituals, and such indicate a whole new order of communication, self-expression, and self-understanding.

Indeed, we humans often overuse our symbol-using consciousness. We get lost in it. We find ourselves living in delusory worlds of our own creation, rather than using our symbol-using consciousness to live more consciously and usefully in the real world. This mode of consciousness is our gift and our nemesis. Because of this endowment we are the most powerful and creative species, but we are also the most destructive and dangerous species on the planet. Our potential to be a powerful form of destructiveness is rooted in this symbol-using consciousness.

Symbols are used by humans in the type of mental process we customarily point to with the term "thinking." Thinking uses both the symbol-using and image-using processes. When our thinking is only symbol-using without being rooted in our imaginal reruns of actual experiences, our thinking has become excessively abstract and potentially delusional. Abstraction is not a problem in itself. It is a great gift enabling the kinds of thinking human can do. Our very best thinking, however, remains conscious of its abstractness and remains attentive to the "grounding" of our symbols in our imaginal reruns. When we work puzzles or do word and number games, we are consciously playing with our symbol-using capacity. Being aware of our capacity for abstraction is also an awareness of our capacity to return to the concretely imaged encounters and responses of our practical living.

Mathematics is the most abstract of all our abstract thinking. We might define mathematics as the abstract exploration of the human mind's capacities for abstraction. Mathematics is so abstract that the mathematician is often the most aware of how abstract all thinking actually is. Because of this awareness, many mathematicians are also musicians or poets. In the arts, abstract symbols are used to evoke rich fabrics of our sensory images and emotional feelings that connect us with our total living. Though mathematics is abstract, our use of it need not be delusional—provided that we are aware that we are dealing with abstractions. We become delusional when we assume that our mathematics has a reality other than the capacities of the human mind for abstraction. The actual cosmos is not mathematical; it is mysterious to our mathematics-ordered minds. The relevance of mathematical order in our understanding of the cosmos derives from the fact that our mind's capacity for order evolved within this cosmos. But mathematics, like all forms of human logic and thought, are human-made and thus finite, limited, capable of being improved, and potentially delusional if we misapply these patterns of order to our experienced reality. So what is delusional is not abstractness itself, but our confusion of our abstract constructions with the processes that are the real world. This confusion can be called "misplaced concretion," seeing the abstract as the concrete.

It is also important to emphasize that symbol-using consciousness includes more than language and mathematics. A painting is a symbol-using creation; it creates a virtual spatial experience that can call our attention to or give meaning to our actual experiences in space. Similarly a piece of music is a highly abstract symbolization of the flow of emotional feelings. Music helps us become conscious of our consciousness of the emotional flow of our lives. It may seem paradoxical that music is both a very high abstraction and yet capable of evoking concrete, emotionally-charged experiences. All the arts are symbolic products that evoke imaginal memories and anticipations.

Important for the central aim of this book is the insight that symbol-using consciousness produced the symbols that constitute what we call "religion." Religious symbols are constructed by taking linguistic symbols and artistic symbols and stretching them into tools of expression for those aspects of human consciousness that can reach into the essential mysteriousness of our experience. Human consciousness has the capacity to reach beyond both images and symbols, beyond emotional and sensory inputs, into the enigma of consciousness itself and into an awareness of the overall, impenetrable Mystery out of which our consciousness comes and into which it returns.

Religion is our temporal, finite, down-to-Earth human attempt to access and express to one another what I will call our wonder-based consciousness. When religious communicators speak of the overarching wholeness of Reality with a capital "R," they are actually speaking of our wonder-filled experiences of actualities that are entirely mysterious to the human mind.

(5) Wonder-based Consciousness

The functioning of image-using and symbols-using consciousness is frequently lumped together under the abstraction "mind." Some psychologists call the image-using consciousness "the reactive mind." Imaginal reruns of previous experience are reactive in the sense that they require no conscious intentionality for them to function. For example, the sight of something dangerous puts our body in motion before we have time to think with language. This is useful for our survival. Thinking is too slow to be useful in many circumstances. Our immediate experience calls upon our reruns of old experiences and our cellular endowments to initiate movement quickly. This is intelligent activity, but it happens quicker than thought. Thought requires a pause in this reactivity. Thought requires "time to think." Only after such responses are already in motion do self-conscious choices begin to take place. At some point we pause to think and make choices. Our symbol-using mind is used to guide these more time-consuming choices. Psychologists often call this "the reflective mind." Image-using and symbol-using intelligence constantly interact in complex patterns we typically call "thinking."

When "thinking" and "mind" are so defined, we can view mind as a very powerful tool; nevertheless, mental functioning is not the deepest layer of consciousness. We have to look deeper to see the true essence of consciousness that undergirds all the other layers of consciousness described above. For example, when we meditate for sustained periods of time, we begin to notice that our conscious being is able to watch the mind function without engaging in its busy patterns. The experience of being the "watcher" points to a truth about human consciousness. We can notice that consciousness precedes reason—is more basic to our existence than thinking. We exist as a conscious being in a way that is deeper than and prior to thinking.

Competent contemplative inquiry can also assist us to be aware of an inability to put into words this experience of being conscious of consciousness. Consciousness has a transrational quality. To speak of this quality we have to twist words into poetry, myth, analogy, paradoxes, parables, koans, and other such constructions that allow us to communicate to one another our consciousness of a consciousness that is beyond words—indeed beyond art, beyond mind, beyond rational understanding. Such communication can only be communicated with persons who likewise possess this transrational awareness. Here are two of my poems that can assist us to notice our personal experience of this transrational quality of our own being.

> I am an alert deer.
> Dread gets my attention
> and I can move quickly
> in many directions.
> I am a surprise
> and hard to predict.
>
> A fear of real enemies
> is the alertness of a deer,
> While my alertness is
> dread of a mysteriousness
> no deer can know.
>
> And I am unpredictable
> in a manner
> no deer can match.
>
> Dread of the Unfathomable
> is my essence.
>
> Surprise
> is my being.

This poem alerts us to our enigmatic alertness. This next poem aims to point us to the enigma of intentionality in our consciousness of consciousness.

"The purpose of life,"
some theologian said,
"is to trust the Mystery
and to enjoy Mystery forever."

Some sage in the East put it this way,
"Those who say what the purpose of life is don't know,
And those who know what the purpose of life is don't say."

The Infinite seems to be silent on the subject.

So I say, "The purpose of life is to ask
what the purpose of life is continually,
but to never know or expect to know –
indeed to know
that the purpose of life is
not to know
what the purpose of life is.

So let us choose in freedom
some finite purpose for our lives,
knowing that we have chosen it
and that we can choose again
when its limitations appear.

Through the aid of such poetry (and other means) we can notice the limitations of our image-using and symbol-using minds. And when we do, we are ready to grasp with our consciousness, if not our minds, how and why religion is part of every human society and how healthy religion is a means of aiding consciousness to journey into the depths of consciousness. Like any social process, religion can be unhealthy; it can provide substitutions for the authentic journey into our real depths. And even the healthiest religion has been created by humans, not by gods or goddesses or God. Indeed, "God," "gods," and "goddesses" are all symbols created by human beings to indicate our experience of transrational Reality. For example, the word "God," as it appears in the Bible, is not an idea that makes sense of anything. The word "God," as used in the Bible, is a word that points to the Final Nonsense, the Final Mystery, the Final Unknowable. Paradoxical as it sounds to our rational minds, we can "know" the Unknowable directly through contemplative inquiry. This sort of knowing is transrational. And, transrational knowing is the deepest kind of knowing; it defines what knowing is. We know Reality with our consciousness. Our mind is just a tool with which we reflect upon what our consciousness already knows. This reflection can make conscious knowing more useful and even expand what our consciousness knows. And certainly our reflective mind is enormously useful in communicating our consciousness to other conscious beings. But the mind as mind knows nothing. Mental knowing is an illusion. "Knowing" as well as "being" and "doing" are categories that describe consciousness, and consciousness in its essence is transrational. The rational is a tool of transrational consciousness.

So when consciousness becomes conscious of its essential nature, it is revealed to be a Wonder-based reality. Consciousness can have a direct experience (a knowing) of the Unknowable. Our rational mind can come to such an experience with all its rational screens still operating, but consciousness, not mind, is having the experience. Mind, we might say, can only "sit by" in infinite bafflement. These statements are not just arbitrary opinions of some weird, anti-intellectual philosopher; they are poetry for an experience that we conscious beings can experience every day as we view deeply the passing flow of our lives. Life is a Mystery, and our consciousness can know that, even while our thinking mind has no comprehension whatsoever of this Mysteriousness.

In addition to pointing to the absolute Mysteriousness, the biblical use of the word "God" includes meanings like commitment, choice, loyalty, and trust. In other words, the word "God" is a relational term like "sweetheart." In the Bible the word "God" means that to which we are ultimately loyal. So to name the Final Nonsense "God," means that we are committed to living realistically within our awareness of this Final Mysteriousness. This awareness is also the awareness of our profound ignorance. Our thinking minds are wondrous, but more wondrous still is the limitation of our minds and the capacity of our transrational consciousness to be aware of the overarching Mysterious Reality within which we and our minds are one tiny part.

Sometimes research physicists and biologists and other empirical scientists become contemplative and thereby honestly tell about the experience of living on the edge of empirical scientific research. Here is a commonly heard admission: "The more we know about the natural world the more we know we don't know." Every new bit of order we discover in nature brings up new questions, new mysteries, new unknowns that we may or may not one day know more about. In post-relativity, post-quantum-mechanics physics, physicists have learned that physical nature is, in the final analysis, unpicturable by the human mind. I have already used the illustration of how the natural actuality we call "light" requires two contradictory pictures to cover all we know about light. Having one mental picture that holds the nature of light may never be found. Nor do we have one picture that fully comprehends an electron or an atom. Surprisingly, we need contradictory pictures to hold what we experience about the basic building blocks of the physical cosmos. Contemporary biology likewise confronts the boundaries of human mental capacity. It remains enigmatic what life is or how life began or how it is related to the pre-life functioning in which it is embedded. All our disciplines of empirical learning silently witness to the Final Nonsense, the Final Mystery, the unknowability of the Overall Reality. The scientific disciplines are customarily silent about such matters, but being human beings, scientists know or can know that their science is an exploration into Mystery. Our conscious knowing of this same Unfathomable Mystery is also the root experience that has made religion a recurrence in every human culture.

Persistent contemplative inquirers in the artistic and religious fields of expression continually witness to the unknowability of Reality. One of the most important mystical writings of Western history is named *The Cloud of Unknowing*. Again and again the Bible indicates that its use of the word "God" points to a Final Reality that is Mysterious beyond human understanding. Here are a few lines from Psalm 139:

> How deep I find thy thoughts, O God,
> how inexhaustible their themes.
> Can I count them? They outnumber of the grains of sand.
> To finish the count, my years must equal thine.[10]

In other words, God's thoughts (Final Reality's intelligent designs) are incomprehensible to the human mind. The Infinite Reality is experienced by the finite mind as unfathomable Mystery. What we call "natural law" is actually human creations of order that seem for the time being to fit our experience of the natural world.

When we human beings (as writers of religious works, or as theologians, rabbis, pastors, mullahs, gurus, shaman, witches, or seers) dare to speak about the thoughts of God, we are speaking in metaphors. We are using the experiences in our finite human minds as metaphors for pointing beyond thinking to the enigmatic processes of Final Mysterious Reality. No human has actually thought Reality's thoughts. When we speak of God's thoughts we are composing a type of poem. We are saying that if Final Reality had thoughts, this is the sort of thinking that Final Reality would be thinking. This is fiction—like Homer or Shakespeare or Little Red Riding Hood. But this can be serious fiction, seeking to express through the limitations of words and fiction an experience of that which is infinitely beyond words.

---

[10] Pslam 139:17,18 The New English Bible 1970

If we picture Final Reality as love for us from a personal father or mother, we are poeticizing our trust in this Final Mysteriousness. We are not describing Final Reality. Some religions do not emphasize personalized symbols for Final Reality. Instead they use more impersonal metaphors like "Tao" (the Way it is) or "Dharma," (the Wisdom). Without recourse to a personalized metaphor, these religions evolve practices that have to do with being devoted to the same Final Reality that is indicated by religions that prefer the intimate metaphors of father-to-son, mother-to-daughter, or I-to-Thou.

A fully "realistic" philosophy of religion needs to begin with some basic axioms: (1) Consciousness itself is transrational. (2) Consciousness of consciousness is transrational. (3) Overall Reality is transrational. Any religion that loses touch with the transrational quality of human consciousness is a perversion of the basic function of religion. Good religion is that religion that is capable of connecting human society to that which is beyond all cultural canopies of understanding created by humans.

Good religion is founded upon trust in that Overall Mystery that never makes sense. Nevertheless, the sense-making function of our human minds can be affirmed as good (as gloriously human) by the same religions that witness to and trust the Overall Mystery that never makes sense. Sense-making is a function of our symbol-using form of consciousness. In order to live within our transrational consciousness, we do not need to negate the task of sense making. We simply need to be aware that our sense making is finite, temporal, provisional, ongoing, never-ending. Our sense of things is never permanent. The Final Nonsense is permanent, and will continually undo whatever sense we have made or will make for the living of our lives. A viable human culture is one that is, to a large extent, supported by Reality, yet in the end Reality undermines all of our cultural, political, and economic creations and challenges us to create better ones.

Once we have noticed this limitation of our thinking minds, we can notice ourselves noticing a much deeper noticing within our beings. We can call it "consciousness." And we can notice that consciousness is Wonder based. As the wondrous 'I' that we each are, we can notice ourselves noticing these basic realms of noticing: (1) our inward body's sensations, (2) the environmental inputs to us through our senses—through sights, sounds, taste, smell, touch—and how these inputs are imaged in multisensory reruns, (3) our emotional responses, (4) the thinking of our symbol-using minds, and (5) the noticing of ourselves as noticers filled with Wonder.

When this fifth layer of wonder-based consciousness is full blown, we can call it "enlightenment." It can also be called "presence," for this awareness exists only in the present in which we are now living. We can also call ourselves "saved," "delivered," "healed" from fighting Reality—for insisting that our self-made sense of things be substituted for the enigmatic glory of What Is. Fighting Reality is despair, because Reality will always win the fight in the end. Here is one more of my poems in which I intend to provoke us to look beyond our symbols to the enigmas of transrational existence.

Words cannot say how words say anything
Words can only point to REALITY beyond words.
"Reality" is itself a word,
a word which points to what is not a word.

And yet, since the word "reality" is itself
    part of REALITY,
there has to be a relationship between
    "reality" the word
    and REALITY which is not a word.

"Can this relationship," the philosopher asks,
    "be expressed in words."
"NO!" is the answer.

In other words, REALITY is a MYSTERY
    not reducible to words,
And the relationship between words and MYSTERY
    is itself a mystery beyond words.

The logic of words is not, no, never,
    the "LOGIC"
    of MYSTERIOUS REALITY.
"Logic," when applied to REALITY,
    is a metaphor
stolen from the experience of
human languages and mathematics.

The world of rational understanding
is a world of made not a world of born.
Trees, squirrels, birds, rainfall, grass,
are a world of born gleaming there
quite beyond our mind-made world of words.

So thinkers, let us think
about these matters that humble all thinkers,
that render us mere children at play,
children who play with words
who play with REALITY
who play with the relationship between
    words and REALITY.

I asked REALITY, this morning,
if what I am saying in words is correct,
    and SHE said, "It is very close."

Visualizing the Whole Spectrum of Human Consciousness

So far in this chapter I have expanded my description of "consciousness" by describing five layers of consciousness. These five layers have developed through the evolution of life on this planet. And all five layers exist and function within the current life of each human being. I have named them: (1) cell-based consciousness, (2) image-using consciousness, (3) emotion-based consciousness, (4) symbol-using consciousness, and (5) wonder-based consciousness.

Instead of picturing these elements as five layers of evolution, we can picture them five aspects of being humanly conscious—five segments on one line that stretches between two limits: *Limit I—The Inanimate Physicality of Life Supports*, and *Limit II—The Absolute Void of Mysterious Every-thing-ness*.

This line of consciousness is pictured on the following chart. Human consciousness is depicted as a line limited by the above two limiting factors. Consciousness arises out of the mud of the physical world and gains in intensity until it meets an internally experienced limit, a sort of "stone wall," a "can't-go-farther" in being conscious. Beyond this point consciousness does not exist. We can be conscious of this Absolute Void of Mysterious Every-thing-ness, but the Void itself devours consciousness just as it devours everything else. In becoming aware of this Void, we also meet the boiling Source of all things, including consciousness. We also meet the tomb of all things, including consciousness. This Void is the Every-thing-ness in which all things coexist. This Absolute Void of Mysterious Every-thing-ness starts us, sustains us, and ends us as the conscious beings that we are.

Our awareness of this Void tells us something about the enigma of consciousness. First of all, such awareness tells us that our fifth layer of consciousness is in close conversation with this Void. As a wonder-based consciousness we are or can be conscious of the presence of the Void, but we cannot consciously enter the Void. We have reached a limit that dramatizes a truth about consciousness: consciousness, like gravity, is a finite field of force within the terrain of temporal nature.

I have already described the five layers of consciousness that appear above the heavy line in the following chart. Beneath the line are companion categories that I will describe next:

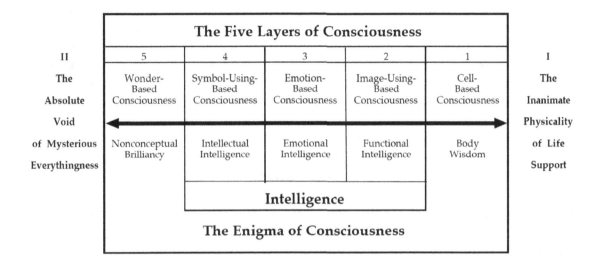

		The Five Layers of Consciousness				
II	5	4	3	2	1	I
The	Wonder-Based Consciousness	Symbol-Using-Based Consciousness	Emotion-Based Consciousness	Image-Using-Based Consciousness	Cell-Based Consciousness	The
Absolute						Inanimate
Void						Physicality
of Mysterious	Nonconceptual Brilliancy	Intellectual Intelligence	Emotional Intelligence	Functional Intelligence	Body Wisdom	of Life
Everythingness						Support
			Intelligence			
		The Enigma of Consciousness				

Body Wisdom

I will use the term "body wisdom" to exemplify how humans can experience the cellular-based aspect of their human consciousness. A common example of body wisdom is experienced by many athletes. It is often called "being in the zone." This happens in many sports, but basketball may be the easiest to understand. Sometimes a player finds himself or herself in a *zone* where it seems that shots just don't miss. This is a state of consciousness that has nothing, or little, to do with the mind. It is as if the body knows what to do; the mind just follows along. When someone is in this zone, his alert fellow players give that player the ball. The defense attempts to do something that will "interrupt" this zone state. This is a deep truth about the game of basketball, one of the things that makes it the unpredictable game that it is.

A similar zone can be experienced in dancing, painting, composing music, even writing. The body knows what to do. Consciousness relaxes the mind into paying attention to this bodily knowing and goes along with it.

And there are more controversial examples of Body Wisdom. Many alternative health practitioners rely on something they call "muscle testing." The practitioner asks yes-or-no questions of the arm muscles or finger muscles or feet muscles of the patient. "Is this herb what is needed by this body at this time?" "Is three times a day enough? The muscles selected respond with strength or weakness as answers to the questioning. The theory here is that the body knows something that the conscious mind does not. So the conscious minds of the patient and the health practitioner devise ways of asking the muscles of the patient about what these cells of the body know. Many reject this entire practice as superstition. But for those who use it and trust it, it may be just another example of what I am pointing to with the term "Body Wisdom." And there are other seemingly "spooky" phenomena that our ordinary, rational, scientific culture tends to finds too odd to consider. Some of these may turn out to be examples of Body Wisdom. Much of what is customarily said about these areas is indeed superstitions. But maybe some of these so-called superstitions are simply Body Wisdom that our scientific and contemplative approaches to truth have not yet incorporated into our categories of common sense.

Intelligence

On the above chart I have labeled the layers of consciousness 2, 3, and 4 as forms of intelligence. I will clarify further our human experience of these three layers of consciousness and what I mean by "intelligence."

In some of our conflicts with other persons, we can notice a conflict between intellectual intelligence and functional intelligence. Those who major in functional intelligence tend to call those who overemphasize intellectual intelligence nerds or egg heads. I am visualizing here the common view of a Texas oil-rig worker of a New York City scientist or poetry writer. Functionally oriented persons frequently view the more intellectual members of our species as lost in worlds of abstraction that lifts them above the needed competencies of ordinary life. On the other hand, those who major in intellectual intelligence tend to view those who overemphasize functional intelligence as dullards, commoners, slugs, or with other demeaning names. The truth is that both ends of this polarity are important, and there are individuals who balance this polarity pretty well. I think of the Nobel-prize-winning physicist Richard Feynman. He was not only a competent mathematician and research physicist, but he was also a quite humorous, practical, approachable person who was a skilled musician on the bongo drums. But balance like this is not all that common. A young house repairman I know could care less about my intellectual pursuits, but he is a genius in creating fixes for anything that goes wrong on our property. At the other extreme I know people with several postgraduate degrees who are helpless with a hammer or with figuring out practical solutions for the simplest of household problems.

Emotional intelligence is another aspect of human consciousness that manifests in a stronger way in some persons than in others. The term "intuition" is sometimes used to mean emotional intelligence. There may be other ways to define "intuition," but it seem to me that most of what we may mean by intuition is indeed the emergence of wisdom for living based on the feelings of the body rather than the thinking of the mind. In intuition, the mind gives form to something discovered with the feelings. Intuition is a truth awareness that can be very quick compared with a logical step-by-step put-together by the mind.

There are many women and men who have accessed deeply both their emotional intelligence (intuition) and their intellectual intelligence; however, it is frequently the case that a friendship or mating happens between a man who has accessed his intellectual intelligence quite deeply, but has accessed his emotional intelligence much less deeply than his woman friend or mate. The woman in this relationship may depend more fully on her emotional intelligence than on her intellectual intelligence. What happens in such a relationship? It may be that each deeply respects the other and uses the other to enrich what is less developed in his or her own self, thereby finding that two of them form a more balanced access of intelligence than either do alone. But it may also happen that tensions develop between them. The woman may become irritated that this man is so emotionally slow or so negligent in noticing when she is simply expressing her feelings. Rather than hear her feelings, the man may view her as putting forth a set of thoughts that cry out to be elaborated or contested. Similarly, the man may become irritated with the woman when she finds some of his finest insights overly abstract, irrelevant, and boring rather than personal enough for her liking. Variations on this little drama are quite familiar to many of us. The truth beneath these conflicts is that emotional intelligence and intellectual intelligence are both important aspects of human intelligence; they are both important gifts, rather than grounds for holding one another in contempt.

Our male-biased, hierarchical, over-intellectualized culture has typically ignored or demeaned emotional intelligence. Some subcultures have even been loath to admit that there is such a thing as emotional intelligence. The emotions have been dismissed as meaningless approaches to truth or exaggerated expressions of the trivial. The truth is that each of us would be severely handicapped without our emotional intelligence. In Antonio R. Damasio's book *Descartes' Error: Emotion, Reason, and the Human Brain* we find the amazing story about a man who lost portions of his brain that enable emotional intelligence. He could move and talk well, but in decision-making he was greatly hampered; in ordinary and practical ways, he was almost helpless. As Damasio illustrates, our bias against emotional intelligence needs to be overcome if we are to enjoy a fully realistic appropriation of human life and consciousness. And we need to end the war between the intellectual and emotional aspects of human consciousness. We need a balanced and holistic appropriation of human intelligence in order to create a grasp of the truth that enriches us and provides us with the intelligence we need to handle the huge challenges we face.

Nonconceptual Brilliancy

In addition to the complexities and conflicts within human intelligence, we also need to access what is being called the "nonconceptual" aspect of consciousness. This aspect of consciousness has been strongly resisted and even denied by many specialists in intellectual consciousness. Indeed, for such "specialists" to admit the importance of nonconceptual consciousness means they have to fully embrace the limitations of their intellectual consciousness. The defenders of intellectual truth frequently oppose the very notion that human consciousness can be conscious of an aspect of consciousness that precedes all thinking and exceeds all thinking in realism. This brilliance, however, is precisely what is meant by the non-conceptual layer of consciousness—a layer I have also described as "wonder-based." The wonder-based layer of consciousness is beyond symbol-using, emotion-using, and image-using consciousness. And it is beyond these important forms of intelligence, not in the sense of being more or less important, but in the sense of being the very essence of intelligence, a brilliancy that lights up every aspect of human intelligence. For a full development of this important point, I recommend a book by A. H. Almaas: *Brilliancy: The Essence of Intelligence.*

Nonconceptual consciousness is more easily accepted by many of the defenders of emotional consciousness, but this is not always the case. Nonconceptual consciousness is also an aspect of consciousness that precedes emotional feelings and exceeds emotional intelligence in realism. So defenders of emotional intelligence are also forced to face the limitations of their emotional clarities and understand that while emotions are extremely useful, they are also limited. Emotions are often useful as guides into the realms of wonder-based consciousness. Nevertheless, the brilliancy of wonder-based consciousness is trans-emotional as well as trans-conceptual. The trans-conceptual realm is beyond emotion in the sense that it reveals the limitations of emotional truth.

For example, our emotional feelings can simply be reactions based on our personality constructions, our self-images, our systems of thought, and other clearly partial perceptions of reality. Fear can arise when we mistake a stick for a snake. Anger can happen in our bodies when we mistake a friend's helpfulness for an attack on our lives. This undependability of the emotions can be very complex. Whatever we *think* is real about the world or about ourselves affects what we feel. Nevertheless, the emotional capabilities of our bodies are doing their best to help us live our lives and in that sense emotions are quite trustworthy. Also, as we move beyond our conceptual and emotional realms of truth into our nonconceptual consciousness, our intuitions (instances of emotional intelligence) become more dependable. Feelings attend each state of Wonder, and these feelings are useful for describing our awareness of Wonder. We might say that Wonder-based consciousness tends to cleanse the emotional aspects of our lives of their unrealism.

In conclusion, the nonconceptual or Wonder-based aspects of human consciousness constitute a brilliancy that both transcends what we usually mean by intelligence and undergirds all forms of intelligence. In Part III, "What is Wonder?" I will use my conceptual mind to chart and describe the domain of nonconceptual consciousness. The fact that a human being can do such a thing is one of the enigmas of consciousness that I will describe. It is indeed a paradox that we can use our minds to poetically describe what is beyond the concepts of our minds. Such poetry-type descriptions communicate to others only to the extent that the others who "hear" are finding within themselves the capacity to be aware beyond the concepts of their minds.

Part Three

Inescapable Wonder?

Table of Contents for
Part Three: Inescapable Wonder?

12. The Thought, Feel, and Choice of Wonder
13. Space/Time, the Eternal Now, and the Enigma of the "I Am"
14. Nine Aspects of the "I Am"
15. Nine Habits of Escape form the "I Am"
16. The Journey into Profound Humanness

Introduction to Part Three

Ancient sages of the Orient found paths beyond the Yang of thought and the Yin of feeling into the Way of Wonder. In Sub-Asia, Hindu and Buddhist seers found methods of concentration that opened enlightenment beyond blinding thought, joy beyond reactive feelings, and liberation beyond fated compulsions. In the West great minds focused on Great Thoughts that carried consciousness beyond the customs of foolishness into experiences of Great Feels and Great Resolves that together with Great Thoughts witnessed to a landscape of Wonder.

Wonder is another word for *awe* and the *numinous*. Wonder lights up thought with new vigor. Wonder cleans feelings of their exaggerated sentiment. Wonder interrupts compulsive behaviors and restores us to the paths of freedom, effectiveness, and persistence. Wonder is a hard experience to talk about, but that has not prevented every era of humans from trying.

Chapter 12
The Thought, Feel, and Choice of Wonder

In her book, *Strange Wonder: The Closure of Metaphysics and the Openness of Awe,* Mary Jane Rubenstein notes that the Greek god Thaumas (wonder) has two types of daughters: Iris (rainbow) and the harpies (ugly birdlike monsters with large claws). All these daughters link heaven and earth. Rainbow fascinates us: we run outdoors to see the spectrum of colors that may arch from north to south as the setting sunlight is split by water droplets into this striking spectacle. As we contemplate such beauty, we may not care about the scientific explanation; we simply stand before this connecting beauty between sky and ground and say pleasant things to each other.

But the harpies are also the offspring of wonder: connecting sky and ground, the Mystery and the ordinary, with connections that prompt us to close our eyes or duck our heads or, like the proverbial ostrich, put our heads into some sort of sand. Wonder is a strange beauty, but also a strange horror.

It was Rudolf Otto who first made clear to me that wonder begins its assault upon us as a trembling, as an upsetting, as a shaking of our foundations (Tillich), as a dread or anxiety that will not, and need not, ever go away. The full experience of fascination, though rainbows, is also accompanied by a sisterhood of upsetting dynamics. It takes courage to be in Awe. Most of the time we are cowards who duck from our potential experiences of wonder.

Rubenstein makes this colorful, but damning, commentary on Western philosophy:

As far as Western philosophy is concerned, however, every aspect of wonder becomes susceptible to erasure, because, whether it responds to that which is fascinating or repugnant, thaumazein *(wonder-ness)* keeps problems unresolved. It renders the thinker incapable of doing the kind of simple calculating, sure representing, or remainder-less opining that might secure himself and his knowledge against the storm of indeterminacy. For this reason, wonder becomes an increasingly problematic ancestor for the increasingly "scientific" Western philosophical heritage. As the tradition progresses, wonder is progressively relegated to something like a temporary irritant: a discomfort not to be endured, but rather cured—or at least tranquilized. [11]

This then is our first block to seriously understanding or practicing a religion. We must open to wonder or awe, however horrible or beautiful or both the awe may be. We must intend a courageous openness in order to be in wonder.

The Direct Experience of Wonder

Though Wonder is unknowable to the human mind, Wonder can be directly experienced by human consciousness. In this sense we can "know" Wonder. If this sort of knowing were not possible, then the word "Wonder" would be meaningless. Some have concluded that the word "Wonder" is meaningless, so they no longer use the word or any word like it—Divine, Sacred, or Holy. But this attitude undercuts our appreciation of the role of religion in human life—namely, the role of binding or connecting humans to that Landscape of Mystery, that River of Enigmatic Consciousness, that Mountain of Compassion, and that Wild Sea or Ocean of Courageous Tranquility. I will explore all that later. It takes poetry and imagination to speak of Wonder. It also takes courage, for security-hungry humans resist Wonder's irrationality, its disturbing subversiveness, and its revolutionary implications.

Nevertheless, every human is close to Wonder, for it is our true nature. Humans, in their essence, are already connected to Wonder. Good religion assists us toward happenings of awakened awareness of this connection to Wonder that has been buried, suppressed, fought, ignored, denied, and unwelcomed by our ordinary states of consciousness.

"Good religion" appears in human life because Wonder is an inescapable human experience. Even though most people spend their entire lives escaping from Wonder, there is no escape. Human consciousness is rooted in Wonder. So, like a persistent bloodhound, Wonder tracks us down and forces us to see its teeth. Wonder is Real, more real than we, in our attempts to escape, can even imagine.

At the same time, this inescapable Wonder is beyond conceptual expression. So how do we even begin to talk about it as an everyday experience in our lives? One very old answer is, "We don't talk about it." One of the ancient Taoist writers

---

[11] Rubenstein, Mary Jane, *Strange Wonder: The Closure of Metaphysics and the Openness of Awe*

put it this way: "Those who say don't know, and those who know don't say." The prophets of Israel on the other hand, felt free to say, "Thus says the Eternal One," and then wax on for 45 verses, hoping that at some point in their discourse the Wonder behind their speaking would break through to some captivated listener. But even these wordy prophets knew that what they were saying was an interpretation of experiences that were un-sayable. There are many biblical verses that basically say, "The Ways of Yahweh are beyond finding out." Jesus also insisted on being cryptic. He spoke in parables and explained that he did so in order that the know-it-all religious experts would not understand what he was saying. I take this to mean that he required of his hearers a deep shift in their lives in order to grasp what his parables were pointing to. We see a similar sensibility in Zen Buddhist teachers when they use what they call "koans." A koan is a cryptic statement designed by a wise teacher who then uses the koan to challenge a student to a shift in consciousness in order for the koan to have meaning to the student. A famous example is "Two hands clap and there is a sound. What is the sound of one hand?" In seeking an answer, the student must reach beyond his standard thinking into deeper awareness.

Great Thinks, Great Feels, and Great Resolves

Being conscious that we are conscious beings is impossible without the aid of the symbol-using mind, but it is also true that the thoughts of our mind are substitutes for the realities they symbolize. Thinking about thinking is a real challenge to our consciousness. Nevertheless, in order to clearly distinguish what we are pointing to with the word "Wonder," we must distinguish the reality of thinking from the reality of consciousness and Wonder. As conscious contemplators of our inward reality, we need to notice and remain clear that thoughts are an important reality (a reality we think about a lot), but thoughts themselves are not synonymous with the Reality to which they point. Just as the finger pointing to the moon is not the moon, so every thought, while a real "finger," is not the object to which that thought points.

The thoughts we think are parts of Reality, but the misidentification of the contents of thought with the contents of Reality is as far off the mark as viewing the words in a dictionary as the same as the objects and relations to which the words of that dictionary point. Our human thinking is a very complex biological gift that we can examine externally as acts of our brain and nervous system and view internally as our thinking mind. The thoughts of that thinking mind are like a wonderful dictionary that each culture of humans has created to augment the handling of Reality. This cultural dictionary is a valuable tool that our consciousness can use, but to use our dictionary well we must be clear that the items in our dictionary are not the same as the dynamics of Reality that these thoughts stand for or attempt to describe. And though thoughts point to Reality, they point to Reality partially. Reality is far more than our mental dictionary encompasses. Seeing this truth is the first step toward true wisdom. Such wisdom includes the insight that mind is not the same reality as consciousness. There has been a tendency in Western culture to see the words "mind" and "consciousness" as words for pretty much the same thing. But I am intent in making a precise distinction. As I am using these two words, "consciousness" is a word that points to the knower and actor of our being. "Mind" is a word that points to a tool that the consciousness "I" uses. Until we have demoted mind to the status of a very complex and wonderful tool, we are not yet ready to enjoy a clear perception of Wonder.

A person who is "lost in thought" is not a true thinker. A true thinker is someone who is aware that his or her thoughts are not Reality, but are only pointers to Reality. A true thinker is therefore open to think different thoughts because of this awareness that Reality is always more than the thoughts we currently think. Reality does support some thoughts better than other thoughts, but no thoughts can be counted on to be the "last word" about Reality.

There are, however, what I am going to define as "**Great Thinks**." A Great Think is a bit of mental poetry that has been derived from our transrational consciousness experiencing some experience of Wonder. It is as if that bit of rational poetry is so imbedded in Wonder that it is capable of communicating an experience of that Wonder to anyone open to the Wonder involved. And because our minds are ever-present, ever-working dynamics, our experiences of Wonder always have (or perhaps almost always have) a Great Think component.

For example the "Great Think" that I have dwelled upon above that "Reality is beyond thought" can communicate to our consciousness a state of Wonder or Awe. I use "Awe" as a synonym for "Wonder." I define "Awe" (and therefore "Wonder") as a primal dread of the Unknown plus a fascination with the Unknown plus an elemental courage to remain conscious of this dread and this fascination with the Unknown.

Dread and fascination are words that point to a vast array of specific feelings in our bodies. These feelings are not thoughts, though we may have thoughts about them. The term "**Great Feel**" can be used to point to whatever feelings attend a specific experience of Awe/Wonder.

The courage it takes to remain conscious of these Great Feels and Great Thinks that attend some experience of Awe can be pointed to with the term "**Great Resolve**." Any specific state of Awe can be communicated by describing the Great Thinks, Great Feels, and Great Resolves that attend that experience of Awe.

This threefold description (Think, Feel, Resolve) is not the Awe itself but modes of description of the Awe. The Awe itself is an experience within some human being's consciousness. The symbol-using mind can be a tool for sharing that Awe consciousness. Our bodily responses of feeling can be indicators of the presence of Awe. Our conscious willingness to be in Awe is also an indicator and component of the transrational experience that Awe is.

I will illustrate these three dynamics of an Awe experience by describing a simple experience of Awe that we have all likely experienced. Each of the following sentences can be said to be a Great Think that associates with this specific Awe experience:

> Life and Death are two wings on the same bird.[12]

> Life is a countercurrent that turns rock, water, and air into living, and living is a fragile quality that death will turn back to rock, water, and air.[13]

> Death walks with us every day of our living. Death walks behind us just over our left shoulder. If we turn our head quickly we might see death walking there.[14]

Each of these thoughts comprises a Great Think if they awaken in us a Great Feel. So what is the Great Feel we feel when we think with sensitivity the just mentioned Great Thinks? We may experience this particular state of Awe as a pain we could do without. Death may come to us as a rawness that we may want to ignore or suppress or find some substitute for. We may say, "Let us think happier thoughts. Surely we need to flee somewhere rather than walk today with the experience of death." But when we take courage to live with our dread, we find that we are also drawn to the experience of death. This draw is what we can point to with the word "fascination." We go to funerals and wakes in order to honor the experience of death. We may tell ourselves that we go to a funeral to hear someone lie to us about the unreality of death, but on a deeper level we go to such rituals as an act of courage to take in the dread and fascination of death and to allow our lives to be realistic in honoring real people and their real impermanence.

Great Thinks and Great Feels about the ever-presence of death do not remain in our consciousness without a Great Resolve, without a choice for Reality over

---

[12] Rumi

[13] my poetry

[14] a paraphrase of a story from Carlos Casteneda

escape. So how do we describe the Great Resolve required to live in the face of the Reality of the ever-presence of death? The Resolve might be described as a solidity of commitment about not being taken in by the superficiality of any assertion or implication that only a life without death is worth living. Real life and real death are worth living: this is the resolve that permits the Awe state we are describing. The mystery of coming into being and going out of being is the life that is worth living. Indeed, it is the only life there ever was or ever will be. In this Great Resolve, I join the animals and the trees in affirming life; I rejoice in my privilege of having this opportunity to live, however short or however long this opportunity may last. As Psalm 90 puts it in the form of a prayer to Reality, "So teach us to count our days that we may enjoy a heart of wisdom." Such words as these enable our consciousness to notice the Great Resolve that enables us to experience and continue living in the Great Feel and Great Think that death walks with us every moment of our living. These three types of indicators describe one of our experiences of Awe before the Awesome Unknowable Reality in which we dwell.

There are an unlimited number of ways of being in Awe. Each Great Think carries us beyond what we think we know to a state of Awe that we "know" with our consciousness. And let us not forget that consciousness knows in a manner that baffles our thinking. Using the analysis of Great Thinks, Great Feels, and Great Resolves is a mode of poetic effort that points beyond itself to the Awe that we humans can experience in a manner that cannot be contained in rational thought.

In a specific Awe experience, a feeling of dread may predominate or a feeling of fascination may predominate. It may take great courage to sustain a particular state of Awe, or it may take only a little courage. Each Awe experience is unique. For example, "I am here and not not here" can be a Great Think that emphasizes fascination. We may feel mostly gratitude for our opportunity to live our life. If our life is quite hard at the moment, the dread aspect of this Great Think may also be strong. In any case, the Great Resolve to be here and be intentionally alive takes courage. Every state of Awe is an act of courage as well as an encounter that occasions dread and fascination and that may be pointed to with some Great Think of poetic creation.

Poems of Awe/Wonder

As already indicated, there are an unlimited number of different states of Awe, each of which can be described in many ways. One interesting way of describing the broad spectrum of Awe experiences can be found in some poetry about living in a Land of Mystery. Joe Mathews, my teacher of many years, discovered the following poetry in Oriental culture and with help from others expanded it into some very interesting charts and spins. Here is my poetic one sentence summary of that "chart" of the overall scope of Awe: *We live in a Land of Mystery that contains a flowing River of Consciousness, a huge Mountain of Care, and a wild Sea of Tranquility.*

My following four-stanza poem is an expansion of the above sentence. Each phrase of this poem can be understood as a Great Think that may be attended by a Great Feel and a Great Resolve.

The Land of Mystery

We live in a Land of Mystery.
We know nothing about it.
We don't know where we have come from.
We don't know where we are going.
We don't know where we are.
We are newborn babes.
We have never been here before.
We have never seen this before.
We will never see it again.
This moment is fresh,
Unexpected,
Surprising.
As this moment moves into the past,
It cannot be fully remembered.
All memory is a creation of our minds.
And our minds cannot fathom the Land of Mystery,
much less remember it.
We experience Mystery Now
And only Now.
Any previous Now is gone forever.
Any yet-to-be Now is not yet born.
We live Now,
only Now,
in a Land of Mystery.

The River of Consciousness

Within the Land of Mystery
flows a River of Consciousness/Freedom.
Consciousness is a moisture in the desert of things,
an enigma in the Land of Mystery,
Consciousness flows through body and mind.
Our bodies are pain and pleasure,
desire, emotion, stillness, and passion.
All these are but rocks in the water
or on the banks of the River of Consciousness.
Consciousness is not the body,
but a flow through the body and with the body.
Consciousness is an alertness that is also
a Freedom to intend, to will, to do.
The mind is a tool of consciousness,
providing consciousness with the ability
to reflect upon consciousness itself.
But consciousness cannot be contained
within the images and symbols of the mind.
Consciousness is an enigma that mind
cannot comprehend—even noticing consciousness
is an act of consciousness using the mind and
flowing like a River in the Land of Mystery.

The Mountain of Care

Within the Land of Mystery
rises a Mountain of Care –
care for self, care for others,
care for Earth, care for the cosmos,
care that we exist, care that we suffer
care that we may find rest and fulfillment,
care that we may experience our caring
and not grow numb and dead.
It takes no effort to care.
It takes effort not to care.
Care is given with the Land of Mystery.
Care is part of the Mystery of Being.

We care, we just care, we are made of care.
Care is a Mountain because care is so huge,
so challenging to embrace, to climb, to live.
Care is a demand upon us that is more humbling,
more consuming, more humiliating,
than all the authorities, laws, and obligations
of our social existence.
Care is a forced march into the dangers
and the hard work of constructing a life that
is not a passive vegetable growth
nor a wildly aggressive obsession.
Care is an inescapable given, simply there,
yet care is also an assertion of our very being.
It is compassion, devotion, love for all that is given
and for all parts of each given thing, each being.
Like Atlas, we lift the planet day-by-day,
year-by-year, love without end,
in the Land of Mystery.

The Sea of Tranquility

In the Land of Mystery
there is a Sea of Tranquility,
a place of Rest amidst the wild waters of life.
The waves may be high, our small boat tossed about,
but there we are with a courageous heart.
It is our heart that is courageous.
We are born with this heart.
We do not achieve it.
We can simply rest within our own living heart,
our own courageous heart that opens vulnerably
to every person and all aspects of that person,
to our own self and every aspect of that self,
to life as a whole with all its terrors and joys.
This is a strange Rest, for no storm can end it,
no challenge of life defeat it.
No loss, no death, no horror of being, no fear
can touch our courageous heart.
We live, if we allow ourselves to truly live

on this wild Sea of Everything in the Tranquility
of our own indestructible courageous heart.
To manifest and fully experience this Tranquility
we only have to give up the creations of our mind
that we have substituted for this ever-present Peace.
We have only to open to the Land of Mystery
flowing with a River of Consciousness
and containing a Mountain of Care.
Here and here alone do we find the Sea of Tranquility –
Here in the Land of Mystery that our mind
cannot comprehend, create, or control.
Here beyond our deepest depth or control
is a Sea of Tranquility in the Land of Mystery.

Chapter 13
Space/Time, the Eternal Now, and the Enigma of the "I Am"

Scientific research, the knowledge it uncovers, the method it uses, and the philosophies it inspires all require the concepts of space and time. Post-Einsteinian physics views the whole of nature as a vast sequence of space/time events beginning with the Big Bang of beginning and then unfolding toward an equally surprising future. Biology also views life on this planet unfolding (evolving) through space and time. Each life is seen as a space/time journey from birth to death. Sociology and history also create their wisdom for us within the story of space/time movement. Psychology likewise sees our lives as a development through space and time. The art we call "music" symbolizes our feelings as movement through time. The art of poetry unravels some eventfulness within the movement of time. Even painting, which might be said to stop time, draws space as space is being experienced in some temporal era of history.

With regard to the inward gaze of consciousness upon consciousness itself, the sense of time and space is different from the notion of time that we take for granted in the sciences. "Contemplative inquiry" takes place in only one time—*Now*, and only one space—*Here*. Nevertheless, in our contemplative inquiry we can notice an *event quality*: feelings change, thoughts change, inward experiences come into being and go out of being. In this way, we experience in our inward gaze a quality of flow that we can also call "time." But this flow of time is flowing through the Now where consciousness lives. Contemplation takes place in the Now and only in the Now. For consciousness, the past is only a memory in the Now, and the future is only an anticipation in the Now. Consciousness as consciousness knows only one time—*Now*.

We also experience this inner flow of time as taking place within an inner expanse we typically call "space." But, inner space is different from the external space that science explores. In our contemplative inquiry we experience ourselves as a solitary subject viewing our own subjective experiences. We watch our mind developing its images and symbols, its sentences and paragraphs, its paintings and music. We watch our body having its sensations, desires, and emotions. We watch choices being made and body muscles moving. And we experience our enigmatic "I" becoming aware of itself. We might hypothesize that the observing "self" is not viewing itself, but only a memory of itself from a few milliseconds before. But when we are pursuing the contemplative approach to truth, the time is always *Now*: so there are no "milliseconds before"! Memory happens in the Now. Anticipation happens in the Now. Consciousness is viewing its memories and anticipations Now. So we have the impression that consciousness is viewing itself in the only time there is—Now. And by "impression" I mean "experience." Inward experience is impressions made on the Now-existing core of consciousness. I experience a flow of impressions—impressions flowing from memory, impressions flowing from anticipation, sensory impressions originating now, and all impressions happening in the ever-present Now. These qualities of inward experience violate a commonly accepted notion that there is always a subjective observer that is observing some object. When we are pursuing the scientific approach to truth, we do deal with "objects" being observed by an observing "subject." And the scientific approach to truth is not illusory. The objective world is encountered as an otherness (object) impacting or presenting itself to me (subject). But when we are pursuing the contemplative approach to truth, the "experience" is different. In the contemplative approach to truth we are the subject that is attending to our own subjectivity. We may attend to that subjectivity truthfully (in that sense, *objectively*), but *there is no scientific-type object involved*.

The very notion of a truth quest in which a subject is observing its own subject provides a shock to the taken-for-granted assumption that is operative in the scientific approach to truth. But every assumption of the mind is just an idea created by the mind. Every assumption is therefore open to doubt, or at least to a limited scope of relevance. Perhaps "limited scope" is the correct consideration in our attempt to differentiate the approach of contemplative inquiry from the approach of scientific research. The mental picture of a subjective conscious viewing its own subjective consciousness is also a picture made up by human minds. This picture has a scope of relevance that is not present within the scientific approach to truth. We have two mental pictures: (1) a subject viewing objects through a passage of time and (2) a subject viewing itself in the ever-present Now. Which of these two pictures applies best to our inner experience of Reality? "Subject viewing subject" is my answer. But this does not nullify the first picture (subject viewing object), which applies best in our experience of Reality as an external environment that confronts our existence.

The answer to any question about which rational picture is best for picturing some specific reality can only be found by looking to see what we see in our ongoing experience. I want to strictly maintain this *commitment*: experience precedes thinking about experience. Of course, we are always thinking something before we experience our experiences, so we tend to see our experiences through the screen of what we already think. Nevertheless, contemplative inquiry includes becoming a watcher of our mind and of our mind's products and activities. We can watch the mind using its current screens and we can watch new screens come into being. We can be aware of consciously occupying a sort of gap between the old and the new screens. The "I" of consciousness is like a mysterious gap between the last screen of thought and the next screen of thought. Indeed, it is consciousness that is creating the new mental screen. A new screen of thought does not arise from the old screen. It arises out of a type of nothingness—the abyss of consciousness itself. So on the basis of our experience, is it plausible that the existing "I" can notice itself in the existing Now, not the self of a few milliseconds before, but in the Now—remembering, anticipating, and choosing on the basics of memories and anticipations a next direction for thought and action?

If these reflections create in you a feeling of shock, it is probably because you want your mind to make better sense of all this. For example, this question may arise: which view of space and time is correct, the one we employ in scientific research or the one we employ in contemplative inquiry? If neither is fully true, where are we? And if both are true, how are they related? And if both are true, can we ever create a consistent and meaningful philosophy? Following is my attempt to provide a bit of further clarity on this topic.

Contemplation and Science

From the viewpoint of contemplative inquiry, the scientific view of space and time is only an idea in our minds. It is a very useful idea; it permits all the assembled knowledge of our minds to be organized for our practical use. But "I," the user of this assembled knowledge, do not exist within the past-present-future timeline of scientific research and knowledge. I exist Now and only Now. The infinitesimal point called "present" on the past-present-future timeline of scientific knowledge is not the same as the "Eternal Now" in which I exist. I am calling this Now "Eternal" because it does not move into the past. The subjective "I" endures through all the comings and goings of my experience.

In the practice of science, this "I," is not observable. "I" is not an object; so "I" cannot be an object of scientific knowledge. Many scientists acknowledge the presence of this "I"; they admit that this subjective observer is assumed in the scientific method. These scientists sometimes say, "We have made an agreement not to explore the 'I,' but to be silent about the 'subject' in our scientific work. Scientific work is about being objective, so we must exclude subjectivity from our scientific work." Other scientists and philosophers of science (those of a positivist leaning) tend to be uncomfortable with the notion of a "subject" that is beyond the scope of scientific knowledge; they hold that this subjective observer is not an "independently real" entity, for such an unobservable entity would disturb the ability of science to build an inclusive view of reality. So these philosophers tend to explain our inner sense of "I" as merely an epiphenomenon of our chemical-electrical-biological mechanics. "Epiphenomenon" means a secondary phenomenon in parallel with phenomena that are primary. Such use of the term "epiphenomenon" allows the positivist thinker to say that consciousness is not a primary phenomenon, but merely an attendant feature of the primary phenomenon that science can observe.

So, if we want to affirm both scientific knowledge and contemplative wisdom, how do we bring order to this discussion? As I have already pointed out in Part Two, consciousness can be viewed as a force in the cosmos—a force that is as independently real as gravity (that is, not an epiphenomenon). Such a view is contradicted by no experience. And if we do not consider consciousness as a primary reality, we reduce our intimate relations from person-to-person relations to it-to-it relations. Also, social reality is seen as a closed system not interruptible by the freedom of an "I" that opts for uncaused choices. It is true that many, perhaps most, of our actions are *caused* by a complex array of genetic coding, social conditioning, and neurotic patterns to which we are habituated. But if we experience ourselves as making even one act in a manner not caused by any other factor than "I" the conscious chooser, then we are experiencing consciousness as a primary force, not as an epiphenomenon of chemical, electrical, or quantum phenomena.

In order to honor the essential freedom that we interiorly experience, we need to make the contemplative approach to truth one of our lenses for viewing Reality. Through the contemplative lens we can view even the scientific approach to truth. In the contemplative approach to truth, we view the human mind and all its products as finite processes. The scientific approach to truth is one of those finite games that the mind plays. It is a very important game; we have no objective knowledge of the environment without the scientific approach to truth. No amount of contemplative inquiry can arrive at our certainty that dinosaurs walked this earth millions of years ago. We can and must view the vast scope of human scientific understanding as wondrous and in its own way true. In addition, we can hold the view that Reality is more vast and wondrous than either science or contemplation will ever be able to comprehend. As good scientists we know that scientific knowledge is approximate and is always open to further emergence. Good contemplative thinkers can have a similar humility about their explorations of inner subjectivity.

The process of scientific discovery involves the inner creation of theories to be tested. This interior theory-creating process cannot be understood within the scientific approach to truth. Only a contemplative approach to truth can view the process of theory creation in operation. The scientific method is one of the mental contents that the subjective "I" views going on in the mind as the "I" sits in the Eternal Now and watches the amazing mind do its stuff. From the "I" perspective, we can notice how scientific reasoning is true; how scientific thinking is one of the ways that mind works to achieve relative but real objectivity about our temporal surroundings. We can watch ourselves experience sensory inputs, watch ourselves create possible order for these inputs, watch ourselves create tests for these creations of possible order, watch ourselves conduct those tests, watch ourselves conclude whether those guesses were refuted or not, watch ourselves guess again if our first guess was refuted or proceed further if our guess was not refuted. Such watching is watching ourselves do the scientific method. The scientific method is a natural method, one that evolved with the human species. The scientific method reflects a true experience of Reality. Part of my subjective experience is the experience of an encountered objective Mysteriousness that challenges me to think more clearly about what I am up against. We cannot conduct our practical lives without the scientific method. This is true even when people are not clear about the scientific method. In a less sophisticated form, many other species use a trial-and-error mode of learning that is a precursor to our more evolved scientific method of thought. Nothing we say about contemplative inquiry needs to minimize the importance of scientifically developed truth. What we have here is two different approaches to truth. Neither can be reduced into the other. Neither is adequate for all wisdom.

A Further Look at the Meaning of Mind

As a still further clarification of the enigma of knowing anything, it may help to say more about what I am pointing to with the word "mind." "Mind," as I use this word, points to the interior experience by the "I" of the brain's (and nervous system's) functioning. The brain can be scientifically studied. The mind is known only to the inward look of contemplative inquiry. Science can study an organism's behaviors and reports, but mind itself is invisible to science. The brain (and the inner mind it supports) comprises a valuable part of our finite biological organism; this brain/mind dynamic has evolved in order to enable us to do what we humans do. Like our feet or hands, the brain/mind is a finite tool for living our temporal lives. When in the typical Buddhist context, we employ the word "mindfulness," we do not mean the functioning of our finite mind, we mean the enigmatic "I" using the finite mind to be attentive to our lives. It is not our brain/mind that is mindful in the Buddhist sense; it is "I" that is mindful. It is consciousness that is mindful. The mind is just a tool for mindfulness. The mind is just a tool for scientific research. The mind is just a tool for contemplative inquiry. Like a screwdriver, hammer, or chisel, the mind is just a tool, a very crucial tool for our conscious living.

Here is another important clarification. What we typically call "artificial intelligence" is not a mechanical augmentation of conscious intelligence; it is a mechanical augmentation of the human mind. Conscious intelligence cannot be created out of anything but consciousness. So in that sense, artificial intelligence is not intelligence; it is merely the augmentation created by conscious intelligence of some of the machinelike aspects of the biologically evolved tool we call "mind."

The Relation between the Temporal and the Eternal Now

Søren Kierkegaard in the early pages of *Sickness Unto Death* provides us with a way of viewing the essence of the "I" which he calls both "self" and "spirit." "What is the self?" he asks. His question implies a *true* self, and Kierkegaard proceeds to spell out his view of this *true self*. Here is my paraphrase of his assertions:

> The self is a relation between the temporal and the Eternal, which relation has the capacity for relationship with itself and in doing so grounds itself transparently in the power that posits it. If this relation is willing to be this temporal/Eternal relation, we experience trust, faith, salvation. But if this relation is unwilling to be this temporal/Eternal relation, we experience despair. [15]

In this his "most perfect" book, Kierkegaard spells out how despair has many forms: it may be hidden in unconsciousness; it may be introspectively contained as a painful inward secret; it may manifest as an escape into sensuality, noble work, or suicide; or it may be defiantly enacted as a self-constructed falsification or as an open rage against our very existence. When we are despairing, it is because we want go get away, and we cannot get away from being this temporal/Eternal relation that we essentially are. So our attempts to get away are experienced as a desperate hopelessness that has no hope of ever realizing the defeat of a Reality that never goes away. Yet, according to Kierkegaard, a different kind of hopefulness is near at hand, for all that is required of us is to surrender to being the temporal/Eternal relation that we profoundly and inescapably are. Kierkegaard

---

[15] See the opening pages of Part First of *The Sickness Unto Death*.

calls this "the turn to faith," the option of trusting Reality rather than despairing over it. It turns out that experiencing our despair opens the door to this different type of hopefulness.

What is interesting to me about Kierkegaard's basic formula for the self is that it preserves the importance of our temporal experience while also asserting the importance of our Eternal experience. That emphasis is deeply Jewish and deeply Christian, according to the best expressions of these traditions. The best of Islam also supports this perspective. The best of these three traditions view the human as a temporal creature with an Eternal relation. Without ceasing to be a finite creature, humans have an I-Thou intimacy with the Eternal Reality. Our creaturely, bodily, blood-and-bone being is not negated by realizing our true self. Following is a diagram that attempts to put temporal and Eternal together into one picture.

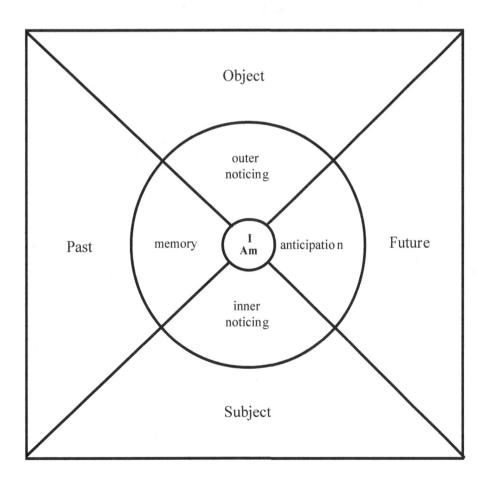

Notice that I have constructed this chart using a double pair: (1) past and future, and (2) subject and object. I have placed "past" in the west (left) with the setting sun. I have placed "future" in the east (right) with the rising sun. I have placed "subject" in the south (below) symbolizing inward depth. And I have placed "object" in the north (above) symbolizing the Earth, the universe, the cosmos, as well as other persons, animals, plants, fungi, microbes, and inanimate things. These four arenas—past and future, self and other—symbolize *temporality*. The "I Am" in the inner circle symbolizes our experience of that *third term*—the true self or "I Am" living in the Eternal *Now*.

Note next the middle circle. The four categories in this circle symbolize the relations of the "I Am" to the four categories of temporality. Memory relates us to the past. Anticipation relates us to the future. Outer noticing relates us to the object aspects of temporality. And the inner noticing relates us to the subject aspects of temporality. The "I Am" is related to temporality in these four ways.

Without temporality there is no "I Am," for the "I Am" is a relation with temporality. Without Eternality there is no "I Am," for the "I Am" is a relation with Eternality.

Using Kierkegaard's formulation of the "I Am" as a *third term* existing between the temporal and the Eternal, we can talk about the "I Am" relating to the Eternal and to the temporal. The "I am" is not the Eternal, but "I Am" participates in the Eternal as a life lived in the Eternal Now. And the "I Am" relates to temporality through memory and anticipation and through inner and outer noticing. Memory and anticipation are direct experiences of the "I Am" in the Eternal Now. Past and the future are abstract mental constructions. The infinitesimal point between past and future that we call "the present," is likewise an abstract mental construction. The Eternal Now is not the same as this abstract point of "present" between past and future. When we speak of an infinitesimal point between past and future, we are speaking of an idea in our minds rather than of a factor of our existence. Our existence is not a mere object in the temporal world, but a temporal-Eternal relation that manifests in objective ways in the temporal world and is a relation with the Eternal. The "I am" is not the Eternal, and the "I am" is not a temporal object. The "I Am" is a third term capable of relating to itself and in doing so grounding itself in the power that is positing it—namely the Eternal.

Scientific thought helps us to be relatively objective about the past and future. Nevertheless, our models of the past are creations of human minds, not to be confused with the full mystery of our origins. And our models of the future are also creations of human minds that have been built by mental effort from our models of the past and our hopes for continuation or expectations of change in the future. The "future" that will actually "occur" within our living Now will be a surprise.

Unless we are blinding ourselves to see nothing except what we expect, the future is always a surprise that happens as we are expecting something else. Only if we expect to be surprised are we open to Reality.

Similarly, inner noticing and outer noticing are experiences of the "I Am" in the Eternal Now. Inner noticing means paying attention to the thoughts of our minds; to our body's sensations, urges, desires, and emotions; and to our capacities for choice and muscle movement. Outer noticing involves paying attention to the inputs of our senses and to the naming, ordering, and interpretation of those inputs by the image-using and symbol-using mind. While both inward and outward noticings are direct experiences of the "I Am," the more abstract concepts of "subject" and "object" are creations of the temporal mind. Our "self," as we commonly conceive of it, is a rational model, made up from some portion of our inner noticings. Being a model created by the finite mind, our "self" is an approximation and an outright substitute for the "I Am" that is truly living in the Eternal Now. Similarly, the objects in our outward vision of the world are made up from some portion of our outer noticing; and being models of the mind, they are fragmentary, approximate, useful for some things, but over time destined to be misleading and in need of replacement. The "I Am," in order to operate a practical life, must value and use these approximate objectifications and must therefore trust them to some extent, but the "I Am" in order to be true to its own authenticity must trust its own noticing more than any of these mind-constructed objectifications. We need to remain somewhat or very much suspicious of all the objects created by the mind and all the patterning of those objects and all the interpretations of those objects that the mind has crafted.

To summarize, Kierkegaard defined the "I Am" as a *relation* rather than a *substance*. He clarifies that the "I Am" is a relation between the temporal and the Eternal. The "I Am" is not the temporal, and it is not the Eternal. "I Am" is a "third term." "I Am" is the relation itself, a relation that does not constitute itself but is constituted by the *power* that posits this relation. The Eternal "posits" the temporal and posits the "I Am" as a relation between temporal and Eternal. This relation that is the "I Am" possesses a strange capacity to relate to itself. It can view itself, know itself, describe itself, enact itself. Unlike a normal set of eyes, the eyes of the "I Am" can see the "I Am." And this "I Am," in relating to its own "I Am," grounds itself transparently in the *power* that posits the "I Am." The "I Am," using the mind, can write books about the qualities and journeys of the "I Am." These books can be more or less accurate, but in every case incomplete. I claim no more for this book.

Kierkegaard's reflections are a different way of talking about these matters than the Hindu way of talking that was developed in the Upanishads. In this antiquity of India, we see the concept of "Atman" which refers to a "self" that is deeper than the ordinary self images created by human minds. "Atman" is the realized "I." The Hindu concept of "Brahman" refers to the Mysterious Overallness of Reality (i.e. the Final That.) With these definitions in mind, we can begin to grasp the meaning of the phrase: "That I Am." This is not a metaphysical statement, but a cryptic pointer to a profound experience. Here is my way of focusing on this experience: I notice that my "Grand I" is just as mysterious as the entire cosmos or Wholeness of Reality. Equally mysterious is the capacity of the "I" to notice the "I" and to notice the "That." These two noticings and what they notice are parts of one Reality—"That I Am."

Nevertheless, I am not at ease when these Hindu insights are used to imply that the "I Am" is simply a drop in the ocean of the "Whole." And I am especially uncomfortable with assuming that I can identify my Great Self with the whole. I prefer Kierkegaard's way of poeticizing this experience. I see my "I Am" essence as in intimate relation with the Whole rather than as an absorption into the Whole. Rather than viewing my "I Am" as the Whole, I identify with an "I am" that is a manifestation of the Whole. This is Kierkegaard's view: the "I Am" is not the Whole, nor is the "I Am" simply a part of the temporal world. The "I Am" is a third term, a relation with temporality and with Eternity, a relation that is neither the temporal nor the Eternal. The "I Am" is simultaneously related to temporality and to Eternality. And this "I Am" is not a synthesis of the temporal and the Eternal, but a "third term" capable of being itself or not being itself. Kierkegaard sets up this profound either-or option: a choice between (1) the state of openness and trust or (2) the state of closedness and despair.

This third term (the "I Am") is posited not by itself but by the Eternal, which means that the "I Am" is not a creation of itself but an essential structure of the cosmos posited by the Eternal. Hence our dialogue with the Eternal is inescapable, necessary, ongoing, for as long as the Eternal sustains the relation with the Eternal that "I Am." So in the Kierkegaardian view of the "I Am," we live in the Eternal Now as an unavoidable dialogue with the Eternal. The All-powerful Eternal meets us through every temporal coming into being, enduring of being, and going out of being. The Eternal posits the self ("I Am") along with the companion positing of the entire temporal world. The true self is the "place" where relations between the temporal and the Eternal manifest.

So, does this dialogue with the Eternal continue after our body goes out of being? This we cannot know, but if it does the Kierkegaardian view requires that a new body be given in which and through which the relationship with the Eternal can be pursued. This is why "resurrection of the body" rather than "immortality of soul" appears in New Testament literature. Both immortality and resurrection are metaphors for the Eternal relatedness that we can sense in our experience of the "I Am." The immortality of the soul is a metaphor that implies a diminution of temporality. The resurrection of the body is a metaphor that implies an affirmation of temporality as an essential part of any life whatsoever, including any possible life beyond death. Kierkegaard's view of the "I am" does not prove or make necessary any life beyond death. The religious issue becomes a quality of life issue for living in the Now, rather than an extension of our consciousness beyond our historical journey.

Even if there is not an "I Am" after the body's demise, it is in our best interest to willingly be this "I Am" in this Eternal Now. Herein is our happiness, our bliss, our rest, our peace, our joy, our authentic life. The other alternative is to fight Reality, a fight that we cannot win, a hope for a life that can never happen, a hopelessness, a suffering appropriately named "despair." So we have a deep interest in discovering fully and identifying fully with this enigmatic "I Am." Doing so is our liberation from the suffering of despair. Doing so is "finding our bliss" as so many teachers advise. Doing so is "being ourselves" as we sometimes say we want to do.

So how do we talk further about this "I Am"? Does the "I Am" have various qualities or aspects that we can talk about? Can we "view" these aspects and talk about them? Yes, but it also remains true that the "I Am" is mysterious, quite beyond the reach of rational imagery or symbols. Many Buddhists typically refer to the "I Am" as being "no self." By this they mean that everything we have thought to be our "self" is not the "Self" of enlightenment. The experience of "no self" means experiencing a disidentification with all our self-images and personality habits: all these common understandings of "self" cease to be identified as "I." Thereby, the true "I" becomes a great void, a great emptiness, a great spaciousness in which nothing "self-like" exists. Some Buddhists go on to admit that this great spaciousness is the "True Self," but they remain determined to point out that this "True Self" is not the "self" we commonly talk about.

So what sort of poetry can we use to describe this unfathomable actuality of the "True Self"? And who is doing the describing? Obviously it will be "I Am" attempting to describe the "I Am." The describer is seeing and describing the describer. Though I have not experienced your "I Am" experiences, only my own, I am assuming that we humans are alike at this profound depth. I am assuming that who "I Am" you also "Are." This is not true on the temporal level; temporally our bodies are unique. And our personalities are unique—even though we may group personalities into types. And our cultures are also unique, temporal creations. But on the level of our Eternal relatedness, human is human. However mind-blowing this may be to much of our common thinking, all that has been said in this chapter implies the underlying presence of an essential/profound human within every human. "Profound humanness" points to a universal life that can shine through all the temporal variety that qualifies human beings. If we mean something essential with the word "Spirit" or "Holy Spirit," then every human is the same when we are dealing with what Spirit fullness means. Finally, let us caution ourselves to keep aware of the difference between our culture's ideals and the profound or essential human that transcends all cultures. Otherwise our talk of an essential or profound human turns into a tyranny of our culture over the other cultures of the world.

In the following chapter I will describe nine aspects of the "I Am." Other models are possible, perhaps better ones; nevertheless, I discern in my own being these nine aspects of the "I Am." I am suggesting that beneath all your unique temporality "You Are" these same nine aspects of the "I Am" that I will describe.

Chapter 14
Describing Nine Aspects of the "I Am"

Giving rational names to aspects of the "I Am" is daring, since by definition the "I Am" is nameless. Even if the names I use are pretty good poetry (good descriptions of something directly experienced), they are only fragmentary descriptions of the experience. So, I admit that my fragments of poetry are flawed lenses through which I am asking you to look.

Furthermore, there are an infinite number of aspects of the "I Am," so grouping these aspects into nine categories is somewhat arbitrary. Therefore, I don't mean for my nine categories to discredit other ways of grouping these experiences. At the same time, I am attempting to draw a comprehensive portrait, one that includes the whole of the "I Am." My descriptions will be brief: each of these nine aspects might have a whole library of books written about it.

Further, I am assuming that all nine of these aspects of the "I Am" can be noticed in each of our lives—that each of us can access these aspects of profound humanness as our very own being. Such sameness can be a shock, for with regard to temporal aspects of our lives, we are each unique, significantly different in almost every characteristic. So, in describing profound humanness, I am asking you to notice that temporality is not the whole story of your life, and that beneath all our differences we are the same in our Eternal relatedness.

The following chart is meant for ongoing contemplation. This chart is a map, a map made from a wide range of experiences found from following many other maps of experiences of the "I Am." Making a good map requires careful attention to what previous maps pointed to and failed to point to, and then making corrections. Humanity has been mapping their most noteworthy and mysterious experiences for thousands of years. I am submitting to you my most recent map for exploring our common profound humanness. On the basis of your own explorations, you may want to make your own map, your own corrections of my map, or at least describe missing elements in each of the areas I visit. Indeed, I have written more extensively about these nine aspects in other books. See especially Chapters 7, 8, and 9 of *Jacob's Dream*.

The pattern of my map incorporates the insight that the "I Am" is a combination of conscious knowing and conscious doing. I will use these next two words to stand for that polarity: **Attentionality** and **Intentionality**. Forget whatever other meanings those two words may have had in our culture. For me these two words are pointers to two inseparable aspects of the nature of consciousness and of the nature of profound consciousness. We pay *attention* to our surroundings, and we initiate or *intend* actions within those surroundings. We know, and we do. We *take in reality*, and we *shape reality* with our choices. "Attentionality" is our direct awareness of our awareness in its temporal setting and "Intentionality" is our action that flows from this awareness into the wide world. As a quality of the "I Am," *attentionality* is related to memory of the past. As a quality of the "I Am," *intentionality* is related to anticipation of the future.

In my mapping, the three aspects of the "I Am" I have placed on the left side of my chart are related to *attentionality*. The three aspects of the "I Am" on the right side of my chart are related to *intentionality*.

The bottom three aspects relate to *solitude* and the top three aspects relate to *being with others*. The "I Am" is both boundlessly solitary and boundlessly related to all things. In *The Courage To Be*, Paul Tillich spoke of the solitariness and togetherness dimensions as (1) the courage to be "apart" and (2) the courage to be "a part."

Finally, the circle in the center of the chart indicates a core aspect of the "I Am" that enriches the other eight aspects. This completes my map—nine inseparable aspects of the "I Am." I will describe them in terms of my experience and perhaps yours:

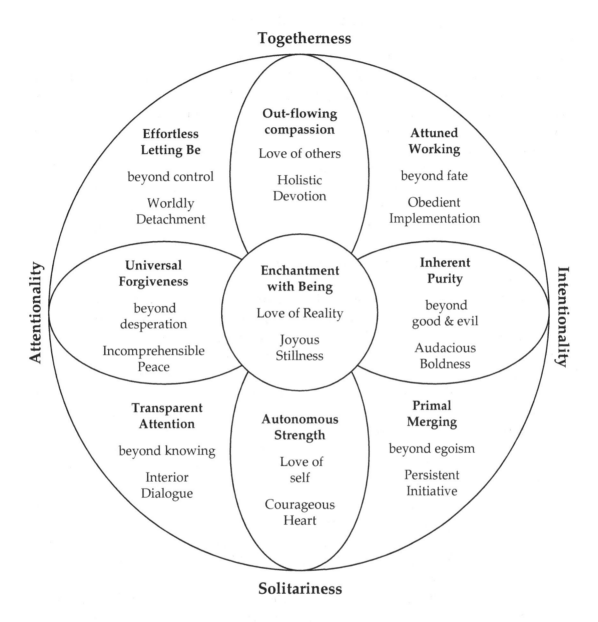

I begin my description on the attentionality side—the left side of the chart. I will start with the solitary aspect of **Transparent Attention** and move upward through **Universal Forgiveness** to the more communal aspect of **Effortless Letting-Be**.

Transparent Attention

Curiosity is a type of trust in Reality; curiosity is a willingness to be open to an ever-deeper vision of Reality. *"Transparent Attention"* is a phrase that indicates a very profound curiosity, a curiosity that begins when we are infants and can remain throughout our lives. Our awareness makes discriminations before our mind begins its work. Before an infant's mind has a name for toe, infant consciousness begins to be aware that its toe is *me* in a way that the crib slat is not. Awareness makes a differentiation between *my* being and *my* mother's being before *my* mind has a name for mother or for self. As the mind learns names and learns to use them, consciousness has a capacity to remain clear that the names are not the experiences named. Consciousness can remain connected to the all-encompassing Reality that is more than the named things. As adults we typically confuse our naming process with the process of Reality, but it is still possible for us to experience *Reality beyond the naming.* This is *Transparent Attention.*

As adults we can find ourselves in a state somewhat like the state that an infant experiences before the symbol-using mind goes to work naming things and building sentences. With the aid of language and the consciousness that the language capacity fosters, we can live our lives more consciously than the infant. But it remains useful to imagine ourselves having a lasting infant capacity to be a consciousness noticing consciousness without a word for consciousness. When we as adults rest in such raw consciousness, we can watch the mind do its work of distinguishing things with names and relating those named things in useful patterns for our living. Such differentiation of individual things from the whole may be relatively true, yet the naming might have been different, and the whole does not disappear. *Transparent Attention* pays attention to the fact that the names are not the realities named. Furthermore, in *Transparent Attention* we can see that the names only imperfectly reflect the realities named.

Let us notice that Transparent Attention is taking place within the contemplative or "I" approach to Truth. We are not being outwardly focused empirical scientists, but contemplators when we describe how *Transparent Attention* can differentiate specific things from the enduring Every-Thing-Ness without losing the awareness that all things participate in an overarching Every-Thing-Ness. As we continue to pay attention to our named things we can also notice that all these things come into being, stay a while, and go out of being. This is true even of our ways of naming things. All things and all perspectives upon those things come out of an enduring No-Thing-Ness and return to that No-Thing-Ness. This No-Thing-Ness can also be seen as the Every-Thing-Ness in which all things coexist. Such awareness is a deep adult experience of *Transparent Attention.* If, however, our awareness focuses only on our mental representations, we can forget that these separately named things are also connected in an all-encompassing expanse of Reality. Forgetting this connectedness is most serious when we assume that the "I" who rationally knows things is separate from the things we know. It is a delusion for us to assume that I am "over here" and the things known by me are "over there." I the knower and the things I know are interlaced. So, "here and there," "them and me," are mental discriminations within an overall inclusiveness. In Reality, each of us is an inseparable, ongoing, flowing part of an All-encompassing Every-Thing-Ness. This awareness we can have, not by mental effort, but by simply paying attention.

Here is another clue for describing *Transparent Attention*: If we read or write perceptive poetry, we can notice that our mind can be used to assist our consciousness to see past the mind into something deeper. An accomplished poet works with the realization that the reader of the poet's poems must see for himself or herself the vision that inspired the poems. Through creating poems, the poet can make contact with the "I Am" of the hearer or reader of the poems. The poems themselves are imperfect vessels of truth, but the fragile poem of the poet can establish an "I Am" to "I Am" connection with the hearer of the poem. Such connections reveals a *brilliancy* of "knowing" that is beyond the ordinary sense of simply sharing between two minds some acquired knowledge that can be stored in another mind.

The phrase *"interior dialogue"* is useful for indicating the communal quality of *Transparent Attention*. Many voices speak to us. Many writers and personally known persons grab us with bits of vision into our own lives. The voices in this inward community have a life of their own—speaking to us constantly. And yet this is a solitary experience. These are our community of voices and we have some power to choose who to listen to and who to "cast back into the abyss." Further, we speak back to these persons of our interior dialogue. And we can talk with them about what they know about experiencing and living the "I Am" of profound humanness. Though this sea of voices comes to us without our consent, we are not their victim. As the facilitator of my inner council of voices, I have considerable power to choose who to talk with and how to talk back to them. I live with a surprisingly large inward company of companions who travel with me into the realization of the "I Am" that we "all Are."

This dialogue of *Transparent Attention* sees both the qualities of the "I Am" and our many escapes from those qualities. We can come to be aware of our own unconsciousness of our "I Am," and we can become aware of our resistance to consciously being the being that we are. In *Transparent Attention* we can also come to notice the trustworthiness of Reality and the futility of our despairing flight from or fight with Reality. Both trust and despair are core topics of *Transparent Attention*.

Transparent Attention can break through the habits of our personality-controlled mind and manifest as a *state of being* that happens to us from time to time. We can also journey into an enjoyment of *Transparent Attention* as an ongoing dynamic of the "I Am" that we never need to leave.

Universal Forgiveness

Universal Forgiveness entails a forgiveness for all—enemy and friend as well as self. It means consent to live with the whole actual situation of living. It means an affirmation of rather than a retreat from or fight with the encountered course of events. Forgiveness does not mean something sentimental or codependent. Built into Reality itself is the possibility of a perpetual *fresh start* in which there is no guilt, no shame, no *despair* over the past, no *closedness* toward the future, no *malice* toward the here and now. Our despair, closedness, and malice are the result of our unwillingness to be who we are in the now of our limitations and possibilities. Despair most often results from clinging to or obsessing about some aspect of the past, whether pleasant or horrific. Despair also results from clinging to future expectations that whitewash the real and that presume no consequences from our continued unrealism. Universal Welcome cuts through all that self-created trash with the Good News of a fresh start in sheer honesty.

When our despair is consciously experienced, we need not flee: despair is a *doorway*. It is through the specific doorways of our own despair that we find the *Incomprehensible Peace* of *Universal Forgiveness*. We can allow ourselves to pass through our doorways of despair into a fresh start of living the "I Am" in the Eternal Now. Or we can go on resisting this dawning in our lives of the abiding Truth of *Universal Forgiveness*. The dawning of *Forgiveness* is not merely an idea in our heads. It is not just a belief that we have chosen to bet our lives on. It is an experience of Truth. It is the experience that the Eternal Power that holds us in being also holds no grudges for our many failures to be our true selves.

We typically power our actions with some supposed truth with which we seek to control the world. Reality defeats us, shows us the limitations of our truth and thereby returns us to a place of needing forgiveness and thereby an openness to new truth. Forgiveness means a return to innocence, a return to a fresh start at being ourselves. This innocence is not achieved by us, but it is imparted to us in spite of our guilt and shame. The consequences of our wayward living may continue on in history, but our inner being is purified. As the father in Jesus' parable of the prodigal son symbolizes, we, the offspring of Being, are always welcome home to authentic communion within the "I Am" family. Our being away was the only penalty, the only hell, the only despair. Having come home, new clothing is issued, a hug and a kiss are given, a ring is placed on our finger, and a feast is prepared to celebrate our return. This is the experience of the state of *Universal Forgiveness*. We can miss this amazing state because it has to be accepted by us.

Universal Forgiveness is a deep challenge to each of us, for to embrace it means embracing forgiveness for everyone else as well as ourselves. Yes, this means everyone—our worse enemies, our unfaithful friends, our stupid advisors, *everyone*. To accept our forgiveness means giving up all blaming and judging of others as a means of rendering ourselves innocent. Innocence ceases to be an accomplishment of our behavior or our thinking. By every criterion we have, we may be guilty, but in the Eternal Now of fresh starts, we are innocent as a complete gift from the Way It Is. This means that forgiveness creates a Void in our self-promotion lust—indeed, this Void is an experience of "No Self," to use the Buddhist insight.

The experience of *Universal Forgiveness* can break through our self-images and personality habits as a *state of being* that happens to us from time to time. At such moments, Universal *Forgiveness* has an "event" quality that includes these three aspects: (1) realizing how forgiveness is needed, (2) seeing the presence of forgiveness, and (3) accepting forgiveness for our particular lives. We can also come to recognize *Universal Forgiveness* as a permanent *gift* of our True Being that we never need to leave. To live in the continuing *quality* of *Universal Forgiveness* means resting in the realization that the quality of the ongoing Now is a continuing fresh start. Such a realization means being open to the future with the certainty that my next deeds, even before they are enacted, are forgiven, however tragically these deeds may work out.

Effortless Letting-Be

Our homecoming to Reality requires nothing of us. It is an *Effortless Letting-Be*—a surrender to our forgiveness and to a fresh start in the living Now. Accepting such forgiveness entails accepting this same *Universal Forgiveness* for all other humans, however flawed they have become. These companion humans may or may not accept *Universal Forgiveness* for themselves. But if we accept *Universal Forgiveness* for ourselves, we accept it for all other humans. So *Effortless Letting-Be* entails surrender to the complex human situation in which we live. It entails surrender to being our true being within what is going on in the whole round of our lives. It means a radical honesty in all our relationships with others and with Reality as a whole.

This surrender is a solitary action, and yet this action includes joining the community of those who are in tune with Reality and are detached from the estranged world. Most of humanity is clinging to the world of temporal things. Those who *Effortlessly Let-Be* the real world are also those who realize that everything in the temporal world is impermanent. They need not be ascetics; they may be in love with the birds and the rabbits and the wolves and the tigers and the grasses and the trees and sex and children and the blue sky and even the hurricanes and volcanoes. But *Effortless Letting-Be* includes letting be death and destruction as part of *That* to which the *Effortless Letting-Be* are surrendering. Most of humanity are not "letting be" both the coming to be and the coming not to be. Most of humanity are clinging to something that is being taken away from them, or insisting on something that is not being given to them. Most of humanity are consumed with becoming more secure in wealth, possessions, knowledge, doctrine, love, friends, children, anything that can seem to promote security. Such absolute security does not exist. *Effortless Letting-Be* lets insecurity be.

As all our securities are shaken, we tend to ask, "Who am I?" We can learn that I am not my body, my reputation in society, my parent's child, my accomplishments, my place of residence, my culture, my race, my gender. And I am not my personality, my set of well-established and well-rehearsed pattern of habits. I am not my ego, my self-constructed image of who I think I am. I am a mystery even to myself. I may experience this mysterious "I Am" as a dreadful challenge or as a fascinating release or as both. If I have been a person habituated to being helpful to others, I may sense some dread in having to give that up. I might be able to assist others to see their choices to be or not to be themselves, but I cannot make those choices for them. In that sense, I am not actually needed by others. I cannot help them be themselves. I am not in *control* in that regard. They are on their own where life matters most. And they cannot help me. I am on my own where life matters most. This may be scary. This may be releasing. It may be both. When I enter into the quality of surrender I am calling *"Effortless Letting-Be,"* I am surrendering to being my "I Am" (my True Self). And I am accepting forgiveness for having not been my True Self. And since accepting forgiveness for myself means accepting forgiveness for everyone, accepting forgiveness means choosing to live among people many of whom are choosing to continue their despairing attempts to be other than they are. Passionately obsessing in my judging of others has to go, even though judging remains a useful tool for living my life.

From time to time *"Effortless Letting-Be"* may break through my busy, striving, helpful, judging, overactive, over-controlling self images and personality and be present as a *state of being* that I enjoy for a while. And I can also come to recognize *"Effortless Letting-Be"* as a permanent *quality* of the "I Am" that I never need to leave.

The above three sections have briefly described the three aspects of the "I Am" on the left side of the chart. These are the aspects most related to the past and to memory. I turn next to the three aspects of the "I Am" on the right side of the chart.

These are the aspects most related to the future and to anticipation. I have named them: **Primal Merging**, **Inherent Purity**, and **Attuned Working**—each of which is an aspect of what can be called *freedom* from ego, *freedom* from good and evil, and *freedom* from fate.

Primal Merging

When we view the "I Am" in its relation to the future, we discover our intentionality, our initiative, our freedom to act *beyond the boundaries of the ego or self image t*hat we have constructed to tell ourselves who we are and what we can and cannot do. If I am by habit a shy person, I may discover my freedom to risk intruding myself into contact with others. If I am by habit a boisterous person, I may discover my freedom to calm down into being sensitive to others. *"Primal Merging"* is the name I am giving to this intensely solitary aspect of what we often call "freedom." By *"Primal Merging"* I mean giving up the ego limitations and merging with the larger, more capable, more true-to-reality "I." The emptiness left by our departure from self-image or ego will naturally fill with a quality we can call *"persistent initiative"* or *"freedom."*

In some religious circles we call this initiative "prayer," but I am not yet talking about prayer as a religious practice. I am simply describing the appearance in our deep solitude of the *initiative aspect* of consciousness. By "initiative" I mean the capacity to influence the future. Though the "I Am" does not control the future (the future almost always comes to us as a surprise), our profound initiatives do make a difference in what the future turns out to be. It is as if our initiatives mingle with the massive forces beyond our control to form a future that is a surprise to us as well as a result of our initiatives. These initiatives can be categorized as many types—four types have dominated the Christian devotions of prayer: (1) confessing our unrealism, (2) giving thanks for our life, our possibilities, and our forgiveness, (3) making requests of Reality for our own temporal being and for its further realization, (4) making requests of Reality for specific others and for the general social conditions that care for whole groups of people. Such initiatives involve more than thoughts in the mind; they are acts of inner choice, and they are proposals for body movement and action in the world. The deep interior acts of *Primal Merging* are intentions to engage in the history of the world. They are internal initiatives that change the course of history.

Such initiatives access the power of being the "I Am"—a power that is not an achievement or a possession of the ego or of the personality. The power of initiative is a gift from the Power that posits us in being. Our access of this power is not an accomplishment but a merging, an allowing of our awareness and action to merge with the essential capacity of an *essential freedom* that characterizes our deep being. This deep initiative is a capacity to create "out of nothing" responses that have no cause except our own initiative. It remains true that many of our responses are automatic actions that derive from our genetics or our social conditioning or personality habits. And we can be frequently surprised about the extent to which some old childhood-developed habit imposes itself inappropriately into our present living. But along with all this past-determined behavior, something more exists for us in this living *Now*: an uncaused initiative that no psychological theory can explain.

Our experience of this profound initiative can break through our personality habits as a *state of being* that happens to us from time to time. And we can also come to recognize this *"Primal Merging"* with our inherent *freedom* as a permanent *quality* of the "I Am" that we never need to leave.

Inherent Purity

Inherent Purity is the central aspect of the "I Am" as an agent of action. *Inherent Purity* means the actions of the "I Am" that originate in the clear space of *Freedom*. This aspect of the "I Am" entails living *beyond good and evil*—beyond the stories of the superego that holds our oughts, duties, customs, and morals; beyond the approval of our parents, offspring, friends and other social peers; beyond all the libraries of ethical thought; beyond all the preferences of our own bodies, minds, and habits. *Inherent Purity* is the *pure freedom* to act out of the spacious emptiness of the "I Am" with uncaused, unauthorized, unprecedented options of creative response.

This confident purity of action is an *audacious boldness*, a *Freedom* so primordially rooted in our deep being that it shocks our personality habits into a sideline share of our living. This *audacious boldness* uses our personality gifts when appropriate, but will also contradict all personality habits and values without qualms. All impulses to be righteous in terms of superego conditioning are bypassed; a new form of righteousness reigns: *essential freedom* itself. We spend most of our lives squeezing our scope of action into some narrow box of morality or social acceptability. Nevertheless, a deep *audacious boldness* is our true being. That we often prefer being guilty before our social norms rather than alive in an innocent liberty does not contradict the truth that living *"beyond good and evil"* characterizes the real "me." In spite of the fact that our parents, our community, our friends, our enemies teach us good and evil, we are each an *audacious boldness* that uses these teachings or leaps beyond these teaching as we deem appropriate to the situation. Within this understanding of our true being, we can recognize how it is true that eating with Adam and Eve from the tree of the knowledge of good and evil is a fall from authenticity, not a step upward.

Engaging our essential *freedom* in temporal action is engaging our *Inherent Purity*. Engaging this *freedom* is the liberation of the "True Me." But because we cling so tightly to our moral certainties and ethical principles, *freedom* may seem dreadful. Indeed, this dread of our *deep freedom* recurs whenever we wish to feel certain about a particular decision. In the real world all our choices are ambiguous. There are many ways to view each choice. There are many values to consider, and some of them will have to be negated in each specific choice. The boldness of such living is truly audacious. Nevertheless, fear of this *Freedom* can turn to glory as we realize that *Freedom* is our *Inherent Purity*, our Righteousness, our Authenticity, our true "me," our "I Am" of profound humanness.

This awesome initiative of *Inherent Purity* can break through our personality habits as a *state of being* that happens to us from time to time. And we can also come to recognize that *Inherent Purity* is a permanent *quality* of the "I Am" that we never need to leave.

Attuned Working

When our enigmatic attentionality pays attention to the "I Am" in its relation to the future, we also discover something about the Overall Reality in which the "I Am" is embedded. Reality is not a fixed fate automatically working itself out like a piece of recorded music. Rather, Reality is an "open-to-options" fluidity that can turn out in a large number of different ways, many of which can seem impossible or miraculous to our self-contained personality and ego establishment. It is in this sense that *"Attuned Working"* means living *beyond fate*. It means giving up all fatalism. This does not mean that we create our own reality, as so many false teachers claim. We do indeed create the worlds that our minds believe to be true, but these creations are all human made and therefore illusory in some or all of their components. The effects of these self-created mind-worlds on the actual course of history are unpredictable and typically tragic in some way or another. These self-created mind-worlds always involve some sort of neglect of Reality and thereby yield disappointments so extreme that despair eventually overwhelms the so-called "reality creator." So I am calling this aspect of the "I Am" not "creating reality" but *"Attuned Working."*

The Jesus in John's Gospel says, "My Father is working still, and I am working." That saying expresses *Attuned Working*—working in the context of "what-is-doing" in the overall course of things. *Attuned Working* pays attention to what is going on and then is obedient to that "working," not in some robotic fashion, but as a free being attuned to the real options. Such living can be very powerful; our tiny little actions can instigate an echo from the whole of Reality.

When out of his deep awareness and honesty, Martin Luther nailed some discussion topics on a cathedral door, he could not have imagined the echo Reality would give to his action. It was as if the whole of European history turned on the pivot of this man's persistent working. Some of Luther's responses may not have been well tuned, but he nevertheless rang a bell of *freedom* that enabled nobles and peasants to break with the stodgy traditions and the oppressive familiarities of that time and place. Many of the consequences of Luther's actions were unintended and some may be judged tragic. Nevertheless, his attunement to what was so in his time joined with the existing trends and potentials, creating an avalanche of historical change. Luther's *Attuned Working,* combined with the *Attuned Working* of others, set in motion a new era of human living that was less estranged from the deep Truth of our human existing.

In the lives of most of us, *Attuned Working* may not be Luther-level dramatic, but each of us has in our essential being this same potential for *Attuned Working* within the times of our lives. We are manifesting *Attuned Working* when we act out of our sense of how the cultural, political, and economic liberation of women is relevant for all of us in today's world. We are manifesting *Attuned Working* when we act out of our sense the relevance for all of us of a serious care of the Earth—its climate, its soils, its waterways, its diversity of species, and so forth. Our *freedom* can manifests as *Attuned Working,* as creative living within the actual challenges of our times. Flight from these challenges is not *freedom*; it is cowardly compulsion, or greedy obsession, or some other cop-out of estrangement from our real lives.

We may also call this aspect of our essential "I Am" *"obedient implementation,"* for it involves the application of our intentional power to the historical circumstances within which our intentional power is to be manifest. By "implementation," I am talking about getting things done—a quiet adding of something useful or perhaps joining a march of protest on some sick Jerusalem that may result in a noticeable uproar. Such placements of our bodies may not result in torture or death, but scorn of some sort can be expected as part of the overall response to any persistent action that is attuned to the actual course of Reality. Illusions are so firmly established in the lives of the multitudes, and especially the lives of most current leaders, that we can expect scorn and surprisingly angry persecution from some members of the well-established "Liars Kingdom."

Attuned Working can break through our personality habits as a *state of being* that happens to us from time to time. And we can also come to realize *Attuned Working* as a permanent *quality* of the "I Am" that we never need to leave.

Three more aspects of this model of the "I Am" remain to be described. All three have to do with what many call "Spirit love," where that term includes compassion, loving kindness, the fire for justice, and deep respect for all people. **Autonomous Strength** has to do with the Spirit love of self. **Out-flowing Compassion** has to do with the Spirit love of others. And **Enchantment with Being** has to do with Spirit love for the power that posits us—a love for the Ground of our existence, for Reality, for Being. We can appropriately call this Ground "God" only when the word "God" indicates a state of devotion or love for this Final Ground of all Being.

Autonomous Strength

Autonomous Strength is the exceedingly deep, solitary aspect of the "I Am" that stands between the quality of solitude described as Transparent Attention and the quality of solitude described as Primal Merging. *Autonomous Strength* is the core aspect of solitude. By *"Autonomous"* we mean that we are realizing the solitary dimension of being who I am, and that we are moving beyond the need for other-directedness of any sort. We see that we have no need for approval from or status among other people. Further, we have no need to be judged in terms of our outward achievements, physical qualities, or mental capabilities. By the term *"Strength"* in this formula, we mean an inward quality of personal invincibility that no outward events can shake.

In the Hindu collection of goddesses, there is a deity named "Kali." She is pictured with a two-edged sword and a belt of skulls. She is seen as a goddess of destruction, but when we access her meaning more fully, we understand her as the slayer of all falsehood. When we arrive at the deep places of our autonomous being, we experience the sword of Kali slicing away every self-image, every habit of the personality, every identification with the temporal aspects of our being, every hope of avoiding the full impact of our finitude or escaping from it. As all these impediments are slain, we find our true strength. We are Kali. We are the invincible truth of our existence. Nothing whatsoever can touch us or oppose us. We are supported by the Ground of our Being —supported as an unstoppable fire of destruction toward everything that is false, illusory, partial, incomplete, weak, silly, sentimental, or foolish. Swinging the sword of Kali is what it means to have the *courageous heart* of loving our true selves.

Too often we interpret "love of self" as an indulgence of our present set of understandings, desires, or patterns of living. Such love is the love of a false self. The true "I Am" is an enigma, a mystery, a vastness of potentialities that baffles us and challenges us and scalds us with the hot flames of overwhelming demand to be more than we are comfortable with being. We cannot claim to love ourselves if we flee from this inherent awesomeness of our being—if we flee to some comfortable self-construction of our own making.

This *Autonomous Strength* can break through our personality habits as a *state of being* that happens to us from time to time. And we can also come to realize this strength as a permanent *quality* of the "I Am" that we never need to leave.

Enchantment with Being

Enchantment with Being is an aspect of the "I Am" that stands between our *Universal Forgiveness* and our *Inherent Purity*. *Enchantment with Being* also stands between *Autonomous Strength* and *Out-flowing Compassion* as the core quality of Spirit love. *Enchantment with Being* is the core aspect of the "I Am"; it is an intensification or enrichment for all the other aspects of our "true being."

To grasp the poetry in the term *"Enchantment,"* we might recall our relation with our first love partner, a person who captivated our enduring attention day and night. Perhaps we have been enchanted with a community we belonged to, with some work we did, with some place we lived, or with some specific time in our lives. With the word *"Enchantment"* we mean an unusually intense attention and intention toward a consuming focus. Our *Enchantment with Being* is the very fullest intensification we can give the word "enchantment." Being is the quintessence of intensity, so *Enchantment with Being* is the quintessence of intensity. It is not quite accurate to call this intensification "ecstasy" if "ecstasy" means strong emotional qualities. Experiences of ecstasy may attend our *Enchantment with Being*, but Enchantment *with Being* is more subtle than ecstasy; it is a more enduring experience than moments of intense feeling. I am proposing the poetic phrase *"Joyous Stillness."* *Enchantment with Being* is also a sort of *Rest*. "Our hearts are restless until we rest in this Rest" (Augustine). It is the "promised land" where all is at rest, where abundance flows with milk and honey (or whatever else symbolizes the good fortune of experiencing such a radical completion). Though we may experience *Enchantment with Being* as *Still* and *Restful*, it is at the same time the presence of the full intensity of our experience of the "No Self."

It might seem that this intensity or completion is very rare, but this need not be true. *Enchantment with Being* most frequently manifests as a glow within one of the other aspects of the "No Self." Perhaps it is transparent attention with a glow, forgiveness with a glow, detachment with a glow, initiative with a glow, boldness with a glow, implementation with a glow, courageous heart with a glow, out-flowing compassion with a glow. And by "glow" I mean nothing more than some sort of Awe being occasioned by the enduring Awesomeness of the Wholeness of Reality.

Enchantment with Being may be experienced as a breaking out of our personality habits into a *state of being* that happens to us from time to time. And we can also come to recognize this as a permanent *quality* of the "I Am" that we never need to leave.

Out-flowing Compassion

Out-flowing Compassion is an aspect of the "I Am" that stands between the quality of other-relatedness I called *"Effortless Letting-Be"* and the quality of other-relatedness I called *"Attuned Working."* *Out-flowing Compassion* is Spirit love in relation to the outward world of others, the Earth, and the cosmos. *"Out-flowing"* means attention and movement away from our preoccupation with inwardness toward whatever is occurring in our actual encounters with the surrounding processes of Reality. The Strength described as *Autonomous Strength* is now experienced as a power moving toward a boundless affirmation of others. *"Compassion"* means the power to be *with* others in all their joy, fun, pleasure, pain, horror, and despair.

Out-flowing Compassion is the opposite of drawing back into our safe and familiar places of inner experience. *Out-flowing Compassion* means the capacity to be fully present with whoever enters our scope of engagement. This includes both our friends and those who are enemies of our deepest values and causes. It is as if our only true enemies are the temptations to withdraw into our own greed, contentment, distractions, and defensive bigotries. *Out-flowing Compassion* does not mean serving our own personality or someone else's personality. It means serving in ourselves and in others the realization of the "I Am" essence of being our true being. The state of compassion can include feelings of anger and sadness toward the corruption, depravity, and meanness of humanity as well as feelings of hope and joy over the restoration of the "I Am" qualities in others and toward the social manifestations of justice and well being. This state of compassion extends to all the living forms of our planet and to all the cosmic forces that support these alive ones. Compassion includes action to change the social structures that care for all humans, all life forms, all processes of the planet.

Out-flowing Compassion is expressed in action, but can also be expressed as a silent presence. *Out-flowing Compassion* is a *singular devotion* rooted in our *Enchantment with Being*. It is not a scattered activism or a series of distractions: it is the unifying of our many tasks into one devotion. It is not other-directedness: it flows from our own being, not from the whims of others. But it flows toward others; it does not focus on our own inward qualities. In that sense it is self-forgetful. And this compassion is also an out-flowing attitude toward our own being as part of the Whole of Being toward which we are flowing. *Out-flowing Compassion* is the fulfillment of the familiar commandment to love our neighbors as we love ourselves.

Out-flowing Compassion may be experienced as a breaking out of our personality habits into a *state of being* that happens to us from time to time. And we can also come to realize this flow as a permanent *quality* of the "I Am" that we never need to leave.

The Implications of "I Am" Description for Interreligious Dialogue

The "I Am" is an inexhaustible actuality, describable in many different religious languages and perpetually filling libraries with books and talks on these many related topics. Dialogue among the adherents of the various long-standing religious traditions can enrich our "I Am" awareness. We have already indicated how Hindu antiquity explored the "I Am" with the Atman concept. Buddhism has used the concept "no self" to make clear that the "I Am" is an empty space beyond self-image and personality habits. Christianity explores the "I Am" through the concept of "Holy Spirit" and its various subcategories—trust, love, freedom, the peace that is beyond understanding, the joy unspeakable, the hope that does not disappoint. Holy Spirit is sometimes likened to the breath of Eternity, a wind that comes from we know not whence and carries us forth to we know not whither. However we choose to make these comparisons, most, if not all, long-standing religions include explorations into the various aspects of the "I Am."

All the long-standing religious heritages require fresh clarity on the "I Am" in order for the greatness of these traditions to be rediscovered and translated for our times. A focus on the enduring qualities of the "I Am" is key for fruitful interreligious dialogue. Interreligious dialogue will flourish if it is about the "I Am," rather than about beliefs or moralities. As each heritage witnesses to its experience of the "I Am," it can enrich the other heritages. Such dialogue can be conducted with interest, curiosity, and respect. When the emphasis is on beliefs or moralities, the result is most often some sort of misunderstanding, disrespect, or even warfare.

The phrase, "That is just your belief" is too often heard in conversations between religious persons or between religious and "secular" adherents. Such a phrase needs to be understood as a statement of disrespect. Interreligious dialogue is not about beliefs; it is about my witness to the "I Am" and your witness to the "I Am." I respect your witness by simply hearing it and then by looking within my own "I Am" to see if your witness points to something that is also true for me. We may have some disagreements about the "I Am" and about how to best talk about it, but such disagreements need not mean disrespect. These disagreements can be received as challenges to each other to look deeper and think more clearly, and poeticize more powerfully about what we each see to be the reality of the "I Am" that we each experience from within our own unique journey.

Such interreligious dialogue leads us to understand that the social process we call "religion" has originated in every human society because religious practices are needed to help us access the "I Am" and give form to living the "I Am" life. Religions can be viewed in all their arbitrary, historical development as manifestations of a social process among all the other social processes: education, life style, economics, politics, etc. And at the same time, religion can be seen in its capacity to point beyond itself to the essential "I Am" which is true for every human being. It has been said that music is a *universal* language understood by all cultures. The same can be said of religion, if religion is rescued from its preoccupation with divisive beliefs and unbending moralities and restored to its true function, assisting us to access the "I Am."

In Part Four I will explore further the nature and function of religion—how healthy religion is an expression of and an inquiry into the unfathomable "I Am" as well as an inquiry into useful methods for the full realization of the "I Am" in the living of our lives within Final Reality or authenticity. But first, I will include two more chapters on the enigma of Wonder. I will describe in Chapter 15 nine habits of escape from the "I Am" that parallel the nine aspects of the "I Am" described in this chapter. Then in Chapter 16 I will describe how humans typically journey from these states of escape to their home base in this "I Am" of profound humanness.

Chapter 15
Nine Habits of Escape from the "I Am"

As we move from infantile immediacy and build our habits of personality, we begin to confuse the habits that we have built with the essence of our nature. The "I Am" is not something we have built or can build or need to build. It is already built with our birth into humanness. Yet as an infant we are only a potential for realizing the "I Am" in a conscious and intentional way. The usual course of development is to confuse our potential to be an "I Am" manifestation with the habits of living we have built to survive. We have learned to call these habits "ourselves." These habits are what we also call our "personality." Having a personality is not bad; it is indeed necessary for the practical living of our lives in the societies in which we dwell. The issue for our consciousness is identifying who we are. We are more than our personality. We are the being that built our personality. We are that mysterious, courageous, awe-filled being that I was describing in the last chapter as the essential "I Am."

So when we identify with our personality or with that part of our personality that we are aware of and with which we want to be identified, we have fallen away from our true being. It is this misidentification that is the core flaw we must overcome to be authentically human. It is this misidentification that is the root of our despair, malice, and compulsions. It is an escape from our essential being, from our best-case scenario for living. We call it an "escape" because we do indeed flee from our true greatness because we find it too demanding, too grim, or too mysterious.

Our functional and dysfunctional personality habits can become a "place" to which we escape. The enneagram heritage has depicted nine types of personality. One of the interesting aspects of this model of nine personality types is that they correspond one-to-one with the nine aspects of the "I Am" described in the last chapter. Each personality type of the enneagram heritage can be viewed as a mode of escape from one of these nine aspects of the "I Am." The following chart is constructed to be an overlay of these nine personality types upon the previous chart of the nine aspects of the "I Am." In each case the escape to personality habits is substituting for an "I Am" essence. On the following chart you will see the personality numbers of the enneagram heritage and by each number is written a few words of poetic description of the way in which that personality type is a falling away from the home base of the "I Am" essence that occupies that space on the previous chart.

For example, identifying with personality type five can be described as a falling away from *Transparent Attention* into *The Greed of Mental Aloofness*. For each of the nine aspects of the "I Am" I will describe a state of falling away, using the enneagram personality types to do this. I will discuss these in the order I used for the "I Am" discussion rather in the numerical order of the enneagam types. So to get this order of discussion in mind, compare the following chart with the chart in the last chapter. Then read the following paragraphs that describe more fully how a personality type can be a fall from an aspect of our true nature—how each of us, as we attempt to identify who we are, substitute personality habits for the "I Am" of our essential being.

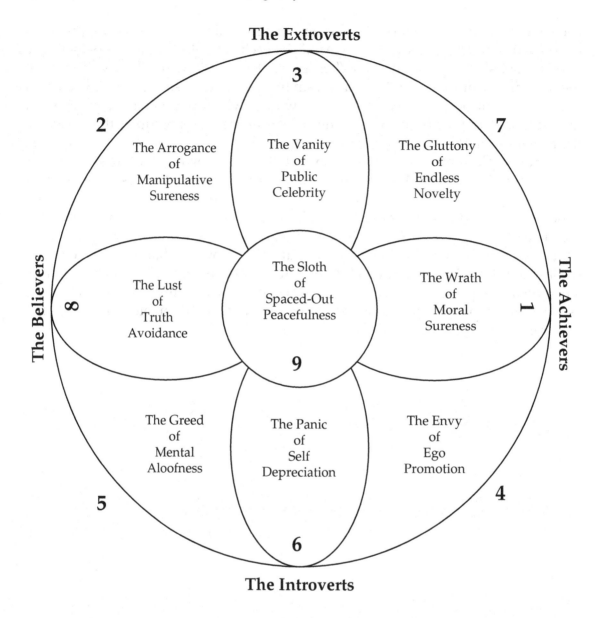

The Extroverts

The Introverts

I will describe each of these escapes from the "I Am" of profound humanness in the same order that I described the "I Am" aspects in the previous chapter. These will only be short spins. For a more thorough examination of enneagram personality types, I recommend *The Spiritual Dimension of the Enneagram: Nine Faces of the Soul* by Sandra Maitri. (New York, Jeremy P. Tarcher/Putnam: 2000). I also work with the personality types as forms of estrangement in *Jacob's Dream: A Christian Inquiry into Spirit Realization (New York, iUniverse: 2008)* Chapters 11 through 14.

Type 5. The Greed of Mental Aloofness

As a mode of escape personality type 5 is an escape from the *Transparent Attention* aspect of the "I Am." Everyone can manifest this mode of escape to some extent, but certain people have a gift for it—even a passion for it. Personality type 5 persons are the shy wallflowers, the recluses who are also busy-minded people. Their busy mindedness can be busy about almost anything. A personality type 5 might be like Howard Hughes busy with airplanes and old movies. A more moderately talented 5 might spend most of his or her waking time with face-in-a-book or scanning several news magazines every month. When challenged to begin an intense, intimate relation, these aloof ones experience a discomforting demand to come out of their shells. This is especially hard if the challenge includes emotional honesty and accurate reporting on their secret lives. The 5's escape has to do with hiding in the forests of the mind. The typical 5 tends to come out energetically only in groups that express interest in whatever is the preoccupation of that 5's mind. Often that mental preoccupation is so specialized or so unorthodox that only a few satisfying companions can be found. And even those companions may feel it necessary to provide most of the initiative to have a real relationship. Type 5 persons may be talkative on many subjects, but they tend to be postponers with regard to putting their talk into action. The exceptions to this, like Howard Hughes or Georgia O'Keeffe, move out into the world in a whirlwind of genius and then retreat almost completely from enjoying the celebrity they may have occasioned.

Having a personality that overemphasizes mental gifts need not mean that such persons cannot access their profound life and use their intellectual gifts in compassionate ways. A. H. Almaas is a good example of a 5 with such intelligent compassion. The escape is identifying with the mental gifts and the mental products of those gifts as a substitute for the type of knowing that is transparent to the deeper matters of consciousness. Living in their minds rather than in their whole mysterious being results in being functionally stupid and also cruel through a neglect of other people, social concerns, and even one's own self.

Greed is a quality of this estrangement because the 5 is hoarding information and because living in the mind requires protection from the slings and arrows of ordinary life. This mode of escape requires some sort of ivory tower in which to retreat from those aspects of life that challenge too deeply a treasured mental construction or perhaps a lack of thoughtfulness in an arena where wisdom was assumed. The 5 personality fears the insecurity of ignorance.

Type 8. The Lust of Truth Avoidance

As a mode of escape, personality type 8 is an escape from the *Universal Forgiveness* aspect of the "I Am." Everyone can manifest this mode of escape to some extent, but certain people have a propensity for it—even an obsession with it. Type 8s are the outgoing, often warlike individuals who seem to live a life in constant conflict with other people's "wrong-headedness," deemed so from the perspective of "their truth." The type 8's truth may not include an openness to new truth that a complete lover of truth might manifest. These persons are in an estranged state because they insist on being leaders in terms of their all-too-confident conclusions. They get things done, but on their own terms. It is difficult to oppose them without engaging in some stubborn argumentation. And however great the wreckage they may cause, they tend to have little remorse, for they see themselves as the truthful ones, however deep their lies may be. They can drop one lie and go on to a next lie without ever admitting fully that the abandoned position was tragic. They don't stop to learn fully from their mistakes or to probe to a depth of truth that would make a significant difference in their living.

Having a personality that overemphasizes strong leadership need not mean that such persons cannot access their profound life and use their leadership gifts with compassion. Martin Luther King Jr. is an example of an 8 who used his leadership gifts compassionately. Susan Sarandon and Franklin D. Roosevelt may be other examples of the compassionate 8. The escape means identifying with this personality pattern in order to avoid the Truth of Universal Forgiveness. Personality type 8 tends to avoid experiencing their own flaws seriously enough to need forgiveness. And the notion of a universal forgiveness for all persons, including the enemies that the 8 is fighting, can be felt by type 8 as a deep offense.

Lust is a quality of this estrangement in the sense that these persons tend to insist upon their success, their pleasure, their way, their goals, their perfection, their leadership, their needs, and so forth.

Type 2. The Arrogance of Manipulative Sureness

As a mode of escape, personality type 2 is an escape from the *Effortless Letting Be* aspect of the "I Am." Everyone can manifest this mode of escape to some extent, but certain people have a propensity toward it—even an obsession with it. Personality type 2 persons are emotionally sensitive, outgoing persons who typically meddle in other people's business. In a Jane Austen novel one meets characters who count themselves matchmakers and fixers for other people's lives but are somewhat blind to their own lives, especially their own needs relative to accessing their more profound potentials. As emotionally powerful and influential persons, 2s make themselves available as helpers of who seems to them to need help. They often become trapped in codependent relations in which needy people lean on the 2, and enslave the 2 with an ongoing neediness and refusal to care for their own selves.

Having a personality that overemphasizes helpfulness and personal relationships need not mean that such persons cannot access their profound life and use their interpersonal gifts with a tough-love type of compassion. Florence Nightingale and Desmond Tutu may be examples of the effectively compassionate 2. The escape is in identifying with their being an emotionally sincere and helpful person and thereby avoiding the strength and realism of "Letting Be" the inevitable processes of Reality.

Arrogance is a quality that describes this estrangement, for the type 2 personality tends toward a delusory arrogation of their "celebrated" powers—attributing to themselves an illusory capacity to fix what it is not within their ability to fix or their business to fix.

Type 4. The Envy of Ego Promotion

As a mode of escape, personality type 4 is an escape from the *Primal Merging* aspect of the "I Am." Everyone can manifest this mode of escape to some extent, but certain people have a gift for it—even an obsession with it. Personality type 4 persons are deeply sensitive people almost to the extent of mixing up their own feelings with the feelings of others. They also tend to be creative people—as musicians or artists or anything that requires emotional sensitivity and expressiveness. Not all 4s are talented, but those who are talented often make contributions to the overall culture that we count as treasures. They often lead us into deeper experiences. They tend to see themselves as special people with regard to personal gifts that most people lack. And if they do not have the personal gifts they want, they tend to be envious of those that do have them. "Self," in the sense of ego strengths, is a big deal for these persons.

Having a personality that overemphasizes personal creative potentials need not mean that such persons cannot access their profound life and use their sensibilities with effective compassion for others. Martha Graham and Paul Simon are well known examples of effective type 4 personalities. The escape is identifying with one's strong ego strengths and thereby avoiding something very much deeper, namely the raw freedom that is beyond ego, beyond personality habits, beyond anything that pertains to promoting or defending self worth.

Envy is a quality that describes this estrangement, for the type 4 personality tends to so focus upon possessing special gifts that they may be envious of others who seem to possess the wanted gifts in more abundance. This can appear as a sort of over-competitiveness toward their gifted companions and an uncharitableness or controlling attitude toward their lesser-gifted companions. All this is a distraction from the real issue of accessing one's own deep freedom in order to shape one's own life in the directions desired or needed or called for.

Type 1. The Wrath of Moral Sureness

As a mode of escape, personality type 1 is an escape from the *Inherent Purity* aspect of the "I Am." Everyone can manifest this mode of escape to some extent, but certain people have a propensity toward it—even an obsession with it. Personality type 1 individuals are principled persons. They may be social reformers. They may stick up for the little guy. Even when they are fairly traditional, they tend to be picky persons who know what is right and do what is right, as they understand it. We often count on them; for they tend to be persons who get things done, and get them done right. Flexibility may not be one of their virtues, or it may be. They are not likely to lie for us, cheat for us, or compromise their core values. They tend to be markedly assertive persons who can seem quite sure about what they are doing. They have no fear about carrying out stern critiques of others. They may be smooth and skilled at promoting what they think is right and true. They may be boring bigots.

Having a personality that overemphasizes moral rightness need not mean that such persons cannot access their profound life and use their tough-mindedness with compassion. Perhaps Ralph Nader and Jane Fonda are type 1 examples of tough-minded compassion. The type 1 mode of escape is identifying with a taken-for-granted rightness resident in their superego, their upbringing, or their ethical thoughtfulness. The escape is seeing such rightness as the "real me," a rightness that is substituted for *the inherent purity* of that essential freedom that knows that all choices must be carried out in a world of ambiguities in which good and evil are always relative to chosen contexts.

Wrath is a quality that describes this estrangement, for the type-1 personality tends to be resentful of violations of their principles and they tend to put the energy of anger into their careful or reckless campaigns of living.

Type 7. The Gluttony of Endless Novelty

As a mode of escape, personality type 7 is an escape from the *Attuned Working* aspect of the "I Am." Everyone can manifest this mode of escape to some extent, but certain people have a propensity or an obsession with this mode of escape. Personality type 7 persons are restless activists who fear that they may miss something or need something different from what has become too routine and boring. They tend to be playful, energetic, always in motion, and often charismatic in their outgoing attention and innovative leadership. We tend to like them until we get a sense of how burned out they can become and how needy they may be for something more. Settling into one thing is seldom their choice. They may astonish us with the number of plates they keep spinning in the air. Like an Albert Schweitzer they may do all these things well, but more often each of their many things tend to be superficial and short lived.

Having a personality that overemphasizes enthusiasm for novelty need not mean that such persons cannot access their profound life and use their enthusiasm with compassion. Carol Burnett and Leonard Bernstein are probably type 7 personalities who put their enthusiasm to good use. The escape here is identifying with the style of experiencing fresh activities that excite and charm and foster enthusiasm. This restlessness is an escape from being attuned in one's actions to the Ground of Being that calls for an ongoing consistency through thick and thin. This entails an obedience that seems to crimp the restless style of personality 7, even as it leads toward a truer freedom—a freedom from restless novelty into the creative persistence that knows itself connected to the deep matters of living.

Gluttony is a quality that describes this estrangement, for the type-7 personality tends to substitute many novel experiences for the richness of staying in touch with that profound humanness that is always fresh because it is being supported by and called for by the Eternal workings of the cosmos.

Type 6. The Panic of Self Depreciation

As a mode of escape, personality type 6 is an escape from the *Autonomous Strength* aspect of the "I Am." Everyone can manifest this mode of escape to some extent, but certain people have an obsession for it. Personality type 6 persons are worried and fearful about being inadequate, not being successful, not being liked, not being accepted by their chosen peers. They are sensitive persons, sensitive to others and sensitive to their own gifts and failures. This sensitivity turns up more and more evidence that one is sub par. So persons of personality type 6 tend to make extra efforts toward being loyal and friendly and useful in order to compensate for this underlying panic about self-worth. Some 6 personalities risk dangerous things to prove to themselves and others that they are not fearful, not worthless, but rather bold, unusual, and worthy of attention. So the 6 personality may manifest as a compliant office worker or as a daring mountain climber, stunt driver, or other impulsive risk taker.

Having a personality that emphasizes sensitivity need not mean that such persons cannot access their profound life and use their sensitivities with compassion. Perhaps Princess Diana and Jack Lemmon show us the outgoing and compassionate 6. The escape is an identification with self-images of depreciation, weakness, unsureness, unlovableness, and so on. These perceptions of self are substituted for the autonomous strength that is the true nature of the profound human. What is lacking is allowing the invincible quality of this deep self to undergird the sensitivities about the inevitable weaknesses and foibles had by all of us finite creatures.

Panic is a quality that describes this estrangement, for type 6 personalities tend to believe they are flawed and limited, weak and poor, and thus not up to the challenges that come to them. What is missing is an enduring experience of that solitary strength for opposing all falseness and genuinely loving the essential, honest, and invincible "I Am" with an affirmation that knows no limits.

Type 9. The Sloth of Spaced-Out Peacefulness

As a mode of escape, personality type 9 is an escape from the *Enchantment with Being* aspect of the "I Am." Everyone can manifest this mode of escape to some extent, but certain people have a propensity for it—a profound acquiescence to it. Personality type 9 persons are the most other-directed of all persons, not out of fear, but out of an anger toward conflict, toward being challenged to manifest the inner energy to participate in the conflicts and struggles of real life. So they make peace with everyone, and they try to enable peace between other persons and among the persons in their groups. They promote peace at the cost of their own integrity or at the cost of not getting done what needs doing. Personality type 9 can be capable and effective in their living and appear to be the most agreeable of all persons. But underneath this outward mask is a rage toward the demanding nature of life. When peace cannot be made in a given circumstance, the 9 personality tends to go to sleep or space out into a trance of inattention.

Having a personality that overemphasizes peacemaking need not mean that such persons cannot access their profound life and use their interpersonal gifts with compassion. Perhaps Abraham Lincoln and Ingrid Bergman show us the compassionate 9. The escape in this instance is about identifying with a conflict-free existence that does not and cannot exist. The escape is from that seemingly uncomfortable energy that it takes to deal with the full realities that humans face. What is missing is the realization of a profound love for that fullness of Being that includes one's own anger, intensity, and passion for truth, as well as the huge challenges and conflicts that characterize real world living.

Sloth is a quality that describes this estrangement, for the type 9 personality tends to "cop out" rather than endure and/or enjoy the full intensity of living.

Type 3. The Vanity of Public Celebrity

As a mode of escape, personality type 3 is an escape from the *Out-flowing Compassion* aspect of the "I Am." Everyone can manifest this mode of escape to some extent, but certain people have a strong pull toward it—even an obsession with it. Personality type 3 persons tend to be (or are at least are committed to be) accomplished persons. They see their outward roles in society as having great importance. They strongly seek the good opinion of others and of themselves in relation to others. This can take many forms, as many forms as there are roles in society. But the roles that most capture the dreams of type-3 persons are the roles that have minor or major celebrity. "Beautiful movie star" is definitely a role that attracts some type-3 personalities. If such extreme celebrity is not feasible, then some form of beautiful, successful, admired, or accomplished style becomes type 3's self-required program for living. A type-3 personality wants to be a star in their own perception of themselves. And they do tend to shine. They make waves in a group. They typically make fabulous first impressions, but as we get to know them they may be found to be without inner substance or at least hiding troubling features that have yet to be addressed.

Having a personality that overemphasizes outward roles need not mean that such persons cannot access their profound life and use their gifts for an outgoing presence with remarkable compassion for others. Perhaps Bill Clinton and Barbara Streisand show us some of the gifts of a compassionate 3. The escape is identifying with their outward roles at the expense of an inward integrity and full development of their profound humanness. The escape is from a full inwardness into the shell of some outward role. This escape is a form of self-forgetfulness, but it is the forgetfulness of failing to nurture the self in its deep inward aspects and thereby not accessing fully one's authentic out-flowing compassion. When that essential compassion is realized, then their outgoingness can be a self-forgetful flow into the tasks of being "with" others in all their sorrow, happiness, despair, and joy.

Vanity is a quality that describes this estrangement, for persons of personality type 3 tend to be vain in the sense of adoring their own outward appearance and the effects they make on others. They do this at the expense of their own inner life and a genuine love for others.

These brief sketches of nine ways of escaping from Reality are only a scratch on the rock of this boundless topic. Nothing is more involuted and difficult to master than the myriad ways that human being have invented to not be human. And the enneagram model provides only one of the many ways that have been invented to organize the topic of escape from Reality. It is not my aim in this chapter to wrap up this subject, but to convince the reader that this propensity we humans have to escape from the "I Am" of our essential human nature is very deep and has a far-reaching impact on all human living. Certainly, we cannot understand the impulse of humans to invent religions and to pervert the religions they invent, unless we have a firm grasp of the propensity of humans to flee their inherent grandeur—to flee from the full challenge of being a species on this planet that is conscious of being conscious and is conscious of the gift that such consciousness can be when fully accessed as a glorious part of the life of the planet.

Chapter 16
The Journey into Profound Humanness

Profound Humanness is our home, but it takes a journey to get there. We are away from home. In Chapter 15 I described what "away-from-home" looks like. In Chapters 12, 13, and 14, I described what "home" looks like. Our true humanity is profound, a life of Wonder, a journey into Awe, a courageous heart of autonomous strength, a joyous stillness of enchantment with Being, a holistic devotion of out-flowing compassion, and much more.

So how do we get "home" from our particular ways of being "away-from-home"? Experiencing the futility, hopelessness, and despair of being away from home is step one. We are away-from-home because we somehow thought a particular "away" was home. As long as that illusion reigns, we will not journey home. The journey home begins with a doorway called "despair," despair over a life of being away-from-home. There is no other doorway home than facing our despair over being away. When conscious despair begins to eat holes in our contentment, we are on our way home, or we might be if two other blessings happen.

Blessing number two is thoroughly noticing the deep truth that we are welcome home, that Reality with a capital "R" does not punish or condemn us for being away. Away was the punishment. In step one, away is consciously experienced as hell. Step two is hearing, noticing, believing that home is forgiveness and a fresh start in being our true being.

Blessing number three is discovering that we can choose to accept this grand gift of being home. Healing our lives is as simple and as complicated as that. We balk at all three steps. We don't want to be conscious of our despair. We can wallow in our despair, rather than see that doorway of forgiveness and a fresh start. We can flee from the intensity for having to choose home and keep choosing it. We can resent this whole set up that human living is either a trap of despair, malice, and compulsion or a demand to live a deep trust, love, and freedom. We can recoil in shock that all we have to bring to the events of our healing is our despair, malice, and bondage. We come always in need of forgiveness, and that forgiveness is our only righteousness. This fresh start in glorious realism is never an accomplishment, but a complete gift, a gift that requires an intense deed of freedom in doing the gift of realism with our whole lives.

Having read this book this far, you may have grasped some of the ways that you are not at home and experienced further insight on what being home might mean. If so, all that is left to be more fully home is to notice that you are welcome home and access the opportunity to choose to be home. You will, of course, need to continue choosing being home over all the temptations to return to some foreign land of estrangement. It was John Wesley with help from Joseph Wesley Mathews who taught me that arriving home is both 100% gift and 100% my choice. Though this does not match my traditional mathematics, this paradox is 100% true. Once I am home, I have to opt to be home and dedicate my life to living at home.

There is nothing more to say except that home keeps expanding in wonder and newness, and that coming home is never entirely over. It has seemed to me that in the early days of this homecoming process, home is like a visitation from some other universe. At first home seems strange, a mountaintop experience, a special retreat, an unusual state of being that interrupts what we have considered to be "normal."

Then somewhere along the way, home becomes "normal," and being away from home becomes the "abnormal." My core identification of myself changes. I begin to see myself as a profound being who also has a personality, instead of being a personality who from time to time has experiences of my profundity. This turning point in the homecoming journey transforms everything. It means experiencing that nothing is more important to me than coming home and staying home, because I see that this profound home is my home, the home that I am made for, the home that is the best case scenario for my one and only life.

But even the just mentioned profound turning point is not the end of the journey home. I still have many recalcitrant elements in my life that do not desire to stay at home. Like unruly dogs, these elements have to be trained to stay at home. Perhaps another metaphor is better—certain elements in my life are still melting into the fires of profound living. In this sense the journey home is never over. That is why we need religious practices. We may have outgrown some religious practices, but we still need practices that enable us to come home and stay home. Being home does not mean an end to the need for religious practices, but the beginning of a whole new understanding of religious practices and why we deeply need them.

I turn now to *Part Four: The Enigma of Religion,* in which I will share a fresh definition of religion and show how the practice of "good" religion can be good for us.

Part Four

What
Is
Religion?

Table of Contents for
Part Four: What Is Religion?

17. The Death of Mythic Space and the Redefinition of Religion
18. The Origin of Religion, a Speculative Story
19. Religion as Practice
20. Religion as a Social Process
21. The Vital Variety of Religious Practices

Introduction to Part Four

"Religion" has become in some circles a synonym for superstition, or at least a suspicion of weak-mindedness. To others "religion" does indeed mean a means of escape from the real matters of living or at least the tragic parts of living. To still others "my religion" is a sort of virtue or status that is more accurately seen as bigotry with respect to other religious practices. For all these reasons and more, recovering a positive meaning for the word "religion" in not so easy. In our time, it takes some effort to recover the work "religion" as a pointer to something dead serious, profoundly real, and necessary to optimal living. So for many people a religious practice is a hard sell.

Nevertheless, this hard sell is my task in Part Four of this book. To do this I will have to clear some rubbish out of the way in order to provide space for a vision of religion that is subversive to the norm, but meaningful to the seeker of a fully realistic life. Perhaps there is nothing more to say except, "Let us begin."

Chapter 17
The Death of Mythic Space and the Redefinition of Religion

Perhaps, the most important historical development in the last 200 years was not the splitting of the atom or the invention of the internal combustion engine or the spread of the computer chip, but the advent of a new religious mode. The old religious mode used the two-story metaphor of heaven above and earth below. What many of us now see more clearly than earlier generations is that this was a metaphor, not a literal truth. This metaphor became difficult for people to use. We can now see it as a temporal human invention that can be replaced; indeed, it is being replaced. But I am getting ahead of my story.

Let us be sure we are clear what this old metaphor was and how it was used in the heyday of its cultural aliveness. Let us picture in our minds what I will call "mythic space" as a top rectangle over a bottom rectangle we will call "ordinary (or sensory experienced) space."

Mythic Space
Ordinary Space

In the top space are angels and devils, gods and goddesses, perhaps one main God or Goddess, as well as fairies, gremlins, and the list goes on. This very old metaphor has died, even though millions of people still use it, take it literally or somewhat literally, use it to support their hope of everlasting life, and in the worst case use it to support a tyrannical attitude—a demeaning of women, a devastation of the Earth, a greed, a meanness, or more. To be charitable, some sincere religious folk simply do not know how to talk about the profound matters of their lives without resorting to a use of this double-deck metaphor. Let us notice that dividing spirit from matter is a subtle form of the two-story imagining.

The current state of decay of this very old metaphor was not always the cultural situation. For thousands of years this metaphor was a taken-for-granted part of cultural life virtually everywhere. A form of this metaphor occurred even in precivilization societies in which the classical up-and-down form of this metaphor had not yet been invented. I am assuming that the dawn of civilization and the dawn of hierarchical thinking were one and the same dawning.

Let us imagine a pre-civilization society in which the male ownership of children had not yet been invented. All humans could see at that time was the wonder of new human life emerging from the womb of woman. Such people used this ordinary experience as a metaphor for Reality as a whole. They envisioned the story of the whole cosmos as a great womb from which all ordinary things emerged. They also viewed this same cosmic womb as a great tomb into which all things returned. Between womb and tomb we humans dwell in the arms of this cosmic Mother whose breasts feed us. We are her children. We owe everything to her. We return to her in our deaths. The myth of the Great Goddess was born. Perhaps the following chart can indicate a sense of this very ancient form of the two-realm metaphor:

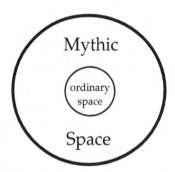

Rather than being "above," mythic space in these early societies "surrounds us." Likely, these very old cultures did not have words for "mythic space" or even "metaphor." They simply housed this basic image in their minds and used this image to talk about their lives. When we civilized people first encountered the Aborigines of Australia, these very interesting people, whose culture was pre-agricultural as well as precivilizational, were talking about "dreamtime and ordinary time." They saw themselves traveling from ordinary time into a trance type reality (dreamtime), and then returning. This ordinary time/dreamtime image of Reality is a form of the two-realm metaphor.

So how old is this two-realm metaphor? There is evidence for the presence of the Great Goddess myth reaching back at least 25,000 years. Perhaps the Old Religious Mode is 100,000 years old. I am asking us to stretch our imaginations back that far in order to underline how astonishing it is for a metaphor that old to die. Most of us now live in a culture whose members no longer honestly believe in the presence of a mythic world of gods and goddesses, or Goddess or God or devils and angels or gremlins and fairies. That once taken-for-granted realm of reality is no longer taken for granted.

All gods and goddesses are GONE. Everything we have meant by religion is GONE. In that sense, religion is GONE, gone forever. Indeed, myth as we once understood myth is GONE.

But that is not the most amazing part of what has happened to us. In the midst of this down-to-Earth world, a realm of Wonder has burned through. And another religious metaphor has appeared that has taken the place of the older one. This new metaphor enables our minds to translate the religious insights of the past into meaningful articulations of those same awareness in our lives today.

The New Religious Mode

So what does this replacement for the two-story metaphor look like? Let me be clear that I am describing something that is already in history. My description of it can surely be improved. My names for it can be changed, but what I am describing is not something I am simply making up. This new metaphor is something that has been emerging in our common societies for at least 200 years. The new religious mode emerged in the wake of the scientific and Enlightenment critique of the old religious metaphor and came into full expression with such writers as Søren Kierkegaard and Friedrich Nietzsche. I will not dialogue with this long history, but I want to acknowledge that I am working in its wake.

I am also working in the wake of the most illuminating person that I have known personally, my mentor for 24 years, Joseph W. Mathews. He first named the replacement for the old religious mode **"the advent of the secular religious."** In a talk called "the secular revolution," he spelled out the manner in which the ancient two-story metaphorical thinking is being replaced by living in one and only one realm of reality. In that talk he also noted how the imagery of angels and demons was being replaced by imagery about historically unfolding relationships. Later, Mathews claimed that we had stumbled upon an even deeper perception of the secular religious revolution. He called this insight the discovery of *"the other world in* *the midst of this world."* [16] He illustrated how in the midst of our ordinary, everyday living we were experiencing the burning through of the same profound *states of being* that were written about in the classical writings using the old two-story way of talking. Mathews gave the illustration of a piece of paper, representing our lives, having a lighted match beneath it. First the paper begins to brown, and then it flames. A state of profound being is like that; it browns and flames the ordinary paper of our everyday lives. This is not supernatural imagery. But even in this image, a trace of the heavenly realm remains: the burning match is being pictured as a sort of second story in this visualization. But if we tell this story right, we are admitting that we are telling a story. There is no literal match. All we experience is the burning through of the depth dimension of this one Reality. And this burning through needs no mountaintop or sacred building; it burns through the ordinary, familiar aspects of our lives. A new sort of polarity is being imaged. No angels and devils are assumed. No divine person is needed. We know that those mental pictures are poetry about an experience that takes place in this one and only realm.

Yet a new sort of polarity does remain: (1) the ordinary and (2) the depth of the ordinary. But "depth" in this sentence does not mean another realm. It means an intensification of this one realm. The extraordinary is the intensification of the ordinary, and the ordinary in its deepest nature is extraordinary. Using this newer poetry we can see with our own one-story eyes what earlier humans were talking about with their two-story poetry of natural and supernatural. We can grant our ancestors the wisdom of using their poetry to talk about their depth experience. But now we have a new poetry—a new polarity of (1) the ordinary and (2) the extraordinary depth of the ordinary. And this is not a reversion to the old polarity, for the ordinary is extraordinary, and the extraordinary is the ordinary fully experienced.

Here is another poetic image that has become part of this conversation. Transcendence (the old mode) is being replaced by transparency (the new mode). The meaning here is that our everyday lives can become transparent, "glass" to the profound dimensions of Reality. What previously was opaque becomes illuminated with light, not from some other realm but from the true nature of this one and only realm.

---

[16] A lecture on this topic, "The Recovery of the Other World," appears in a book of Joe Mathews' talks, *Bending History* (John Epps: editor, Resurgence Publishing: 2005). I count this talk as one of the most important talks in that book.

Translating from the Old Religious Mode to the New Religious Mode

Here is an example of how a very old text can be translated into this new religious mode. Moses, so the story goes (Exodus 3), saw an ordinary bush burn with an ethereal flame. But he did not have our secular religious metaphor to think with. His mind appropriated this experience as a Divine Being speaking to him. He attempted to find a name for this Divine Being, but all his two-story mind could fathom was that this "Divinity" had no name comprehensible to the human. Some unfathomable I AM THAT I AM was speaking to him in imperatives that his consciousness was already brooding upon. He heard speech that said, "Let my people go."

Even though we cannot see ourselves talking with Divine Beings anymore (except in a poetic manner), we can grasp what Moses was talking about when he tells us about his talk with *we-don't-know*.[17] In our own ordinary life among our own "bushes," we can also experience an ordinary part of our lives burning with surprising heat. Like Moses, we may have felt called to some atypical task of living in which we surprised ourselves with our own daring that we may have resisted, but did the task anyway. We may still count such moments as the most important events of our lives. This important, ancient story is not diminished by stripping it of its two-story language. Indeed, its essential meaning only becomes clear to us when see it in the light of our recently dawned one-realm, transparency mode of understanding.

I will demonstrate a more involved example of metaphorical translation from the Old Religious Mode to the New Religious Mode, using this story from *Luke 9: 28-36*:

> About eight days after these sayings (about the son of man coming in his glory), Jesus took Peter and James and John and went off with them to the hillside to pray. And then, while he was praying, the whole appearance of his face changed and his clothes became white and dazzling. And two men were talking with Jesus. They were Moses and Elijah — revealed in heavenly splendor, and their talk was about the way he must take and the end he must fulfill in Jerusalem. But Peter and his companions had been

---

[17] Please note that it does not matter that this story about Moses has been elaborated by later generations. Using mere historical empirical thinking, it is difficult to prove that Moses even existed. But in our memory the Moses figure, whether literary or empirical, still lives as a source of insight into the way WE-DON'T-KNOW-HIS-NAME interacts with humans.

overcome by sleep, and it was as they struggled into wakefulness that they saw the glory of Jesus and the two men standing with him. Just as they were parting from him, Peter said to Jesus, "Master, it is wonderful for us to be here! Let us put up three shelters—one for you, one for Moses, and one for Elijah."

But he did not know what he was saying. While he was speaking a cloud overshadowed them and awe swept over them as it enveloped them. A voice came out of the cloud saying, "This is my Son, my chosen! Listen to him!"

And while the voice was speaking, *they found there was no one there at all but Jesus.* The disciples were reduced to silence, and in those days never breathed a word to anyone of what they had seen.[18]

First of all, to translate this wonderful poetry we have to notice that it was written years after the crucifixion. The whole thing is fiction — not a word of it is actual history except for the names of the people. "They never breathed a word to anyone of what they had seen" was an admission by the storyteller that he or she was making it up. The truth of this story only happened to resurrected persons after the horror of the crucifixion became a door for them into the deeps of life.

The teller of this tale knows that "there was no one there at all but Jesus." All the rest of the story is told in a sort of dream imagery. The dazzle of Jesus' garments is something seen only by transformed people who see the dazzle of Jesus along with the dazzle of Moses (first author of the law) and the dazzle of Elijah (grandfather of the prophets). We can translate this dazzle as an experience of awe, a dread and fascination moment that is mysterious, that requires courage, and that in the end redirects our lives.

No tape recorder would have picked up the voice from the cloud. In fact the cloud itself is a symbol used to indicate the heavenly source of the message. And "heaven" is also a symbol for what we would call the realm of Mystery that penetrates every ordinary moment, if we have accessed our capacity to notice such things. And what did this dream-world "voice" say? It said to pay attention to Jesus, for he is revealing the nature of the Mysterious Every-thing-ness/No-thing-ness, by which Moses and Elijah were also dazzled.

The disciples were reduced to silence. There were literally no words for what they, in this story, were experiencing. They were experiencing the resurrection, that rebirth on the other side of having all their illusions crucified in an event so shaking

---

[18] Luke 9: 28-36 J. B. Phillips translation.

of the foundations of their lives that they never got over it. Only when this shaking of the foundations is complete, does the dazzle appear. Only when all our illusions are exposed for what they are and we have died to all our egoistic projections upon Reality, does the dazzle of Reality appear.

Peter's first response was to build some booths or altars at this place. In other words he wanted to invent some religion. Peter did not know what he was saying; he only knew that he was experiencing Final Things, appropriate for marking this place with some sort of humanly invented religious something. The story begins with the words "they (the disciples) were struggling into wakefulness." This is a story about what it is like for us today, here and now, to struggle into wakefulness of our true being.

Such a commentary is an example of what it means to translate an old double-deck story like this into a single-realm story that calls forth Awe from the profound depths of our own lives today.

Many people dismiss ancient stories like these because they are so imbedded in two-story language. Metaphorical translation is the answer to rediscovering the "juice" in our ancient religious texts and memories. And this metaphorical translation process applies not only to biblical stories and other Western stories and teachings but also to Hindu and Buddhist stories and teachings; to the two-realm stories from ancient Australia, Africa, and America; and indeed to the religious forms from every place and generation of those thousands of years that were culturally characterized by the two-story religious mode. Students of Christianity must do metaphorical translation in order to correctly understand a fifth century Augustine; a twelfth century Aquinas; a fifteenth century Luther, Calvin, Teresa of Avila, and John of the Cross; an eighteenth century Wesley and Edwards. Even recent theologians like Dietrich Bonhoeffer and H. Richard Niebuhr had one foot in the two-story metaphors of the past. Nevertheless, all these luminaries were talking about our profound humanness, doing so in the language of the Old Religious Mode. The core meaning of most of the religious expressions of humanity are hidden from us until we see that the old metaphors they used are not essential to what they were saying. We can point to the same core experiences by employing our transparency, one-realm, mode of interpretation.

The place where many people are most reluctant to give up their two-story metaphors has to do with "life after death." Reincarnation, immortality of soul, and the resurrection of the body have been the two-story metaphors most used to talk about life-after-death. For our sanity we need to be blunt with ourselves that these three stories are metaphors, not literal biological or psychological processes. But the metaphors have meaning; they point to something. They point to the realization that our essential consciousness is an enigma that does not fit into the laws of physics that we normally accept. We can actually experience ourselves watching from that deep well of consciousness the processes of our physical bodies. We know or can know that we are an "I Am" that can view this "I Am" in a calm and curious way. We quite naturally ask the question, "What then becomes of this "I Am" after the conclusion of our historical presence and the apparent eclipse of consciousness that personal death entails? The reincarnation heritages theorize that we continue our incomplete journeys toward full realization in yet another physical body. The immortality of the soul heritages theorize that we go to a nonphysical or spiritual realm for reward, continuing purification, or perhaps a punishing experience of no hope. The resurrection of the dead heritages theorize that a future life will be embodied, differently, but in a new physical creation given by the same power that created and is creating the current creation.

The literalization of these three stories renders them unbelievable to increasing numbers of contemporary humans. And the use of these stories to threaten and control a population of people is now seen as insidious by freedom loving people. Nevertheless, we are left with a witness to something profound in all three of these stories: human life is deeper and more wondrous than the ordinary eye can see. In this one life we can experience ourselves killed and resurrected many times. In this one life we can know that we are somehow related to the Eternal in the everyday processes of our lives. In this one life we can know that we are part of a "realization journey" that preceded our birth and will continue after our death.

The Redefinition of Religion

The death of the two-story or transcendence metaphor is also the death of most of our old images of what we point to with the word "religion." If religion is not about gods and goddesses, God or Goddess, what is it about? If religion is not about preparing for life after death, what is it about?

As the etymology of the word indicates, "Re-ligion" is about reconnecting. It is about reconnecting with something from which we have become disconnected, namely our essential "I Am." Religion is about accessing an experience of our profound humanness. It is about restoring us to our true nature from the myriad of substitutes we have invented to take the place of that true nature. Religion is about Great Thinks that call forth awareness of our true nature, including Great Feels of our true nature and Great Resolves to live that true nature.

Religion is a practice. It is not something we think: it is something we do. Some thinking will be part of that doing, but religion is a doing, a practice, a practice of meditation, a practice of prayer, a practice of contemplation, a practice of ritual, a practice of service, a practice of devotional reading, a practice of dance, and so forth. I will look at these many practices in detail in Chapter 19, but for now I am dwelling on the basic definition of religion as practice and what this means.

A core truth about religious practice is revealed in the short conversation that some student had with his meditation teacher:

> Student: Does meditation cause enlightenment?
> Teacher: No, enlightenment is an accident: it happens or it doesn't happen.
>   Meditation makes you more accident prone.

This understanding applies to every sort of religions practice. Accessing our essential being, our "I Am" quality, comes to us on its own terms in its own way, and in its own good time. We do not cause it by our religious practices.

There is a wonderful story at the end of the movie "Little Big Man." The old Indian chief takes Little Big Man with him up to the top of a hill to ritualize the old chief's death. The old chief goes through an elaborate ritual and lays down expecting to be taken up in death. The clouds merely drizzle rain on him. After a time the old chief get up and tells Little Big Man, "Sometimes the magic works, and sometimes it doesn't." And they walk back down the hill to live a bit longer.

I have had experiences of this grand lesson while preaching sermons to a local congregation. Sometimes the magic works and sometimes it doesn't. Sometimes the sermon grips people, releases them, and sends them out the back door in a buzz of refreshment. And sometimes a sermon just lies there on the ground with rain drizzling on it. This could have to do with the quality of the sermon, or the quality of the delivery, or the receptivity of the hearers, but none of these considerations provide a full explanation. Enlightenment, healing, the resurgence of profound humanness is a gift, a mysterious happening that happens or it doesn't happen.

We have sometimes called religion a means of grace, but this "grace" must not be understood as some sort of dependable magic. Religion simply makes us more accident prone to accidents of realization that we cannot control.

Another way to approach this truth is to notice in our own experience that religion is created by human beings, while profound humanness is given by mysterious Reality. Our profound humanness is a gift, and only when we see this giftedness can we accept it and resolve to live it. Nevertheless, religion is an important part of human society. Religion is as important and as widely present as education, healthcare, farming, housing construction, and waste disposal. Religion, in some form or another, tends to arise is every culture. If what is commonly called "religion" is absent, something else takes its place. Members of communist societies often claim they do not need religion, but communism itself functions as a religion for many people in those cultures. And communism is not an entirely dysfunctional religion as some would claim. For example, here is a quite valid "religious" realization within communist thought: the course of history must be understood and obeyed and humans can take responsibility for participating in directing that history. Such themes are shared by the great prophets of the Hebrew Scriptures. The dysfunctional aspects of the communist "religion" reside in not seeing deeply enough into the wonder of history. I will not elaborate further on this topic; I only want to point out that every society develops some sort of religion or quasi-religion—some way of connecting to the deep matters of life. If a society makes that Eternal connection poorly or has no religious processes that perform the service of making that connection, then that society will eventually become a form of madness and disintegrate.

* * * * * * * *

In conclusion, here is a summary of this redefinition of religion that appears on this side of the death of mythic space: Religion is a practice, a symbol-using practice along with language and the arts. Religion is a symbol-using practice that provides a means for us to become more accident prone to the accidents of realizing our profound humanness.

Chapter 18
The Origin of Religion, A Speculative Story

Any discussion of the origin of religion is a speculation, a piece of poetic fiction. My aim here is not to explore with scientific carefulness the probable historical facts, but to further explore the nature of religion through contemplative imagination.

In my speculation, the origin of religion precedes language and art. Indeed, it is the very first dawning of the consciousness of being consciousness. The origin of religion precedes the evolution of the human brain to its current size. The origin of religion took place on the same day as that great dawning that makes our species qualitatively different from other forms of mammalian life.

Here is my piece of fiction about that grand day. A small tribe of hominids, perhaps 500,000 years ago, were walking across the African Savannah, when a deeply valued member of their group suddenly died. Everything that gave enduring unity to their group seemed to unravel. They gathered around the dead body. One of the women began moving in a sort of rhythmic way, a sort of dance, a sort of (dare we say) ritual. One or two others copied her. This very simple ritual implanted itself in the memory of this group. It came to be repeated when others died. Doing this ritual called to consciousness the experience of loss of a valued member. What was new here was not death itself, but the ritualizing of the deep experience of death. The ritual was new. This ritual was the existence of a mental form that stood for something, that allowed a certain distance from that something and from the feelings that went with that something. It allowed a reflection upon that something. It was the dawn of a new form of mental entity—the symbol.

Before that dawning this species of animal life had gotten by, like all smart apes, dogs, cats, zebras, and elephants get by, with images, not symbols. Images are multi-sensory mental reruns of previous experiences. The image-mode of intelligence is very powerful, but it is not capable of reflection upon the experience of experience itself. Image-intelligence is intensely practical for survival, food, affection, sex, danger avoidance, and so on. But a ritual is something different than an imaginal rerun of multi-sensory experiences. That first ritual had no practical use whatsoever. It allowed reflection upon experience. It allowed consciousness to be conscious of being conscious. It allowed or began to allow the awareness that each of us is going to die, that each of us has been born, that each of us was or could be conscious about birth and death. As this sort of reflection evolved, it enabled the raising of questions. Perhaps the word "why" was the first human word. Then again, perhaps "why?" is too sophisticated a word to be first. Perhaps that first word was just "waaeeee" as a sort of curious pointer to the overwhelming Mystery of it All.

The initial rituals of this new awareness became more useful as these new mental forms (and their attending consciousness) expanded from simple rituals to art forms and then to language. With the dawn of art, the simple rituals could be elaborated with icons. With the dawn of language the simple rituals could be elaborated with stories or myths. I imagine this development took hundreds of generations. It survived because it came to be an advantage for survival, a tool useful for group bonding and an aid to teamwork. It may also have survived because it made existing more fun, experiences more interesting, living more conscious. As pointed out in Part One, consciousness has an inward propensity to become more conscious. Also, it may have survived because such consciousness was a sexual draw or helped in child rearing.

This is my story about the origin of religion. Don't take it too literally. The meaning of my story is that the practice of religion is basic to human culture. Religion is the foundation beneath language and art. And religion-art-language is the foundation of human culture as a whole. Culture is the foundation beneath politics and economics. Religion is thus the rock upon which the human form of society rests. A sick religion spawns a sick society. A healthy religion spawns a healthy society. This understanding is needed to counter the crass notion that economics is the prime driver of human affairs. Economics is a driver in the historical process of humanity, but it alone does not explain the origin, development, and historical transitions of our species. Economics does not explain the wild adventures taken by our species into the often costly deepening of our consciousness of consciousness.

Being religious and being human is one and the same adventure. Humans have intensely explored being human and being religious for at least a hundred thousand years. There have been many huge turning points in our religious and social history. We are currently engaged in another huge turning point in our awareness of consciousness and in the religious forms that nurture this expanded consciousness. We are beginning to see the elemental nature of religion and to build our new societies accordingly. We are beginning to know that an open, honest, affirming relation to the Mystery-of-it-All is the solid ground on which new cultures, polities, and economies can be built. We are beginning to know that our ever-busy language-using and art-form-producing minds can separate us from our true and glorious lives. To heal from our falling into horrific forms of depravity and despair and to maintain ourselves in our deepest actuality and glory, our cultures need solid roots in illuminating rituals, icons, and stories that access profound humanness. When healthy, these humanly invented but deeply rooted symbolic forms can enable our consciousness to be conscious of our consciousness and thereby be conscious of the Ground of Being that posits us as conscious beings.

Chapter 19
Religion as Practice

Religion is too often misunderstood as a collection of thoughts. Religion is a practice; it is something we do. It is something we do in order that our awareness of the Deep Self and the Awesome Wholeness of Reality may be more vivid. Our awareness of Reality is not caused by our religious practices. Rather, religious practices make the dawning of this awareness more likely.

Religion is also too often misunderstood as a set of ideas brought into our minds from some long-established heritage. But a religious heritage is more than furnishings for the mind. A religious heritage is about doing—doing a daily, weekly, yearly practice of specific activities. We use our minds of course, but it is the doing of the practice, not the thinking about it, that makes it effective religion. For some philosophers of religion the following statement would be a big paradigm shift: *religion is a practice before it is a set of accompanying thoughts*. We might say, "Worship precedes theology." Or, "Ritual, icon, and myth precede religious theoretics." Our theology or theachings can purify our worship. Our religious theoretics can enrich our religious practices, but the action of doing religion precedes enriching our practice with thinking about it. We might put it this way: doing theology is a religious practice. Once we see the primacy of practice, then we can also see that the practice of thinking about our religious practice is part of the practice. Religious thinking need not be scorned. Indeed, it takes a practice of thoughtfulness to practice a religion well. *But practicing, not thinking, is the essence of being religious.*

So what do we mean by "religious practice"? We mean things like sitting in silence for twenty minutes or an hour. We mean things like reading a good book that provokes Spirit awareness. (I will use the word "Spirit" with a capital "S" to mean the profound humanness explored in earlier chapters, the Awe, the numinous, the qualities of the "I Am.") By "religious practice" I mean things like praying passionate requests or passionate intentions in the face of onrushing challenges. Religious practice can also mean dancing, singing, or performing some ritual observance or pageant. Religious practice can mean sitting in a circle of peers and sharing the glories, tragedies, remorse, guilt, and fears of our daily lives. Religious practice can mean listening to good words about our welcome home to Reality, a welcome that Reality is always offering to our specific states of historical existence. Religious practice can mean listening to prepared talks from those who have in some way accredited themselves to us as persons of Spirit awareness. As we will discuss later, our engagements in history, our washing dishes, our building community life may also be viewed as religious practices. Religious practice can mean many things, including reading these words about religious practice.

And here is an important sub-point about seeing religion as practice: religion is not something you wait around to have happen to you. Religion is something you do. Religion is something that human beings organize, pay for, and spend time doing. Religion is a part of the practice of being social beings, including the coming apart from other people for solitary practices.

Thinking about religion is important; it may even play a big role in giving ourselves permission to do religion. But religion as religion begins with doing, action, performing, engaging in the seeming silliness of standing, sitting, kneeling, dancing, chanting, drumming, meditating, reading, dialoging, journaling, vowing, singing, ritualizing, socializing, engaging in social justice, and more. Theological study and reflection are part of our religious action. Ethical thinking and practical love of neighbor, society, and planet Earth are also part of religious practice. *When we retreat into our minds from "religion as practice," we retreat from the very essence of religion.*

So what are the basic practices of religion? How do these basic practices of religion relate to the nine aspects of the "I Am" described in Chapter 14. The following chart associates nine basic types of religious practice with the nine aspects of the "I Am."

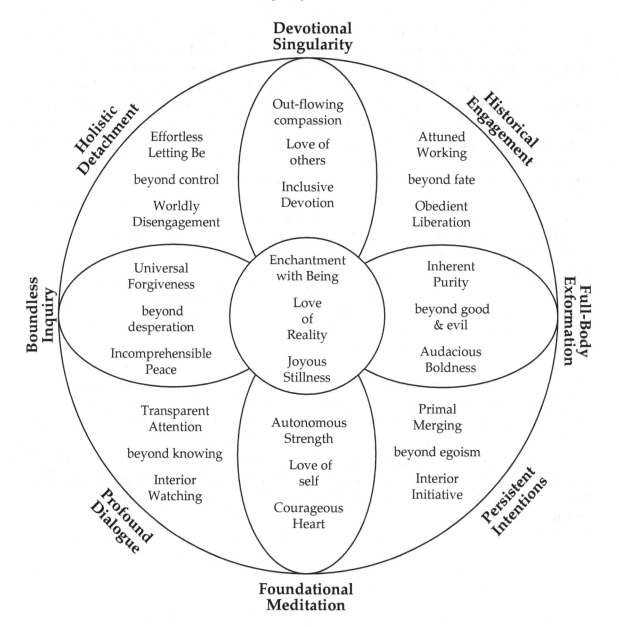

With each of the large bolded words add the modifiers:
The Practice of_____

**Corresponding with the center Circle associate:
The Practice of Visionary Trance**

I will begin my descriptions of these types of religious practices with the bottom three, which I will call the "solitary practices." These are the religious practices that we do alone. Every long-standing religious heritage has developed solitary religious practices.

Solitary Practices

There are three distinguishable types of solitary religious practice. I am calling them "Profound Dialogue," "Foundational Meditation," and "Persistent Intentions." Some Christian groups have called these "Meditation, Contemplation, and Prayer. The first, *Profound Dialogue,* has to do with developing an *inner council* of persons with whom to dialogue. The second, *Foundation Meditation,* is about what we might also call *contemplative consciousness*, the practice of "viewing" the dynamics of consciousness with a concentrated focus on consciousness itself. And the third, *Persistent Intentions*, has to do with *petitioning Reality*, initiating our interior programming with respect to Reality and the many realities that we confront.

Profound Dialogue

The practice of *"Profound Dialogue"* includes what we have called devotional reading, meditation on Scriptures and other "sacred" texts, and interactions with "saintly" persons both personally known and known through their writings and/or art. Dialogue is a helpful name for this arena of religious practice, because the key to this practice is hearing deeply the voices of other persons and speaking back to them. We all tend to have an interior council of "great people" with whom we dialogue: a parent, a teacher, an author, an artist, an activist, a personal friend, a person in the distant past, a contemporary, and many others. As a solitary religious practice, Profound Dialogue means bringing those "great people" to mind through reading or remembering their words —hearing their voices, their music, their poetry—seeing their paintings, their sculpture, their architecture. These people are "great" because we have found them inspiring, evoking Awe within us, assisting us to access our "I Am" greatness.

While all the voices that have spoken to us have taken up a place in our memory and tend to talk to us more or less all the time, *Profound Dialogue* begins when we take charge of this interior council of "great voices." We can seat these speakers as we want them seated. Some of them are on the front row of our circle of council members. We consult them first or most often. Others we have seated further back. We consult them with reservations or infrequently. We can order our interior council in accord with various subjects or topics or ways of aiding us. This is our council, our creation, our interpretations of our personal history of being inspired. It is also our future resources for further inspiration. We have the power to listen or not, accept what they say or not, correct them, enrich them, or shut them up. This religious practice is dialogue! We are not passive pawns of our inspiring voices, nor are we closed to what these voices have to share with us. In a practice of dialogue, we go to these "great people" willingly and actively for the enrichment of our lives. We may disagree with them, fight with them, and even unseat them from our interior council.

Profound Dialogue makes us "accident prone" to experience that aspect of the "I Am" described in Chapter 14 as *Transparent Attention*—an interior watching that unites mind with Being in a form of knowing that is more profound than our customary forms of information gathering and knowledge mastering.

Foundational Meditation

The second of these three overarching arenas of solitary religious practice, I am calling *"Foundational Meditation."* In Christian heritage this arena is often called "contemplation." But I am honoring the Buddhists who call this practice "meditation." As a collection of religious practitioners, the Buddhists stand out as our planet's chief experts on meditation practice. Whatever name we call it, meditation distinguishes itself as a pre-rational, post-rational, or transrational practice. In this practice we are not thinking or dialoguing, we are simply noticing. And this noticing is not a mental sort of noticing, but a concentration of our consciousness upon the activities of aliveness as we experience them in our inner being. For example, in the elemental teachings of most Buddhist practitioners, we are advised to begin by noticing our breathing. This is not a mental game; it is a discipline of concentration on an aspect of our aliveness that is always taking place. In-breath and out-breath, air moving across our upper lip, the rise and fall of the abdomen, these are the sorts of noticing that Buddhist meditation practices emphasize. If thoughts arise, we are advised not to resist those thoughts, but simply notice them, and allow them to come and go rather than engage in them or let them carry us away from our concentration on the immediate aliveness of breathing. Faithfully maintained over periods of time, this practice creates an awareness of how we are aware of our living in the actual here and now. It teaches us that this aware consciousness can be present no matter what programs of thought or projects of action may also be going on. It teaches us that we have intentional power over our thoughts and actions rather than being the victim of whatever stories we have habituated or whatever reactionary behaviors we are obsessing. And *Foundational Meditation* is a practice that prepares us for noticing our "I Am" essence. We are not in control of the enlightenment journey that accompanies meditation practice; the enlightenment journey unfolds in its own way, unique to our own psyche.

The practice of meditation can be most associated with that aspect of the "I Am" that I describe as *Autonomous Strength*, as the *courageous heart* of true love of self. Buddhist meditation or Christian contemplative practices do not exhaust what I mean by *Foundational Meditation*. Many of the yoga practices of Hinduism qualify as *Foundational Meditation*. The Orient has given us Qi Gong, Tai Chi, and other forms of bodily movement that can be viewed as contemplative activity. Islamic Sufi chanting and dance traditions can likewise be viewed as practices of *Foundational Meditation*. Any practice that focuses consciousness upon our conscious experience can be called *Foundational Meditation*. All types of *Foundational Meditation* make us "accident prone" to experience an "accident" of that aspect of the "I Am" described in Chapter 14 as *Autonomous Strength*, the courageous heart of love for our own "true self," or "no-self" as many Buddhists prefer to call it.

Persistent Intentions

The third of these three arenas of solitary religious practice, I am calling *"Persistent Intentions."* In Christian heritage this practice is often called "prayer." The term "prayer," however, needs to be cleansed of its magical meanings. We need a wider and more secular title for this practice in order to assure an understanding of the universal, and down-to-Earth nature of this practice. *Persistent Intentions* means taking an active relationship with the Awesome Wholeness that Awes us. Yes, this interior action changes things, but it does not radiate out as a spooky influence that finds its way to some Majestic Controller or to some other person's psyche. *Persistent Intentions* means our initiative, our freedom operating in our own being. Awakening and employing this capacity in our solitary time does make a difference in the way we live our lives, and thereby it makes a difference in the course of history. Such historical effects can be understood without any spooky or magical explanations. The Christian community has conceived at least these four types of prayer: confession, gratitude, petition, and intercession. Describing these four aspects of prayer is a useful means for illuminating the universality of this practice. This dynamic of solitary practice appears in virtually all religions.

Confession as an aspect of solitary practice means owning up to some reality in our behavior, our attitude toward life, our feelings, our thoughts, whatever. It means admitting the ways these bits of living are escapes from the "I Am." Confession is an important initiative on the part of our consciousness because it is a beginning toward being where we are in our living, rather than pretending to be where we are not.

Gratitude as an aspect of solitary practice means choosing to affirm the Reality we are being given instead of lusting for some unreality we might desire to substitute for the given Reality. In so far as the given Reality always includes forgiveness and the option of a fresh start in our living, we may experience grateful feelings for this welcome release from self-incrimination, self-underestimation, or self-victimization. But whether we have grateful feelings or not, the practice of gratitude is restorative to our solid here-and-now openness toward life. Life, openly lived, does provide its joys and exuberance, but the practice of gratitude does not mean forcing such states of feeling. Gratitude is an intention that allows our real lives to produce whatever feelings and potentials life naturally produces.

Petition as an aspect of solitary practice means choosing specific directions toward some augmentation of our own existence. Where do we want to go in our life journey? What do we what to have as states of being or worldly opportunities? Petitionary prayer is a courageous thing because we do not always receive exactly what we ask for, or what we thought we were asking for, or what we thought having our request would actually mean. A petition puts our life out there to be disappointed or surprised or amazed beyond all expectations. Petition is a powerful practice, it readies us to receive a future which contains that for which we are asking. Petitionary prayer programs our psyche to pursue opportunities as they present themselves. Petition is a powerful thing: it changes history. But petitionary prayer is not a magical means of controlling the future. Our petitions seldom work out exactly as we expect. History is a surprise, a surprise that can be intensely disappointing as well as overwhelmingly gracious.

Intercession as an aspect of solitary practice means choosing what to intend with regard to other people, social systems, ecosystems, and the planet as whole. To intercede means to stand between a value and the threat to that value. To intercede means to put our body, our wealth, our reputation, our very being in the breach of creating solutions that handle the threats to what we value. Intercessory prayer is a solitary practice that is intending our being. Intercession is not asking some divine Power to do something for someone. Intercession means requesting with our whole body that the trends of Reality change on behalf of some specific value that concerns us. In making a solitary intercession we do not need to have a clear plan about how this change in history can happen or what our role is in making this change will be. We can intercede for something that may be impossible. An intercessory prayer is simply the programming of our psyche in a specific direction. We set up our own being to be on the lookout for insights and opportunities that pertain to the value that is the topic of our intercession.

All four of these types of prayer are *Persistent Intentions*. And all four types of *Persistent Intentions* make us "accident prone" to experience an "accident" of that aspect of the "I Am" described in Chapter 14 as *Primal Merging* with our own essential freedom.

Following is a triangular chart of what I will call *Core Religious Practices*. These are the same religious practices listed on the previous chart, but now in a triangular array that shows something more about the relationships between these nine arenas of religious practice. In particular, the chart groups together three groups of practices: *Solitary Practices*, *Corporate Practices*, and *Transparent Practices*.

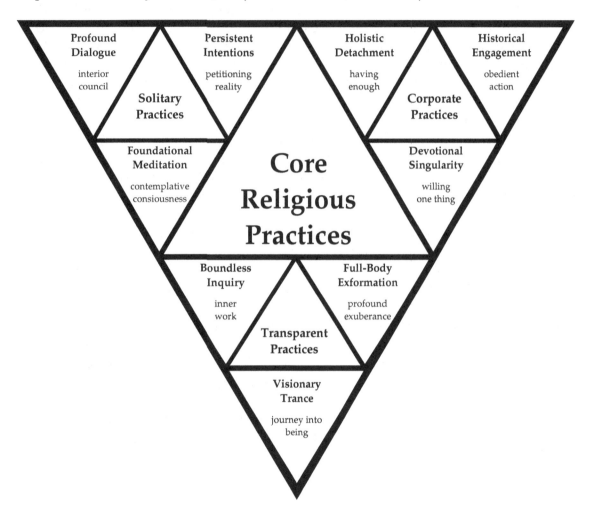

In addition to the *solitary practices* already described, the above chart pictures three *corporate practices* and three *transparent practices*. Can we be confident that these nine practices encompass all religious practices? No, we can't. I am simply drawing my model of what I have observed about religious practices. Such a model is little more than a teaching tool, hopefully a thoughtful one. In any case, the model is just a model, and any model can be improved. We may want to include more practices or to see these relationships differently. So bear with me as I describe what I am calling "Corporate Practices."

Corporate Practices

By "corporate" I mean practices that are done together with other people rather than done alone. This includes practices that would go on in the life of a religious order as well as practices that characterize a worship service, an intimate circle, a study group, and so on. I am not going to examine the details of the wide variety of corporate religious practices. I am suggesting a typology of three major arenas of corporate practices. Our "life together" can include intentional practices that calls forth profound humanness. The monastic orders of Christianity came up with these three categories: Poverty, Chastity, and Obedience. Properly interpreted, I find these to be useful categories, but for this chapter I want to use categories that have a wider reference—categories that can include non-Christian and non-monastic communal applications. My three categories will be *Holistic Detachment*, *Devotional Singularity*, and *Historical Engagement*.

These categories can also point to inner states of being. But I will emphasize how these three categories can point to religious practices. I will use these categories to point to three types of vows (or promises) made to a group of religious practitioners. Members of such groups make vows to live lives of *Holistic Detachment*, *Devotional Singularity*, and *Historical Engagement*. In order to do this, the group may write a covenant and create rules that spell out how these practices are to be done by their particular group. For example, the rules might be as simple as: come to a weekly meeting on time and be prepared. In a more extensive practice, the rules might include selling all your possessions, living together in the same buildings, wearing a monastic garb, doing a share of the daily work of the group, and relying on the group for your lifelong subsistence. In the next three sections I will be describing group practices as well as indicating the inner states of being that these practices can help us access.

Holistic Detachment

Holistic Detachment is rooted in a vow a group of people make to live simply and carry out a life of simplicity in order to access detachment from the general culture of neediness for more, and more, and still more goods and status. ("Are we all more-ticians?" asks e. e. cummings) Holistic Detachment need not mean a strict asceticism, but it does include a commitment to a style of "enough already." Food, shelter, health can all be affirmed while still manifesting a style of living that renounces the obsessive consumerism and frantic climbing of economic and status ladders into the stratospheres of self-indulgent delusion. This vow or promise to live a simple style of life typically includes a commitment to live beyond the common obsessions: sex, emotional love, acceptance by others, status, celebrity, family ties, partners, friends, social expectations, philosophical systems, states of peacefulness, and more. All these ties are valuable in limited ways, but they are not infinitely valuable. A vow of *Holistic Detachment* is a promise to live in a loose relation to all these "limited" values, and thereby remain open to the change of and the inevitable negations of such values. Indeed, *Holistic Detachment* means being open to death itself. Life is a factor of indescribable value, but *Holistic Detachment* includes a willingness to lay down our lives (time, treasure and bodies) for the causes and persons that call upon us for our service. This style of living opposes the common style of thoughtlessly backing into the grave. We can intend our deaths. *Holistic Detachment* includes living our deaths, expending our deaths along with all other aspects of our living.

The practice of *Holistic Detachment* implies communities to whom we vow our vows of simplicity and who assist us to fulfill those vows, rescue us from our failures, pronounce our forgiveness, and challenge us to continue in the life style of *Holistic Detachment.* Maintaining the religious communities in which such vows are made and practiced is part of the religious practice of *Holistic Detachment.* Humans are communal beings. We seldom manifest our profound humanness entirely alone. Solitude is a sacred practice, but communal practice is no less sacred. *Holistic Detachment* is a communal practice of belonging to a community of people who practice detachment and thereby conduct a fresh relationship with the entire community of humankind. Indeed, this practice can lead us into as a fresh and open relationship with the entire community of Earth beings and with the Earth itself.

The practice of *Holistic Detachment* can make us more "accident prone" to experience an "accident" of that aspect of the "I Am" described in Chapter 14 as *Effortless Letting Be*—letting our finitude and our aliveness and our possibilities be what they are.

Devotional Singularity

This communal practice has to do with the disciplined use of the images and symbols, stories and pictures with which we nurture our lives. Every religious community has a religious culture in which its members are educated and with which they are cared for in the depths of their beings. If *Holistic Detachment* is the "economics" of corporate religious practice, then *Devotional Singularity* is the "culture" of corporate religions practice. *Historical Engagement* will be described as the "politics" of corporate religious practice.

The essence of *Devotional Singularity* is not easy to state, for it is more than being familiar with a tradition; it is finding a heartfelt devotion to the states of being alive that a specific religious tradition is capable of accessing and nurturing. The very idea of committing to a specific religious tradition is threatening to many people, for they have been burned by so many experiences of perverse religious community. Nevertheless, it is necessary to select or create some sort of religious community in order to have a religious culture whose images, symbols, stories, and icons can form a disciplined nurture. In order to wholeheartedly commit ourselves to such a discipline, it is crucial for us to understand the state of being that *Devotional Singularity* is aiming for.

Søren Kierkegaard wrote a book he called *Purity of Heart is to Will One Thing*. His core insight was this: we do not will one thing when our core devotion is less than the Whole of Reality. Our devotion to finite causes always ends up duplicitous: we are willing two or more things instead of one. Our only purity of devotion is to will the Whole of Reality. Then all the smaller realities take their relative places within that wholeness of devotion. I will not attempt to summarize Kierkegaard's intricate development of this topic. I merely want to indicate that the state of being we aim for with *Devotional Singularity* is happening when we are willing one thing, when we are willing devotion to all the actualities and possibilities that confront us.

Here is a story from the New Testament that helps us to get a feel of the state of being that the practice of Devotional Singularity aims for.

> Jesus came to a village and a woman called Martha welcomed him to her house. She had a sister by the name of Mary who settled down at the Lord's feet and was listening to what he said. But Martha was very worried about her elaborate preparations and she burst in saying, "Lord, don't you *mind* that my sister has left me to do everything myself? Tell her to get up and help me!"
>
> But the Lord answered her, "Martha, my dear, you are worried and bothered about providing so many things. Only a few things are really needed, perhaps only one. Mary has chosen the best part and you must not tear it away from her."[19]

---

[19] Luke 10:38-42 J. B. Phillips translation

There is nothing wrong with the thousand and one finite causes with which life is filled, and Martha was just doing some of them. We need to be thankful for the many Marthas that are doing the many things that make our lives possible, including our times of religious practice. But for Martha or Mary or you or I to be scattered in our devotion among the many things of temporal life is to miss what Mary has chosen—namely, the purity of heart that wills one thing. Martha is anxious and troubled about many things. One thing is needed. The Martha in each of us may cry out, "Oh for the glorious tranquility of willing one thing with all my heart and all my mind and all my strength." Mary is focusing upon this very *Devotional Singularity* that must not be interrupted. Rather, such a practice needs to be enabled for both Mary and Martha. Mary is just one more Martha who has chosen to practice what needs to be practiced to become a tranquil person in the midst of her own busy round of living.

Paradoxical as it may seem, the practice of *Devotional Singularity* can assist us to access the profound humanness aspect of *Out-flowing Compassion*. When we sit at the feet of profound humanness long enough, we learn to act from an inward authenticity that includes *Out-flowing Compassion* toward others.

Historical Engagement

Typically, we do not think of historical engagement as a religious practice. But many of us have had experiences that witness to why and how social engagement can be religious. Walking down the main streets of Jackson, Mississippi with a crowd of white and black citizens in the 1960s was for me a religious experience. It was not the walking that made it a religious experience, though walking can certainly be good for us. It was not the revolutionary thoughts in my head that made it a religious experience. It was the engagement with people on their porches watching us go by. It was the engagement with the conservative establishment of Jackson, Mississippi, dramatized in their police forces. It was the "we" feeling within that specific group of people walking and thereby tangling with the actual forces of history in that time and place. This engagement was the source of our Awe. This engagement was an encounter with the Awesome Upagainstness that one might, with a specific brand of theology, call "God." This engagement was a request to the power that posits us to give us a better world.

There are many ways to be historically engaged. Sitting at my computer writing this book can be experienced as historical engagement, in so far as I genuinely feel that I am engaging the religious communities of the planet with insights that can matter in the broad course of events for my generation. Much of our historical engagement takes place in quite simple ways: stuffing envelopes for a mailing that matters, staffing a booth at a county fair, facilitating a meeting of an ecological planning council, attending a hearing about not licensing a coal-fired power plant. What makes any of these activities *Historical Engagement* is that history is being actually engaged. History is being understood as a pliable flowing that human effort can redirect. And such engagement directly involves or indirectly implies a group of people with whom we are engaged in solidarity and communion. Surely, all this can be viewed as religious practice.

Not all religions emphasize *Historical Engagement* as a religious practice. The best of Judaism, Christianity, and Islam do emphasize *Historical Engagement*. And we can view the life of Mohandas Karamchand Gandhi as an example of engaged Hinduism. And we find many folk today who explain their religious practice as an engaged Buddhism. It is becoming meaningful for many people to view *Historical Engagement* as a religious practice right alongside solitary meditation, devotional ritual, and so forth. *Historical Engagement* takes its place alongside *Holistic Detachment* and *Devotional Singularity* as a *Corporate Practice* of religion.

The practice of *Historical Engagement* can assist us to be accident prone to the "I Am" aspect of *Attuned Working*. Rather than being forever preoccupied with trying not to miss out on something, we can be wholehearted focusing on real historical imperatives and thereby experience the satisfying adventure of relevant action.

Transparent Practices

The solitary practices and the corporate practices are the most obvious of the religious practices. They seem to have "substance" to them. The *Solitaries* have the substance of our psychological life, and the *Corporates* have the substance of group participation and historical relations. The practices that I am calling *"Transparent Practices"* are not so directly grounded in obvious "substance." The *Transparent Practices*, though being practices that involve our minds and bodies, are practices that focus exclusively upon the "I Am" enigma of profound consciousness. The transparent practice on the left side or knowing side of the above chart, I am calling *Boundless Inquiry*. The transparent practice on the right side or doing side of the above chart, I am calling *Full-Body Exformation*. And the transparent practice in the center of the first chart and at the bottom of the second chart, I am calling *Visionary Trance*.

Boundless Inquiry

"Inquiry" is a word that has been carried into new levels of meaning by A. H. Almaas, by many Buddhist teachers, by many forms of depth therapy, and popularized by innovative celebrities such as Byron Katie, Gangaji and Eli Jaxon-Bear. All these innovators encourage us to use our minds to work beyond our thoughts into conscious inquiry about consciousness itself.

Perhaps many of us have discovered something about *Boundless Inquiry* through doing a practice we have called "journaling." As a religious practice, journaling is a step beyond diary keeping, but like diary keeping, journaling is reflecting upon and recording insights about our own lives. If diary keeping means recording memorable events, journaling goes a step further into inquiring into our real experiences of lasting truth about our lives. Such inquiry can be called "Boundless" because it is not bounded by the philosophical or religious teachings that have influenced us so far in our lives. *Boundless Inquiry* is a process of self-discovery in which the self itself is both the discoverer and the discovered. We inquire into our own being with an intensity of disciplined openness that we expect of a good physicist inquiring into the structure of the atom or the patterns of gravity.

Boundless Inquiry is, however, different from empirical science. It is operating within the contemplative approach to truth. It is even a purification of the contemplative approach by the invention of methods for making the contemplative approach more effective in dodging our illusions and limited ideas and thereby opening ourselves to the convincing truth that arises from within our own inner lives.

Boundless Inquiry can be a solitary method, but it is actually more effective when conducted with the aid of teachers who can assist us to track our own experience more accurately. This brief description of the wide spectrum of practices is, of course, sketchy, for without direct experiences of doing "inquiry" into our own life and coming up with revelations that matter to us, this entire category can seem opaque. To make this category of religious practice "transparent," we will have to do the inquiry.

The practice of *Boundless Inquiry* can assist us to be accident prone to the "I Am" aspect of *Universal Forgiveness*. Rather than being preoccupied with promoting our last best ideas and defending them from Reality, we can journey deeper through inquiry into the surprising details within our own consciousness and thereby have a fresh taste of the abiding treasure of being welcomed home to Reality.

Full-Body Exformation

The "doing" aspect of *Transparent Practice* I am calling "*Full-Body Exformation*." I have had three teachers who have contributed most to my grasp of this religious practice and its effectiveness. The first was a meditation dance teacher named Dunya. She is a retired professional dancer who has combined her dance experience with a Sufi mystical sensibility and a selection of fabulous Arabic-oriented music.

What I learned from her was that I could move my body from the feelings evoked by the music in my body rather than moving my body from the ideas or habits that I had in my mind. The experience was one of consciousness and body movement without the "control of what we might call "mental will." We spend so much of our time driving our bodies around with our mental will that we do not often slow down to realize the direct connections between consciousness and body. Such improvised dance movement can lead us to experiencing aspects of our being that we do not often access through other practices.

Two other helpful teachers of *Full-Body Exformation* are Cynthia Winton-Henry and Phil Porter. These two innovators created the term "exformation" which I am using in my title for this category of religious practice. By "exformation" they mean experiencing the opposite of what we normally mean by "information." We take *in* so much information that we can become "chock full." We need to *"exform"*—put the inner into outward expression. Specifically, this practice includes both bodily movements and innovative talking. Phil and Cynthia are founders of a movement they call "Interplay." They have created scores of exercises that enable people to "exform" effectively and imaginatively.

One of my favorite exercises they call "Dance-Talk-Three." In groups of three or more, each person performs for the others a brief improvised dance and then talks about something going on in their lives. (No advanced thought about this is necessary, just exform whatever comes to mind.) Then that person does a second short dance movement and another brief talk session. Then he or she dances a third time; then talks a third time. Each person does this three-part process while the others witness. This exercise moves the participants beyond needless secretiveness and comfort zones and gives them an experience of sharing their lives instead of holding them in. I call this a religious practice even though it is done in a secular context. Some of the Awe of living is accessed no other way than through some form of full-body exforming.

The practice of *Full Body Exformation* can assist us to be accident prone to the "I Am" aspect of *Inherent Purity*. Rather than being preoccupied with doing the right thing and knowing for sure what the right thing is, we can find our truly good life by honestly sharing in active ways what is actually happening to us.

Visionary Trance

Of all the nine types of religious practice, *Visionary Trance* can seem the most kooky to many people. Actually, all religious practices tend to manifest what some think of as kooky elements, but with visionary trance we are observing practices that move us into a full departure from our mental sensibilities. *Visionary Trance* is a practice that is very old. It was perhaps the favorite religious practice led by the shaman in very early tribal life. In more recent times we also see instances of Visionary Trance in the practices of Pentecostals, Holy Rollers, Shakers, early Quakers, as well as in Sufi twirling, Hindu chanting, and much else. When encountering both recent and ancient forms of this practice, many people have typically dismissed such practices as ignorant superstition. We need, however, to find a plausible explanation for the continuation of such practices for thousands of years. What is the validity so many have experienced in these practices? Perhaps we skeptics have opened ourselves to a number of practices that can be also included in this category. For example, practices that promote ecstatic, mind-blowing laughter might seem OK to us. To "lose oneself in laughter" is a sort of trance. A certain kind of songfest can also be trancelike. Some songs are written to promote trance. Ecstatic drumming and dancing is another trancelike practice. Those who have experimented with dream interpretation and waking dreaming are touching into this arena. Yes, even the use of certain drugs has been an exploration into trance. However uncomfortable we highly-mental members of society may feel about exploring *Visionary Trance*, we can perhaps begin to appreciate this tradition of practice by simply noticing that all direct consciousness of the enigma of consciousness is a sort of trance in which the mind is somewhat set aside even though the mind may help express and interpret these trancelike experiences of our raw consciousness.

Ancient shamans typically understood themselves as enabling their youth or adult "clients" to take a "trip" away from their familiar thoughts and patterns of living into an "other world" of conscious experiences from which the "client" was then enabled to return and report, and then with help from the shaman learn something of value for the pursuit of their ordinary lives.

Many of us have been on religious retreats of such length that a similar departure-and-return experience was had. We found a new context in basic consciousness about our lives during such a "trip." Afterward, we returned to our ordinary lives with a challenge to integrate the trancelike trip into the quality of our ordinary living. This is the essence of the practice of *Visionary Trance*: to go away for a time from our ordinary thoughts, patterns, anxieties, distresses, despairs, apathies, etc., and then return to our ordinary lives with a fresh ability to be our being in a more transparent, victorious, and effective fashion. Perhaps we can see why this religious practice can be associated with accessing that central aspect of the "I Am" that I have named *"Enchantment with Being."*

The practice of *Visionary Trance* can assist us to be accident prone to the "I Am" aspect of *Enchantment with Being*. Rather than being preoccupied with avoiding conflict and making everybody happy, we can rediscover our profound intensity through making trips into the unusual frontiers of Reality.

* * * * * * * *

My aim in writing this chapter has not been to wrap up the immense topic of religious practice, but to spread out and intensify our imagination about what "religious practice" includes. Obviously, religious practice includes more than what has been mentioned here. Each of these arenas of practice is a deep well of possibility. And it is likewise plausible that there may be still unmentioned arenas of religious practice. But to this insight I cling: religion is practice, practice, practice, practice, before is it anything else.

Chapter 20
Religion as Social Process

Religion is rooted in practice, but it is not limited to practice. In addition to practice, a religion develops a religious theoretics (in some religions it is called "theology," in others "teachings"). Religious theoretics does not take the place of religious practice; it supports practice, perhaps criticizes practice and recreates it. Studying theology together can even be viewed as a practice. The relationship between practice and theoretics is a close one, but practice remains the core aspect—I call *practice* the *being* pole as compared with the *knowing* and *doing* poles of religion. Theoretics is the knowing aspect of religion. We need to know the meaning of our religious language and we need to know how to use and lead our various practices. Theoretics plays a supporting role to practice, but an important role.

In addition to practice and theoretics every religion develops religious bodies—social organizations that house the practices and the theoretics. These bodies have all the elements of any social body: economic processes, political processes, and cultural processes. Religious bodies are cultural institutions, but like all cultural institutions they have political and economic processes that make them viable as functioning bodies. By political processes for a religious body I mean things like membership structures, the basic covenant and rules, the leadership designs, decision-making processes, foreign relations with other bodies, and the overall missional patterns for engaging the world at large. By economic processes I mean how teachers or leaders are paid or not; how shrines, temples, and meeting places are built and cared for; and how to handle the other expenses that emerge from being a particular social body. Membership dues, sale of products, and support from the general society may figure in. In other words, all the worldly aspects of being a functioning group have a place in the definition of "religion."

Religion is a social process along with healthcare, education, life styles, political systems, economic systems, waste disposal, and so on. The following triangle of social process is a picture of the essential social processes that comprise any whole society. I have broken down the cultural processes to show where the social process of *Religious Formation* shows up in relation to every other social process.

In the logic of the following chart, the economic side of this triangular map of social processes has to do with taking in the Earth for your society, the more political side has to do with putting forth choices and actions, and the more cultural side has to do with the identity of the people for whom resources are taken in and by whom human effort is put forth. In each set of three triangles the upper left triangle is the *taking-in* aspect of that whole. The upper right triangle is the *putting-forth* aspect of that whole. The lower triangle in that set of three is the *identity* that glues the set of three together.

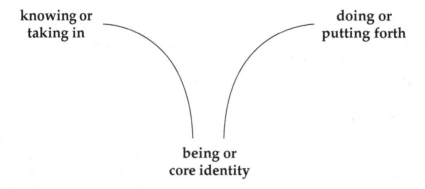

knowing or taking in

doing or putting forth

being or core identity

In the following mode of organizing the social processes, *taking in* is associated with *knowing* for knowing is a way of taking in reality. *Putting forth* is associated with doing for putting forth implies initiative. Core identity is associated with being, for identity means the grasp and expression of some "we" who know and do. It will take some practice with this method of organization and some intuitive familiarity with the essence of each social process to fully catch on to this organizational method. So if this mode of social thinking is new to you, simply contemplate this model for a while realizing that it is just a model and all models can be improved.

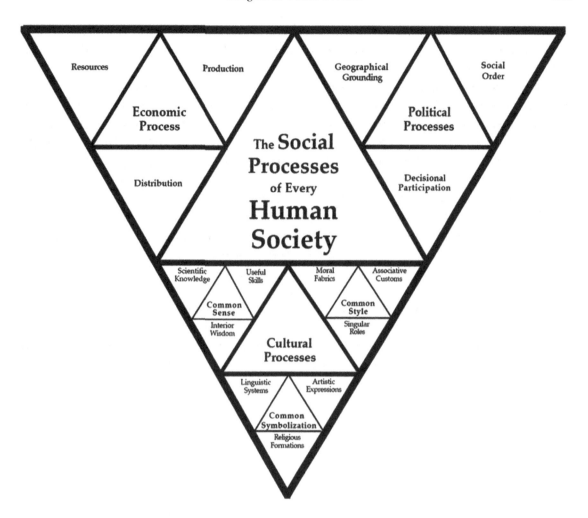

The social processes called *"Religious Formations"* is pictured in this chart as the core identity of the *Common Symbolization* processes which are the core identity of the *Cultural Processes* which are the core identity of all the social processes. This understanding is not commonly held in sociologies of both Capitalist and Marxist origins. In both of these camps of thought, the economic processes are thought to be the primary element of a society, while the political and cultural processes are thought to be subsidiary. In fact, classical Marxists typically viewed the cultural processes as merely a rationalization for the economic organization of the society. From the Marxist point of view, the values for a cultural revolution are chosen on the basis of what is expedient to support economic vision and strategy. The traditional Marxist view does not include the idea that the cultural processes provide the core identity of a society, and thus also a core revolutionary component in social change.

Nevertheless, many current Marxist thinkers are coming to a deeper appreciation of the revolutionary role of culture and religion. Alain Badiou is a vivid example of this in his book *Saint Paul: The Foundation of Universalism.*

So let us inquire further into how the history of social change is impacted by how a society formulates its basic relations with Reality—that is, its Religious Formations. A religious formation need not be opium that numbs the psyche to social responsibility; it can be a core source of revolutionary fervor. Marx is correct that most religion, both in our century and much earlier, has been an opiate. Marx says somewhere that "the critique of religion is the foundation of all critique." Such statements bring into focus how "bad religion" is a powerful factor. "Good religion" can also be viewed as a powerful social force in the opposite direction from an opiate. Though the classical Marxist view of religion as incomplete, the Marxist critique of decayed religion has played a role and can still play a role in the renewal of the religious aspect of social existence.

I turn next to a breakdown of the social process of *Religious Formulations* into 27 subsidiary processes. The following chart is the small triangle at the very bottom of the previous chart, broken down by the same organizational method into my current picture of the 27 subparts of the social process of *Religious Formations*:

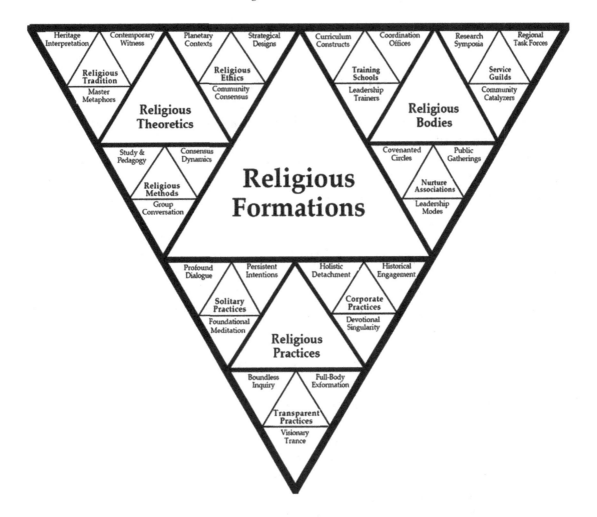

In the last chapter I discussed the *Religious Practices* third of the above chart. I will comment now on the *Religious Theoretics* third and the *Religious Bodies* third of this whole triangle. Perhaps I should warn the reader that many may find this chapter boring or disagreeable. Why? Because many people in typical contemporary cultures have come to yearn for a "spirituality" that is devoid of institutional embodiment. It is hard for many of us to accept the challenging fact that a vital religious practice is needed for our Spirit maturity, and that a religion with cultural, political, and economic processes is needed to house that vital religious practice and its theoretic underpinnings. So bear with me as I comment on each small triangle in the upper two thirds of the above chart. Such a detailed look at what is entailed in renewing an old religion or inventing a new one, may call to your consciousness old hurts you have endured from bad religions and current fears about forging a good religion or belonging to one.

Religious Theoretics

Every religious community does some thinking and forges some teachings. (1) Those teachings form an ongoing heritage that needs to be interpreted for each generation. (2) Methods have to be devised for studying those teachings and conducting life together in the "culture" of that religious community. And (3) the question of right action or ethics comes up for still further thinking and guideline creation.

(1) Religious Tradition

Below are three paragraphs—one on each of the three subparts of *Religious Tradition* in the triangular chart above. The teachings of a religious community gather over time and become heritage. This heritage may become cryptic or at least require recasting for a next generation.

1a. Heritage Interpretation

Typically a religious community wishes to both honor the truth in its founding breakthrough and speak relevantly to the contemporary experiences of the humans within its influence. In times of rapid change, the work of heritage interpretation can become controversial. Part of the community hangs on to past formulations of the heritage and part of the community reaches forward for more relevant ways of understanding the heritage. Both directions can lead to "bad religion." The backward lookers can become rigid in ways that turn old teachings into convictions that are contrary to the original fire of that religion. Similarly, the forward lookers can lose contact with the original fire by becoming accommodated to currently popular escapes from Reality. The challenge in *Heritage Interpretation* is to remain true to the essence of the heritage while also making contact with contemporary humans. For example, Christians interpreting the virgin birth of Jesus go in all three of these directions. The backward lookers insist that the virgin birth was a literal biological event proving Jesus' special standing. The forward lookers give the virgin birth a very shallow meaning or ignore it all together as an ancient superstition. The virgin-birth heritage is being genuinely recovered only when we see ourselves as capable of a "virgin birth"—that each of us can join Jesus in finding our true parentage in Eternity rather than in our earthly parents.

1b. Master Metaphors

The meaningful interrelation of all long-standing religious traditions has become unusually challenging because of the huge changes in human culture during the last couple of centuries. As spelled out in Chapter 17 we are experiencing a shift in a master metaphor, the shift from double-deck transcendence to one-realm transparency. For example, when Jews, Christians and Muslims read about the call of Isaiah in Isaiah 6, they cannot grasp the meaning of the angels with six wings and the shaking of the foundations of the temple unless they can work their minds loose from that two story-mythology into a realization that the author of this passage was talking about a shaking of the foundations of his own life and how we do not confront Eternity directly but through a cloud of Awe that hides the Awesome with its "flapping wings." Isaiah knew that this extreme poetry was about his personal life, but for us the meaning of this old poetry can be accessed only through a use of the transparency mode of interpretation.

1c. Contemporary Witness

The extent to which religious communication is conditioned by the contemporary culture is about equal to the extent that it is conditioned by the heritage. For the essence of an old religious heritage to come alive in our times that essence has to be communicated to our own lives and to the lives of others who are living in the contemporary world of sensibilities and challenges. We experience this very strongly in these times of vast and rapid change, but it has always been so. For example, among the New Testament writings the Gospel of John differs greatly from the Gospels of Mark, Matthew, and Luke. This difference is due to the fact that whoever wrote John is addressing a different time and culture. The earlier Gospels were still speaking to Hellenistic Jews, and the Gospel of John was written near the turn of the first century for people who possessed a more thoroughly Greek-oriented mentality and who needed to have simple Hebraic matters explained to them.

(2) Religious Methods

Below are three paragraphs—one on each of the three subparts of *Religious Methods* in the chart above. Methods are a very important aspect of religious formation that has been too little explored. The power and popularity of many contemporary Buddhist movements can be credited to the thoroughness with which effective methods of meditation are being taught. Western religions would also be empowered by upgrading their religious methods.

2a. Study and Pedagogy

For most people today the study of religious writings has to overcome both an anti-intellectualism that only scans written material and an intellectualism that cannot move beyond bare ideas into personal-life experience. So teaching religion requires a study method that enables the student to grasp the author's structure of thought rather than simply selecting agreeable bits and ignoring the overall address of the author. Secondly a good study method enables students to move from mental statements to the grounding of those statements in their life experiences. Study is not complete until we can draw on one page our picture of what a piece of writing is actually saying. And teaching is not complete until each student knows what the rational content of the material studied means in terms of his or her own life experiences. Scientific historical knowledge is important for understanding the original meaning of an ancient text, but our understanding of that text is incomplete until we have achieved a connection of the material with our own contemporary lives. This will require translating the old language and metaphors used in that ancient time into language and metaphors that are alive for us in our own time.

2b. Group Conversation

Lengthy talks can be important if they are crafted by informed teachers and made deeply relevant to our actual lives, but there is no substitute for conversation in which each person in a relatively small group is challenged to share profoundly their life experience and their edge questions. Good group conversations require good methods. For example, here is an effective method for discussing art. A painting or movie or poem or music can be powerfully reflected upon by using a group process that organizes the conversation in this order: (1) each person says something objective about what they actually saw or heard, (2) each person shares how they reacted or felt about the viewing or hearing of this piece of art, and only then (3) ask selected persons to share interpretive statements about what this artistic expression is saying to us today. Ancient writings also require special conversation methods. I have found that each style of religious writing requires a different method to discuss it effectively. Effective group conversation methods are needed for an optimal communal life among members of a relevant future religious formation.

2c. Consensus Dynamics

Methods are also needed to make group decisions and to think together as a group. To meet the challenges of our times, our next expressions of religious community need to be far more democratic than the religious practices that have characterized most religious formations in the past. So, it seems obvious to me that we need to teach a thoroughgoing means of consensus decision making. The Quakers pioneered consensus methods many decades ago. Many recent ecological and justice movements have also developed skills in consensus processing. In order to be fully relevant, religious groups will need to learn the best of these methods and use them throughout every layer of their decision-making structures. This is not easy to do. We find that the value of full participation needs to be balanced with disciplined and effective decision making. Also, what we can do in small groups with a consensus method can have an easy informality, while large groups will need a more formal ordering. However difficult all this may seem, effective consensus methods is another important topic for the optimal ordering of a vital religious formation.

(3) Religious Ethics

Below are three paragraphs—one on each of the three subparts of *Religious Ethics* in the chart above. A religious community is never entirely about the nurture of its members; it is also an active presence in the general society. *Religious Ethics* means discerning how that religious community can with integrity be a gift to the general society. And this gift is given as a group as well as through the life quality of each of its members. Religious formations are one of the social processes that comprise every society. So when we are practicing a religion, we do this not only on our own behalf, but on behalf of the whole society, the whole of humanity, the whole natural planet. *Religious Ethics* are the guidelines we create for that outreach into the wide world.

3a. Planetary Contexts

An important clarification about *Religious Ethics* has happened in recent decades: our ethical guidelines do not emerge from our religious teachings or written Scriptures but from our living experience of the "I Am" in our times. It is out of the basic experience of the "I Am" of profound humanness that we envision (choose with thoughtfulness) general guidelines for the future of human life on planet Earth. In former times religious ethics did not have the awareness we now have of the whole planet, but there was always a sense of something larger than "my village, or "my tribe" or "my civilization." Because religious ethics begins with an awareness of the Wholeness of Being, responsibility for the whole of social and natural reality follows. When religious people do their planetary ethical thinking from the beginning point of profound humanness rather than from some specific sectarian principles, every religion tends to come up with similar guidelines. Indeed, we no longer have a Christian ethics or a Jewish ethics or a Muslim ethics or a Hindu ethics or a Buddhist ethics. We simply have ethics created by humans upon the foundation of the "I Am" experiences from a wide variety of religious groups. Religious ethics today is becoming interreligious ethics. This is a profound point to which I have devoted the whole of Part Six of this book.

3b. Community Consensus

In our local places we begin with guidelines that are being created through the consensus building of many religious people on a planet-wide basis and for the whole planet. Each of us who is accessing our "I Am" profundity can share in building that planetary consensus, but we are also a small part of that planet-wide league of guideline building. So we find ourselves engaged in an attitude of obedience to the ongoing consensus building that is taking place in the planetary scope of discussion. Living in our local place we build further consensus among our aware neighbors on how that emerging planetary context applies to our local place. To do this we need to train one another in consensus building, inform one another about this planet-wide consensus already in process, and initiate vision and strategies that apply to taking action in our local place. As we move out into our geographical regions (whether alone or in groups), we provide leadership among others not in the name of some religion, but in the name of the truth that we are discovering as we live the "I Am" in awareness of the planetary realities and the local realities in which we live.

3c. Strategic Designs

Strategy is an important ethical category. Understanding strategy delivers us from the crime of imposing our idealistic beliefs upon situations that we may not even understand. A love-Reality strategy begins by understanding and accepting the challenge of the given situation with all its injustices, foolishness, bad thinking, prejudiced feelings, sheer meanness, and more. Strategy is a loving interaction between what now is and what needs to be according to our planet-wide and community-wide guidelines for change. Strategy is envisioning the soft points in the current conditions where change can most likely begin and devising the actions that can move the whole in a series of appropriate steps toward the type of social structures and care for one another that our "I Am" profundity is enabling us to conceive. Obviously, the "I Am" does not provide the social specifics; we have to create those through the trial-and-error guessing that characterizes all creative activity.

Religious Bodies

The thought of creating or recreating a religious body for a next expression of religious practice will be, for many people, the most disagreeable of all the topics in this book. There is a wide spectrum of people who want to be what they call "spiritual," but want to have nothing to do with any more religious bodies. This fear of a religious body is understandable, for having been injured, mistreated, and offended deeply by perverse religious bodies, it may be hard to believe that we need a religious body even if that religious body is an outgrowth of the "I Am" Truth. There is an illusion involved in the hope of being "spiritual" as a way of avoiding consideration of the need for a religious body. If "spiritual" means accessing the "I Am" profundity, we need a religious body within which and through which we express and share our "I Am" profundity. And we also need a religious body to assist us in completing our access of the "I Am" profundity.

(1) Training Schools

Below are three paragraphs—one on each of the three subparts of *Training Schools* in the chart above. If we look around we can see that almost every person or group of people who have accessed a bit of the "I Am" profundity have created some sort of Training School through which to share their discovery with others. They sometimes call these "workshops" or "retreats," but whatever we call them the basic dynamic is about creating a set of group exercises that enable people to get a taste of or a furtherance of their journey into the "I Am" realization.

1a. Curriculum Constructs

When we Christians read the New Testament dramas we call "The Gospels," we get the impression that Jesus did his teachings only once, but likely he had a set of teachings that he did over and over in village after village. There is a story in the Gospel of Luke about how he trained 70 disciples to go out two-by-two and teach his "curriculum" of core "teachings" in all the villages they could. Again and again in every age of history, curriculum constructs have come into being that were used extensively because they worked in enabling people living in that time and place to be delivered from some escape and returned to their true nature of "I Am" wonderment. Creating a curriculum for our specific time and place turns out to be an ongoing part of being a member of some group in which the "I Am" essence of human life is being recovered.

1b. Leadership Trainers

While there are circumstances in which any person might provide leadership for others with regard to realizing their true nature, the Training Schools of a vital religious formation require a leadership core who have in some measure accessed their "I Am" essence and have learned well the *Curriculum Constructs* that are making a difference in the current culture. In addition, this leadership need to become competent in the *Religious Methods* that are needed to teach those constructs in a manner that leads others toward accessing their true nature. In other words, skilled leadership is needed! Nevertheless, to be effective in the emerging cultures of our times, the formation of religious leadership needs to be done in a manner that does not establish a two-class organization. The *Leadership Trainer* is just a member of the community doing a servant task on behalf of the whole community. This trainer is training others in the means of accessing their own true nature as well as in the skills for using the effective *Curriculum Constructs* and *Religious Methods* to assist still others in accessing their true nature. Such training is best done in face-to-face groups. The use of e-mail, the internet, the telephone, and the postal services have serious limitations that go along with their advantages for easily reaching large numbers of people and the saving of transportation costs and time. But fully effective *Religious Formation* cannot be done without eye-to-eye, body-to-body communication between those who are learning and those who are leading. The less intimate means are subsidiary to the intimate means. In order to deal with the transportation costs and still have intimate associations between leaders and new members, a religious formation will need a large number of leaders and a large amount of leadership training.

1c. Coordination Offices

Coordination Offices will be required for bringing together qualified *Leadership Trainers* with an ongoing stream of learners of the vital *Curriculum Constructs* of that religious formation in its time and place. As we view this picture we are viewing how it becomes necessary for a fully developed *Religious Body* to come into being. Whether we are viewing crowds of people following an itinerant teacher walking through the villages of ancient Galilee or the more complex organizations that are typical of our 21st Century cultures, we are talking about creating religion as a social process within the other social processes of our down-to-Earth human societies. These *Coordination Offices* will require economic processes and political processes that enable and support the cultural processes that are basic to vital and continuing *Religious Formations*.

(2) Nurture Associations

Below are three paragraphs—one on each of the three subparts of *Nurture Associations* in the chart above. Not only are *Training Schools* an obvious emergence for expanding a breakthrough of "I Am" realization, also obvious is the truth that awakening persons need regular meetings with their peers. Awakening individuals enter a process of emergence that has no end. A retreat or school may occasion a fresh beginning of "new" life, but this new life is then lived daily, weekly, monthly, yearly. Daily and weekly practices of religion are implied from our experience in living the "I Am" life within our estranged cultures. Our efforts to live the "I Am" life teaches us the need for regular meetings with our peers in order to sustain this ongoing "I Am" emergence.

2a. Covenanted Circles

Whether we call them sanghas, base communities, house churches, resurgence circles, support groups, or something else, intimate groups are springing up in almost every vital religion. Perhaps one of the reasons for such interest in small groups is that intimate associations beyond the nuclear family have to be arranged in contemporary culture where both individualism and collectivism squeeze out deep personal relations. This felt need for regular small group meetings I interpret as a sign that the next stage in *Religious Formations* needs to emphasize small intimate group associations. This does not require us to devalue larger gatherings, but it raises questions about what those larger gatherings need to be. We also need to raise questions about what small group practice needs to be, if we are to emphasize religious formation aimed at the access of the "I Am" profundity. To begin with, the small groups of the next religious formations need to emphasize *Universal Forgiveness* (the welcome home to Reality of every person). This will tend to make the members of a small group feel safe to do open sharing of their lives. Also needed is a willingness to face fully our escapes from Reality and "enjoy" the eyes of others upon us to assist us to see those escapes and to work through the recasting of the entire round of our lives toward manifesting all aspects of our "I Am" being. In order for small group life to maintain such a commitment to depth, we will need some sort of covenant that outlines our responsibility for regular attendance, care for one another, and upfront clarity about the purpose of the group and the methods and curriculum to be used.

2b. Leadership Modes

Also needed to maintain depth in our small group life will be two or three members in each circle who have been trained in the *Training Schools*, in the *Curriculum*

Constructs, and in the *Religious Methods* that each small group will need to learn and use. These small group leaders need not see themselves as the only leaders in the group, but the importance of their presence and service to the group will need to be rather explicit. The role of those leaders in anchoring the group in a religious practice that has depth will need to be carried out in a style that is neither dictatorial nor permissive. In our contemporary culture our ideas of leadership flip back and forth between encouraging our groups to do whatever their whims desire or controlling the group with an iron hand of imposition. It will be an ongoing challenge to discover how we combine (1) a respect for the autonomy and decisional participation of each person with (2) a disciplined ordering of activities that honor the agreed upon purpose of these group meetings. What is most clear is that a leadership that honors these challenges is a necessary part of our emerging patterns of religious formation.

2c. Public Gatherings

Another way that small group life can be enriched is regular associations with other small groups doing the same religious practices. These larger gatherings will need to be well organized by competent leaders and held regularly enough to be a part of the ongoing pattern of religious practice. If the *Covenantal Circles* meet weekly, the *Public Gatherings* might meet at least quarterly. The *Public Gatherings* might gather only those who are members of Covenantal Circles or these gatherings might also gather persons who are interested in exploring Circle life or organizing new Circles. I am attempting to describe guidelines that can apply to many different religious practices, but each set of religious practices within each culture will be different. The core point of this paragraph is that some sort of balance between *Public Gatherings* and *Covenantal Circles* will need to guide the future organization of a *Religious Body* that supports a relevant religion on planet Earth in century twenty-one.

(3) Service Guilds

Below are three paragraphs—one on each of the three subparts of *Service Guilds* in the chart above. In these next three paragraphs I will insist that in order to be a full manifestation of the "I Am" profundity, the next *Religious Bodies* will need to develop a balance between nurturing "inreach" and contributing "outreach" to the whole of humanity and planet Earth. A best-case religion is both a personal discipline and a social process that moves outwardly, taking its place of responsibility within the other social processes of the society.

3a. Research Symposia

The ethical manifestations of our "I Am" experiences will result in an ongoing process of consensus building. We can no longer accept the notion of permanent principles dropping down from a divine realm, so we are cast into the ongoing task of creating our ethical guidelines through consensus building conducted by well informed persons who are also grounded in their "I Am" being. This means organizing groups of persons who are committed to work on selected topics throughout a period of time communicating with each other regularly and meeting face-to-face at least once a year. The results of such *Research Symposia* will then be published or in some way taught to all the *Covenantal Circles* in a given Network of Religious Practice.

3b. Community Catalyzers

When we imagine several *Covenantal Circles* in the same local community, we can imagine select members from a number of those Circles taking on specific issues that arise in their local place. *"Catalyzers"* is a term meant to communicate that these Circle members do not act in the name of their Circle or their religion. Rather they join local community organizations and play creative roles within those secular groupings. Also, they may organize new secular groups. And the persons who do these sorts of things may come from "Circles" that practice different religions. For example, some members of a Buddhist Sangha may join with some members of a Christian Circle to protest some malpractice or advocate for some key change in community life. As indicated earlier, *Religious Ethics* do not derive from a religious practice, but from the "I Am" profundity that all effective religious practices attempt to access.

3c. Regional Task Forces

If "Regional" means a wider scope of geography than local community, region-wide social responses will look different from *Community Catalyzers*. A *Regional Task Force* would need to be a rather formal organization spending the time required to research the needs of some planetary region, design an inclusive vision for that region, and create the strategies needed to make the envisioned changes. Again, members of such a task force may come from a wide range of religious practices but still be working from the same base in "I Am" realization. One of the gifts brought to social action from the presence of vital religious groups is skill in working with people and skill in avoiding burnout during the long struggles that it takes to deal with powerful opposition. Fostering hope in seemingly hopeless circumstances is a core service that effective religious formations can bring to Regional Task Forces.

Recapitulation on Religion as a Social Process

My description of these 27 subparts of my chart on *Religious Formations* has been far less than exhaustive. My aim in this chapter has been to paint a comprehensive portrait of what is involved in viewing religion as a social process within the whole pattern of essential social processes that make up a whole human society. To be religious in the deepest meaning of that term is something more than a private, psychological avocation. A "healthy" religion assists members of a society to access their true being and to live that true being for the benefit and enrichment of the entire society as well as for the well-being of the planet upon which every society depends. The election to be religious is more like a vocation than an avocation. A vital religion spawns a *calling* or life quest from which our set of finite vocations can emerge and become rewarding. And our set of finite vocations can include the finite vocation of organizing and renewing the next expression of the religion that we choose to practice.

Seeing religion as a social process provides us with essential clarity on how to reinvent vital religion. A religion is just another social process; it is not more divine than waste disposal. But if a religion is fulfilling its role as a means of accessing our true being, it is assisting us to access That which may be called "divine"—the Every-thing-ness in which all things cohere that is also the No-thing-ness out of which all things come and to which all things return, both of which comprise the Awesome that Awes us profoundly.

Chapter 21
The Vital Variety of Religious Practices

Because religions are created by human beings and because human beings live in numerous and very different cultures, religion takes on a huge variety of practices, beliefs, and moralities. This variety is so great that it may seem at first that little can be said that applies to all religions. And that would be true if we were looking at specific beliefs, specific practices, or specific moral guidelines. It has been my aim in Chapters 17-20 to talk about religion in general terms; nevertheless, it may seem to some readers that my description of religion as a general category excludes some of what is often called "religion."

Part of such difficulty may stem from my aim to describe universal qualities that I claim apply to all *good* religion. I have thereby implied that there is such a thing as *bad* religion, religion that functions in ways that are opposite or almost opposite to the essential functions I have described for good religion. We humans unavoidably apply criteria of good and bad to all humanly formed social processes. We speak of good education and bad education, good economics and bad economics. We assume that there are ways of evaluating these aspects of society—such as workability, justice, effectiveness, truthfulness, etc. We experience a similar need to evaluate "religion." I am assuming that credible ways exist for evaluating each specific manifestation of the essential social process I have named *"Religious Formation."* For example, I have written essays on how so much religion has fallen into intellectualism, moralism, and sentimentalism. I mean this as criticism.

Clearly, I am assuming that each and every religion can be evaluated good-better-best, or bad-worse-worst. And my criteria for this evaluation is how each particular religion corresponds with: (1) the realism of the scientific approach to truth, (2) the realism of the contemplative approach to truth (especially, does that religion attempt to express and open us to our true nature—that profound humanness that I have explored through the concept of the "I Am"?) and (3) the realism of the workability approach to truth (especially, does that religion enable us to be more prone to the "accident" of realizing our true nature?).

Nevertheless, it is still a credible possibility that I could be using *my* religion as the criteria for the judgment of all religion. It is my aim, however, to avoid using my specific form of Christian practice as the definition of all good religion. I am attempting to articulate a philosophy of religion that is broader than "my religion." I am attempting to provide my own religion with a philosophy of religion that applies to all religion. Whether I am succeeding with this intent is open for examination, but I firmly believe that such a philosophy is needed and possible. We need such a philosophy because we now live in interreligious communities, cities, nations, and planet. We must learn to think and work interreligiously. To do so we need a definition of religion that is broader than any one religion and that provides us with ways to honor all religions in their always-fragmentary means of assisting people to access their profound humanness.

With my adventures into universal statements about what religion is and what makes religion good or bad, I do not want to slip into any implication that this universality is a subtle version of my religion that I am using as criteria for the judgment of other religions. I count such a view as bigotry and view such bigotry as the source of much needless conflict and violence in the world. I am seeking criteria that are deeper than my religion, criteria that judge my religion as well as every other religion. Even the word "criteria" is misleading if it means a set of rational statements. I am using the word "criteria" to indicate a baseline in human experience about experiencing our experience of the profound roots of human consciousness. This is a pre-rational "standard" that also transcends the word 'standard." Applying this experiential consciousness as our "standard" is not the same as applying a set of rational principles. I am envisioning a sort of enigmatic "un-standard standard" that we can apply intuitionally, based upon our own experience of our own profound experience.

I am assuming that Buddhist practices can access the same profound humanness that Christian practices can access. These two religions (actually two groups of religions) open us to slightly different aspects of profound humanness, but it is the same "elephant" that is being touched by all the various "blind men" in the wide variety of Buddhist practices and in the wide variety of Christian practices. Whether any of these practices are good depends on whether they actually put us in touch with the "elephant" of our profound humanness. And if any of these practices are judged "bad," it needs to be because they cloud or escape from or prevent our consciousness from touching the "elephant." I am attempting to develop a sense of profound humanness that stands in judgment of all religious practices. Religious practices are not good or bad because they are finite human creations, for such finitude is true of all religions. The issue is whether each finite human creation of religion has the power (or even the intent) of making us more prone to the "accident" of profound humanness discovery. If you grant me the statement that good religion (true religion) is any practice that assists humans to access the "I Am" profundity of our true nature, we clearly face a vast variety of religious practices that are *good* and an even greater variety of religious practices that are *bad*.

Furthermore, each religion comes into being within an ongoing dialogue with the vast religious diversity that surrounds it. Religions quite commonly learn from one another. A huge "borrowing" is going on between Buddhism and Christianity at this moment in history. Christians are enhancing the contemplative qualities of Christianity with help from Buddhist meditation practices and theoretics. And Buddhists are enhancing the social engagement qualities of Buddhist practice with help from the ethical intensity that Buddhists are learning from the best of Christianity and Judaism.

Christians who argue that Christian ideas and ways of practice dropped down from heaven are clouding the fact that the New Testament formation period was doing wholesale borrowing from Judaism and Mediterranean Paganism, as well as from sophisticated forms of Greek religion and philosophy. Some have argued that early Christianity was so eclectic that it can claim nothing unique to itself. I believe that to be an exaggeration: I believe that the religious elements that those first Christians adopted from their surroundings were given a unique cast that flowed from the breakthrough in awareness that was initiated by Jesus' life, death, and the resurrection taking place among the bodily lives of his followers. But however that may be, it stands as factual history that all religions take elements of religion from the planet-wide religious treasury; they take whatever assists them to enable their unique formation of religion to become what works for them as an assistance toward the maturation of the profound consciousness that they are discovering. And we do well to continue doing such interreligious swapping today.

The above insights are important for undergirding what we now call "interreligious dialogue." We now live in a planet-wide ferment of interreligious cultures. We live on one planet, mixing the antiquities and futures of all expressions of human culture. Furthermore, this dialogue has become more than swapping ideas or moral principles. For example, many Christians now realize that to be fully engaged in interreligious dialogue, they need to meditate with the Buddhists, attend festivals with the Jews, pray head-on-the-floor with the Muslims, sit in sweat lodges with the Pagans, and so on. It is these down-to-Earth practices that make a religion a workable religion. So the aware ones among us are already trying out practices on a planet-wide scale and adopting what works for us into our chosen religious emphasis.

The vast variety of religious practices is a vital treasury precisely because of its variety. It is understandable that the many finite approaches created by religiously creative humans have been and will continue to be various, multiple, many, and continually creative. While each of us may focus our creativity on one religious heritage, we do so within a planet-wide interreligious dialogue. In doing so we learn not only to honor more our chosen heritage but also to discover greater respect and cooperation among all the varieties of human religion and human society.

Part Five

Six Ways to Imagine the Unimaginable

Part Five: Six Ways to Imagine the Unimaginable

22. Six Primal Metaphors for Religious Formation
23. The Primal Metaphor of Sub-Asia
24. The Primal Metaphor of Arabia
25. The Primal Metaphor of Europe
26. The Primal Metaphor of the Orient
27. The Primal Metaphor of Sub-Saharan Africa
28. The Primal Metaphor of Native America
29. Spirit Completeness beyond all Metaphors

Introduction to Part Five

When we push the essence of interreligious dialogue to its deepest places, we discover that different geographical places on the planet developed in their classical periods different basic ways of framing their religious talk. This can be examined by attempting to describe the primal metaphors that underlie these different types of religious thought. There have been at least six quite distinct primal metaphors. Describing them is a challenging task, and my efforts here may be open to oversimplification, big misunderstandings, and even strong arguments. But the importance of this basic vision is worth the risks of sharing this admittedly elementary beginning on a highly complicated study worthy of many lifetimes of work by scholars wiser than I.

Also, our understanding is complicated by the fact that all six of these primal metaphors are now becoming consciously heard and used in all parts of the planet. We live in an interreligious era. Every large city houses bits of almost every cultural creation from the entire planet. This fact is, however, one of the reasons why this discussion is important. Being religious today in a responsible way entails expanding our view of what religion is.

In the following chapters I will often look back historically in order to clarify the essence of these six primal metaphors. We can often see a primal metaphor most clearly when we view it before that culture was impacted by the primal metaphors from other sectors of the planet.

Chapter 22
Six Primal Metaphors for Religious Formation

My interest in world cultures began under the tutelage of Joseph W. Mathews as he, other colleagues, and I were teaching International Training Institutes all across the world. It was plain to us that being a Christian in India or Japan or Africa was different from being a Christian in Europe or America. Christians have tended to bring to nonwestern cultures a Westernized form of Christian witness that implied contempt for nonwestern cultures. This has tended to make Christians in these nonwestern cultures needlessly alienated from the religious wonders of their native places. As part of our attempt to promote a form of Christianity that was respectful of all cultures and religions, we attempted to understand these world cultures in relation to their quite different ways of giving form to the basic religious impulse.

Mathews came up with a model of six basic cultural areas, each of which is rooted in a uniquely different way of giving religious form to profound humanness. He characterized these six cultural symbols as "Ur-images." In this book I have defined "image" in a particular way, namely as the mental recording of multi-sensory reruns that is common to all animal life. That understanding of "image' was not what Mathews was pointing to with his term "Ur-image." Rather, his Ur-image was a very basic kind of religious symbol. So, I will use the term "primal metaphor" rather than "Ur-image." There is something poetic about the term "Ur," (reflecting as it does an ancient city by that name), but perhaps "primal" is more clarifying. And "metaphor" is also quite descriptive of the cultural form that Mathews had in mind.

Mathews saw six distinct cultural areas of the planet, about which our reading and our visiting indicated were geographical expanses with a similar primal metaphor: (1) Sub-Asia—especially India and its close surrounding places, (2) Arabia—from the old Babylonian Empire that is now Iraq through Egypt to the rest of North Africa. (3) Europe—the upper Mediterranean all the way to Scandinavia and Ireland. (4) The Orient—China, Japan, Korea, Vietnam, and adjacent places, (5)

Sub-Saharan Africa—the wide variety of ancient cultures dating back to the primal origins of humanity, and (6) The Americas—before European settlement. There have been questions raised about this model, such as: Is there a seventh primal metaphor characterizing some of the Pacific Islands? But I will go with Mathews' six-primal-metaphor model, recognizing that it is a model—a very useful one for making the basic point that religious formations have developed in different ways in different places with different primal understandings of what it means to be profoundly human.

The insights that I will share in the next six chapters are only sketches for a research project that could take generations to complete, and that is clearly beyond my competence. I have not studied and do not have time to study in the remaining years of my life what would be needed to in order to do an adequate job of fully exploring these topics. I do, however, experience enough intuitive wisdom about these cultures from my readings and my visits and conversations to propose this basic hypothesis that can at least encourage further research. I am willing to go out on a limb about this, because I am convinced that this topic is important for every person living on this planet of thoroughly interacting cultures and religions.

My basic hypothesis is that a unique and primal cultural metaphor has conditioned the development of the resident religions of each of these six geographical areas. This metaphor has been largely unconscious or simply taken for granted by most members of these cultures. We now live for the first time in an era of human history in which many of us have had encounters with these various peoples and can therefore understand and need to understand the basic differences in these six zones of human religious formation. We now have a need to become more and more aware of how significantly different the formations of religion have been in different parts of the planet. And we need to know that the taken-for-granted primal metaphor of our own culture turns out to be a human creation, not a "truth" appearing from some universal realm. We can hold that the primary essence of being human is everywhere the same, and yet see that our ways of understanding, nurturing, and enacting that primal humanness have been and still are fundamentally different from at least five other regions of the planet. When we are confused about those differences, we can become arrogantly oppressive, supposing that our taken-for-granted cultural uniqueness is the universal by which other cultures are to be judged. Such unconscious oppressiveness is one of the roots of our malice toward one another that we surely need to overcome. So I have dedicated these chapters to calling attention to these very deep cultural differences.

Here is a poetic summation of the Chapters to follow:

Chapter 23. The Primal Metaphor of Sub-Asia–Uniting with the Infinite Silence
Chapter 24. The Primal Metaphor of Arabia–Intimacy with the Eternal Communicator
Chapter 25. The Primal Metaphor of Europe–Ordering the Absolute Wonder
Chapter 26. The Primal Metaphor of the Orient–Balance within Inclusive Community
Chapter 27. The Primal Metaphor of Africa–Attunement with the Final Rhythm
Chapter 28. The Primal Metaphor of Native America–Designing the Unstoppable Flow

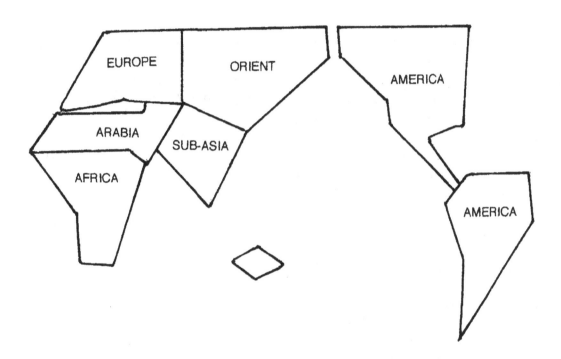

Chapter 23
The Primal Metaphor of Sub-Asia

Hinduism and Buddhism are not the only religious formations that originated in Sub-Asia, but they are the largest ones. They have spread, especially Buddhism, to other areas and adapted to those cultures while carrying with them the inner logic of the Sub-Asian metaphor for approaching Final Reality. I am naming that metaphor, *Uniting with the Infinite Silence.*

The Hindu saying, "That I Am." is one of the clearest expressions of this primal metaphor. That (Infinite Silence) I (Profound me) Am. That (Eternal Brahman, beyond all temporal passing things) and I (the Atman or Great Self) Am. In other words, That and I are of one Reality. In the final realization of myself, I experience a union with the Infinite Silence. I am one with that Absolute Stillness beyond all the busy, noisy things of life. Part of what this means is a highly exalted view of personal being. My essence cannot be understood as a psychological pattern or a sociological conditioning. I am a Mysterious Part of that equally Mysterious Whole. In this sense, I transcend my culture, my body, my biology, my personality, my ego, my whatever I have typically referred to as "my self." The route to experiencing this essential "me" entails a detachment from all these temporal things. This freedom from all things enables a consequent "return" or "engagement" in all temporal things in a free and nonchalant fashion.

Buddhism perfected methods of sitting in alert silence and stillness, watching the inflow and outflow of the living breath as well as achieving awareness of the coming and going of sensations, thoughts and feelings. The final aim of this intense concentration was to experience the union of the concentrator with this Infinite Silence/Stillness. This means experiencing an "I" that is something more than my coming and going sensations, thoughts, and feelings. I am that Silence. I am that Stillness. I exist not merely in the temporal comings and goings, but as one with the entire cosmos of Every-Thing-Ness, indeed the Stillness beyond all that moves or sounds. The Hindu foundation for Buddhism is clearly retained. Buddhist enlightenment resonates with the experience pointed to by the phrase "That I Am." Many Buddhist teachers teach that their "enlightenment" is an experience of "no self." But this "no self" does not mean having no inner life or no responsibility for living my temporal existence. I find it clarifying to view "no self" as an expression of the loss of everything we normally take to be our self. We are not our ego. We are not our personality. We are not our social conditioning. We are not our reputation among humanity. We are a mysterious at-one-ment with Being as a Whole.

I am not attempting to give a complete description of the vast variety of Buddhist and Hindu practices and reflections, but simply to note a metaphor that is operating in this complex set of ancient religions originating and functioning within this Sub-Asian cultural zone.

Uniting with the Infinite Silence can be understood as a conscious experience in the living here and now. This experience is Timeless. This experience is wholly Now. The Infinite "That" and the deep "I" are both Timeless. The realized no-self or Atman Self is timeless. In the depth experience pointed to by the metaphor *Uniting with the Infinite Silence,* the temporal world stops. I exist in the Now. The past is only memory. The future is only anticipation of not yet. In this Now I am liberated from both memory and anticipation. I live in Freedom, and within this Freedom I return to my temporal world. I have memories and anticipations. I have a body with its sensations, emotions, and thoughts. But I am living within a liberation or detachment from the temporal flow. I live in the temporal flow as a non-temporal union with the Timeless.

With the aid of many competent Buddhist and Hindu teachers, this basic motif for religious practice is making an enormous impact on Europe and the Americas. These revitalized forms of Sub-Asian practice are challenging Westerners to inquire beyond the psychological and sociological views of themselves into a grounding in conscious experience that is more basic to who they are as human beings.

As we will see, this primal metaphor is also a human creation, and thus it is finite and limited like all the other primal metaphors. It is a primal metaphor that is no better than the other primal metaphors. But it is a powerful and useful metaphor, and its current revival of clarity challenges all religions, from whatever zone of culture, to pay attention to the depths of consciousness that this metaphor encourages. Every area of the world deals with the enigma of consciousness, but Sub-Asia specializes in a research of consciousness. In being so focused Sub Asia has pioneered treasures that can deepen all the other heritages. Many Westerns are already experiencing an important deepening through their respectful dialogue with this zone of inquiry.

Chapter 24
The Primal Metaphor of Arabia

Arabia is the cultural geography that initiated Judaism, Christianity, and Islam. All three of these religions have traveled beyond their place of origin, and they took their Arabian primal metaphor with them. The primal metaphor of Arabia is distinctly different from the primal metaphor of Sub-Asia. I have chosen the name *Dialogue with the Infinite Communicator* to illuminate the contrast with the Sub-Asian *Uniting with the Infinite Silence.* The Arabian religious formations are characterized by a more passionate attention to the details of history and an emphasis on interpersonal relations among humans and between humans and Final Reality.

Arabic stories sound something like this: "In the beginning the Infinite Communicator Spoke and the temporal cosmos appeared." Every aspect of temporal reality is the Speech of this Infinite Communicator. "In the beginning was the Word." This Word is not a set of Hebrew, Greek, Arabic, or English words. It is the speech of the Infinite. We can state the nature of this Word in a starkly paradoxical manner: this Word is the Speech of the Infinite Silence. How do we experience this Speech? We experience it in the events of temporal history. Our birth is a first Word to us. The presence of the entire natural world is a Word to us. The ups and downs of social history are all Words to us. The end of society is a Word to us. The end of our own historical lives is a Word to us. This is how Reality is visualized: a conversation: Thou-I-Thou-I-Thou-I-Thou-I-Thou. This is a temporal picture. It is not timeless. It is a dialogue taking place through time. Time is important in the Arabian primal metaphor; it is where Final Reality is met and responded to. Time is where we fall away from our loyalty to Final Reality and where we are restored to the family of those who are devoted to Final Reality. This is the metaphor of Arabia. Time has a meaning not given to it in the Sub-Asia primal metaphor.

The following diagram lays out some contrasts between these two primal metaphors:

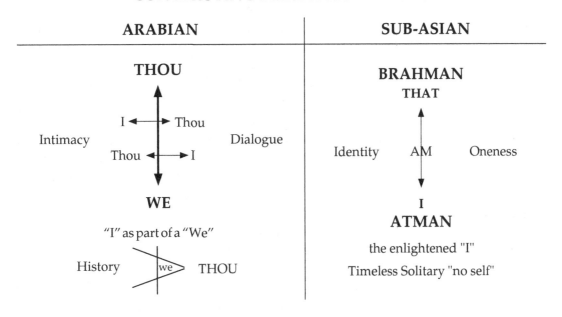

CONTRASTING PRIMAL METAPHORS

Notice the emphasis on solitary identity in the Sub-Asia primal metaphor compared with the emphasis on intimacy (I-Thou and WE–THOU) in the Arabian primal metaphor. By "intimacy" among humans I mean the experience of looking into the eyes of another human being and seeing a conscious being looking back. Of course, Sub-Asian cultures are not oblivious to intimacy experiences, but in the Arabian cultural antiquity this intimacy experience became basic to its primal metaphor. The relations among humans and between humanity and Final Reality are drawn as an intimate dialogue through time. The Almighty "Thou" calls us into conversation. Too often in our scientific age this metaphor has been dismissed because its interpreters have understood it literally. Of course, Final Reality is not a big person who inserts Hebrew, Greek, or Arabic words into our passive heads. "Dialogue" is a metaphor for understanding the actual eventfulness of our lives. We are called out of Egypt to be an un-Egyptian experiment in social law and communal life. We are taken into Exile to learn that our devotion is not limited to simple nationalism. We return to our Promised Land to reestablish our treasury of living wisdom for all nations. This deep communal and historical emphasis of ancient Judaism is also present in Christianity and Islam. I have used the terms "We–Thou" in the above diagram to signal this primary emphasis on being a people—a people of God, a Divine Kingdom, a Holy Commonwealth, a communion of saints, a "We" commissioned by this "Thou" to bring healing to all peoples.

But in spite of these fundamental differences in emphasis between these two distinct cultures, members of these two cultural groups can speak to and understand each other. Indeed, they possess some important common ground. Both primal metaphors have enabled deep clarity on the "truth" that whatever is born and dies is not Eternal—that temporal "things" are not worthy of our absolute devotion. Our nations come into being and go out of being. Our families come into being and go out of being. Our own bodies come into being and go out of being. Our feelings come into being and go out of being. Our thoughts come into being and go out of being. Our personalities are developed by us and die with our bodies. Indeed, our view of who we are may die sooner than our bodies. We may see in this present moment that our personalities are finite, built by ourselves, a pattern of habits that imprison us. We may see now that in our profound depths we are more than our personalities, more than the egos that our personality habits imply that we are. Sub-Asian Buddhists may speak of realizing our "no self." Arabia speaks of dying to self in order to find our true self. Both groups of religious traditions imply that what we truly are is beyond personality and ego—and beyond all the temporal relations that comprise our ongoing historical lives. We are Eternity-participating beings.

Also, both primal metaphors include a strong emphasis on freedom. Judaism, Christianity, and Islam all witness to an awareness of imprisonment in the patterns of finite selfhood as well as an awareness of the possibility of realizing our deep freedom—the freedom to break out of the habits of the past, the freedom to choose freedom as our mode of operation rather than continuing in our addictions to what we desire or want to flee. The Arabian saint sees that each of us, instead of embracing this freedom that is our real lives, have been enslaved to the temporal in two ways: (1) we are attached to things that are passing and (2) we flee from the fullness of life and its responsibilities. The deep self, the true self, the essential soul of a human being is a boundless freedom that is not determined by our circumstances, our bodies, our emotions, our thoughts, our habits, our personality. We can access that freedom or we can lose that freedom into an incarceration in personality patterns that we have invented and with which we identify and passionately defend.

"Plant your feet firmly therefore within the freedom that Christ has won for us, and do not let yourselves be caught again in the shackles of slavery."[20] This was a core teaching of the apostle Paul. According to the first witnesses of the Christian breakthrough, our estrangements from Reality have formed a prison of bondage. The meaning of the Christ happening in the human story is that bondage has

---

[20] Galatians 5:1; J. B. Phillips translation

been broken open; we can walk forth as free beings. We have "idolized" things that are born and that die, and thereby lost our loyalty to both Eternity and our time-embodied lives. But when we have died with Christ (the profound human) and been raised up into this profound humanness, we manifest a freedom from estrangements. Similar teachings about freedom appear in Judaism and Islam.

After such "liberation," we find that both Arabian and Sub-Asian cultures describe the freed person returning to live freely within the temporal flow. That does not mean a full control of the flow of temporal events. We still face limitations as part of the external realities of life. But this inner freedom is a freedom to accept limits as well as to engage in possibilities that have a limited but relevant and surprising impact upon the course of events.

The contrast between the primal metaphors of Arabia and Sub-Asia is most vivid in how this temporal living is pictured. Sub-Asia emphasizes a sort of timelessness that tends to minimize the significance of specific temporal events, while the Arabian sensibilities tend to see each temporal event as a Word or Communication with the Final Reality that calls "the hearer" into the freedom to respond to that Final Reality in the flow of history. Arabian worshipers see themselves called to make history. Sub-Asian sensibilities focus on liberating individuals from the karma of history.

Both of these emphases are meaningful, and these two cultures are learning from one another (made possible by this interreligious era). For example, a number of contemporary Buddhist teachers now advocate an "engaged" Buddhism that seeks to enthusiastically define justice and social action. In Christian circles it would sound strange to speak of an engaged Christianity, for Christianity, at its prophetic best, is always engaged in history. In Christian circles we sometimes speak of a contemplative Christianity that helps to ground our social action in our true beings. But in Buddhist circles, they need not speak of a contemplative Buddhism, for such a focus is assumed.

Seeing that both the primal metaphors of Sub-Asia and Arabia are metaphors rather than literal truths brings the "dialogue" between Sub-Asia and Arabia into a deep level of lucidity. Like viewing light as both *wave* and *particle* in the domain of physics, *dialogue* and *union* in the domain of religion are two inventions of the human mind—neither of which can fully comprehend the human participation with Final Reality. Light is neither *wave* nor *particle*; it is both. And Final Realty is more than a "Thou" with which we *dialogue through time* and Reality is more than a *timeless union* in which the ordinary self disappears. Our experience of Final Reality is both of these perceptions, and it is more.

Chapter 25
The Primal Metaphor of Europe

When I speak of the primal metaphor of Europe, I am thinking of the Greek or Athenian-impacted Europe. Europe has now become the home of many primal metaphors, so I am really focusing upon the Hellenism that drove the Alexandrian and Roman Empires. In the ancient Athenian city-state, this primal metaphor had already reached sophisticated expression in the teachings and writings of Socrates, Plato, Aristotle, the Greek Playwrights, and others. Like all primal metaphors, this metaphor has roots that disappear into antiquity. The Homeric and pre-Homeric literature was evolving this metaphor. When we look carefully into this emerging flurry of creativity, we find a primal metaphor that has most to do with order and chaos, with reason and mystery. I will name it *"Ordering the Absolute Wonder."*

The Westward spread of Judaism, Christianity, and Islam carried the Arabian primal metaphor into Europe and combined it with the European metaphor to such an extent that it is not easy to sort out the ancient European metaphor in its pure form. Also, Plato and Aristotle wrote sophisticated philosophies that may cloud the simplicity of the ancient metaphor that these philosophers assumed. Nevertheless, the following description will surely resonate with European people and with European migrants to the Americas. For all these lands are now deeply characterized by this basic way of relating to Final Reality. The explosion of contemporary science was spawned and nurtured by a society rooted in the ancient primal metaphor described in this chapter.

The key dynamic we need to notice here is the tension between chaos and order. Does Final Reality have an order, or is chaos the essence of things? And what do we mean by order? And what do we mean by a lack of order? Clearly the human mind has evolved with a capacity to conceive patterns in our experience of nature and use our awareness of those patterns to enhance our survival and well-being. So is there, we might ask, a Final Pattern toward which our human patterning may be trending. Scientists like Newton and Einstein have thought so. Einstein's patterns were seen by him and by the generations that followed him as a more valid approximation of the way physical things work than what was previously envisioned in the Newtonian system. In spite of such vast changes in scientific knowledge, it has seemed to most scientists, as well to Plato and Aristotle, that the cosmos is intelligible or is in large measure intelligible. So many people have postulated a Final Intelligibility toward which obedient, thoughtful, human inquiry can trend.

Yet there has always been a minority report, currently stated in this sentence endorsed by many contemporary physicists: "The more we know about nature, the more we know we don't know." Thomas Aquinas, that great synthesizer of Aristotelian and Hebraic wisdom, posited an Eternal Law, but went on to claim that this Eternal Law was beyond the capacity of the human mind to grasp. This implies that Mystery or Chaos is the real essence of things and that order is simply what the human mind can put together as wisdom about an overwhelming Reality that the human mind can never hope to encompass.

But whatever has been the optimism or pessimism about the human mind's capacity for some sort of Universal Intelligibility, chaos and order, mystery and reason have been the preoccupation of this segment of the planet.

Europe and Arabia, Athens and Jerusalem

Through the centuries, Christians as well as Jews and Muslims have sought to synthesize the Arabian metaphor of *Dialogue with the Infinite Communicator* with the European metaphor of *Ordering the Absolute Wonder*. Christianity arose in a sea of Hellenistic Judaism. By the end of the first century, New Testament writings like John's gospel and letters were using Greek metaphors and addressing Greek culture directly. Toward the end of the fourth century and the beginning of the fifth, Augustine synthesized the "ordering" of Plotinus' Platonism with the historical import of the I-Thou dialogue emphasis found in Hebrew and Christian Scriptures. Thomas Aquinas constructed another synthesis in the 12th century, when his religious order was learning Aristotelian-impacted philosophy arriving from the Muslim world. At that time Europe had forgotten Aristotle and followed Augustine's preference for Plato and Plotinus. Thomas was attracted to Aristotle's manner of finding order in the empirical data of material happenings. He assumed that the natural laws that Aristotle discerned could be reconciled with the more Hebraic elements retained in the heritage of the Catholic Church.

Thomas's synthesis was not sustained by all of those who came after him. Some have made *Ordering the Absolute Wonder* paramount and dismissed *Dialogue with the Infinite Communicator* as superstition. Others have gone in the opposite direction, fighting with science whenever it seemed to contradict with what they thought they knew from their *Dialogue with the Infinite Communicator.*

This war between fanatics of Western science and fanatics of Western religion has persisted to this day. I call them "fanatics," because there need be no irresolvable conflict between *Dialogue with the Infinite Communicator* and *Ordering the Absolute Wonder.* Each of these primal metaphors can be seen as poetic expressions drawing attention to experience, rather than seen as literalized systems of rational beliefs.

Today we are experiencing some fresh synthesis of the wisdoms of these two primal metaphors. We know more clearly than some generations have known that Mystery surrounds us and only grows deeper as we learn more. Furthermore, natural reality in its deepest and broadest scopes is so unimaginable to the human mind that even order-loving research scientists are carried into experiences of extreme wonder at the shocking Mystery of it all. So, the best of research science can be viewed as a religious practice and as including a religious perception in terms of the definition of religion that we have been elaborating. An openness to deep Awe before the truly Awesome has happened in the very heart of science.

In the more Arabian side of Western culture, literal understandings of Final Reality's "Speech" are being abandoned under a bombardment from the sciences. For example, a literal creation of the Earth in seven days has been given up by all but the most belligerent defenders of a magically revealed knowledge. Western religious thinkers are learning how to distinguish mythic expressions of contemplative experience from literal statements of scientific fact. Such thinking sees the creation story not as a scientific theory or a rigid dogma but as a story about the goodness of the natural world and its Mysterious Source. The creation story is now widely seen as a poem about that first Word of the Infinite that brings nature and humanity to be and thereby initates the conversation between the Actions of Reality and the actions of humanity. The response of humanity to this first Word is symbolized in the story of Adam and Eve naming the other creatures. The Infinite Silence "speaks" the existence of these creatures, but they do not have names until humanity names them. This I-Thou dialogue continues in the story of a "fall" in which illusions, forbidden by Reality, are eaten (taken in) by humanity. We can understand these stories as stories about our actual lives only if we understand these ancient stories as mythic tales rather than literal science or factual biography.

When such innovations in science and in religion are thoroughgoing, there is no conflict between science and religion. And it is also true that *Ordering the Absolute Wonder* and *Dialogue with the Infinite Communicator* are primal metaphors that can exist side by side as two complementary modes of accessing Final Reality. Our Athenian and Jerusalem roots can mingle together as two perspectives on the same Final Reality. We can thank science for showing us some of the wonders of this "creation" as well as acknowledging the Mysteriousness of nature's Source. We can recast our Hebraic/Arabic inheritance with an understanding that "Yahweh," "Allah," or "God" mean nothing more or less than a devotional dialogue with Mysterious Reality. "The Mind of God" is likewise a poem pointing toward our awareness that any Intelligent Design of the cosmos is unknown and unknowable to our mind while nevertheless present to us as Awe in our enigmatic consciousness. Our personal experience of Reality and our I-Thou dialogue with Reality reveal to us an ever-expanding sense of amazing richness.

The combination of these two antiquities has taught us that Reality is experienced by human consciousness as an impenetrable Blackness. That Blackness may shine with Awesome Power and provide those who experience it with a Peace that passes all understanding, but encompassing that Blackness with the human mind does not occur. We can love that Blackness and even celebrate our perpetual ignorance, an ignorance that persists no matter how deep our actual experiences of Reality become. And this same love of Reality can also fully embrace the pursuit of knowledge, but with the awareness that our knowledge is forever partial.

In such an enriched and limited way, *Ordering the Absolute Wonder* remains for many European and American citizens today a viable and powerful primal metaphor for relating with Reality. But the viability and vitality of this metaphor is only operative if we remember that this exalted ordering is only a poem, a metaphor about a Mystery that the human mind never encompasses.

Europe and Sub-Asia

The metaphor of *Ordering the Absolute Wonder,* which found its first glory in ancient Greece, had little contact in ancient times with Sub-Asia's *Uniting with the Infinite Silence.* These two primal metaphors seem quite opposed to one another. Europe has emphasized the intelligence of the human mind and the intelligibility of Reality while Sub-Asia has emphasized states of consciousness that transcend the human mind, states of being that are entirely transrational. For Greece, truth is a discovery of the Mind of Reality through the openness and action of the inquiring human mind. For Sub-Asia truth is a participation in the transrational Unity of Reality, the mind being only a tool for describing this experience. Sub-Asia emphasizes the inward look of consciousness upon itself, and Europe emphasizes the outward look upon the objects of this world. The European primal metaphor has also encouraged an emphasis upon the inward magic of mind to comprehend outward things as well as its own mental functioning. Europe has spawned a love of wonder that witnesses to transrational experience, but this was seen to happen alongside its basic thrust for practical truth. Sub-Asia has not entirely neglected practical truth;

but the truth that mattered was the result of an inward inquiry that finally dissolved inward and outward perceptions into an apprehension of the Oneness of what is Real. This relativized the whole of practical life. Reality and consciousness merged into a shining Blackness of Absolute Mystery and a Silence or Stillness of Absolute Peace. From this enduring and cleansing "place," the Sub-Asian "sage" returns to the practical realms of endeavor and lives there in a fresh and free manner.

As a member of the Arabian/Athenian synthesis, the Western "saint" never leaves the temporal world, but sees a sacredness that is filling all of nature because of its Source in the Final Sacred Mysteriousness. Every rock, river, mountain, and historical event becomes intimate Speech from this Vast and Shining Blackness. This vision inspires the inquiring mind to speak back with new creations of order.

Chapter 26
The Primal Metaphor of the Orient

Uniting with the Infinite Silence, Dialogue with the Infinite Communicator, and *Ordering the Absolute Wonder* are three unique and distinguishable primal ways of approaching Final Reality. There are others. The cultures of China, Japan, Korea, Vietnam, Laos, and a few other places share another unique primal metaphor. I will call this region "the Orient" and name this primal metaphor *Balance within the Inclusive Community.*

When we call all of Asia "the East," we tend to overlook the vast difference between the primal metaphor of the Oriental cultures with the primal metaphor of Sub-Asian cultures (*Uniting with the Infinite Silence*). The primal metaphor of the Orient focuses on communal life, on the yin and yang of communal interactions, on saving face within the communal whole, on communal type relations with nature and the Final Community-ness of Reality. *Uniting with the Infinite Silence* focuses on transrational concentration upon states of consciousness within the solitary individual. Sub-Asian cultures tend to structure communal life to assist that solitary quest. In spite of strong community expressions, Sub-Asian persons are hermits of solitariness compared with life styles of the Orient.

The primal metaphor of Oriental cultures existed before the coming of Sub-Asian Buddhism to the Orient. Buddhism brought with it the Sub-Asian primal metaphor and affected the Orient greatly, but Oriental cultures did not give up their primal metaphor. Rather they adapted the practices of Buddhist meditation to their oriental cultures. So Buddhism in China, Japan, Tibet, etc. turned out quite different from the original Sub-Asian Buddhism. In order to explore the uniqueness of the Oriental primal metaphor, we need to examine the Confucian religious practices and especially the Taoist religious practices that preceded the arrival of Buddhism.

The religious practices of the ancient Orient focused on styling or balancing communal life in a way that fit the *WAY* that the Whole Community of Reality is balanced. For example, as I, a male human being, confront female humans, I am to style my life in a way that honors the truth that men and women share a common humanity. Similarly, humanity as a whole is part of a large community that includes nature. One cannot honor humanity without honoring nature, and one cannot honor nature without honoring humanity. We have here an inclusive perception of Reality in which all life is a polarity of *taking in* and *putting forth*. There is the *yin* of taking in and the *yang* of putting forth. Humanity can be seen as a type of yang to nature's yin. And men can be seen as a type of yang to women's yin. In a full honoring of the *WAY* of Reality male yang is not better than female yin. And women are not without their yang, and men are not without their yin. Civilization with its rigid, hierarchical ordering of male-female relations is moderated somewhat by this yin-yang vision. Of course oriental cultures, as well as Western cultures, have managed to be quite patriarchal in spite of this yin-yang wisdom. Still it is possible to argue that patriarchal behavior is a departure from the depth wisdom of the primal metaphor of oriental cultures.

Our contemplation of the following familiar icon may assist us to reflect further on the essence of the primal metaphor of the Orient.

The white color is the yin, and the darker (often red) color is the yang. We see a spot of yang on the yin side, and we see a spot of yin on the yang side. We see that the yin and yang are the same size and are contained within a circle of wholeness that is incomplete without both complementary parts. One cannot be a yang quality in defeat of the yin quality, for the yin quality is part of the larger whole within which the yang exists. Each yang and yin exist together and nowhere else.

The stylistic subtlety of this depth awareness is manifest in the etiquette practice known as "saving face." In order for my own honor to be saved, I need to include a saving of the honor of the other in my actions. Perhaps we can observe the power of this ancient metaphor in the quality of Mao's communist thought. Mao's strategic thinking differed from Western communism by beginning with an appreciation of the whole situation of the society. Then he sought to see what he called the contradiction within that whole. He sought to know what two main forces were operative and which side of that polarity needed to be advanced next. We can guess that some of the unique power of Maoist thought reflects this ancient yin-yang Taoist wisdom.

In the primal metaphor of the Orient, the community of nature is present within the community of society, and the community of society is present within the community of nature. This whole drama is my being. I find my full truth only by styling my living to reflect this primal communal polarity. We can see an obvious relevance for our current ecological challenges. Instead of ruling nature, contemporary society might move toward honoring nature as an equally important partner.

Taoism carries this manner of visualizing into its perception of Final Reality. The Infinite *Way*, the Wholeness within which all parts cohere, is called the *"Tao."* The Tao is the *Way* Reality operates. Here is part of a poem about this Infinite *Way*.

> Being and non-being create each other.
> Difficult and easy support each other.
> Long and short define each other.
> High and low depend on each other.
> Before and after follow each other.[21]

The following portion of a poem by Chaung Tzu indicates that the Tao is not a set of moral principles or metaphysical ideas, but a word of devotion that points to the same basic experience of Final Reality that other cultures have pointed to with Allah, Yahweh, Brahman, and so on. In all these cases, Final Reality is an awesome shock or break with human beings' more ordinary sense of reality.

> Tao is beyond words
> And beyond things.
> It is not expressed
> Either in word or in silence.
> Where there is no longer word or silence
> Tao is apprehended.[22]

---

[21] Michell, Stephen; *Tao te Ching: A New English Translation* (New York: 1988, Harper Perennial) page 2
[22] Merton, Thomas, The Way of Chaung Tzu (New York: 1969, New Directions) page 152

Such poems have to be read a few times before the truth of their transrational logic breaks through. This Oriental sense of the transrational mysteriousness of Final Reality overlaps with the sense of transrational mysteriousness emphasized in Sub-Asia's *Uniting with the Infinite Silence.* Both the Oriental and Sub-Asian primal metaphors challenge those of us who are embedded in the Arabian and Greek primal metaphors. Transrational consciousness has not been easy to understand or accept as valid by the more rational emphasis present in the Greek primal metaphor, *Ordering the Absolute Wonder.* Similarly Arabia's hearing the Word of Majestic Reality and speaking back is a different emphasis than we find in the Orient or Sub-Asia. Let us examine these comparisons more fully.

The Orient and Sub-Asia

Balance within the Inclusive Community differs from *Unity with the Infinite Silence* in this way: the Orient focuses on transrational communal balancing and Sub-Asia focuses on transrational solitary inquiry. Buddhism changed significantly when it migrated to the Orient. It turned from being a practice primarily for solitary monks and nuns into a religious practice for the whole people. In the Oriental context Buddhism became an element of the whole culture. It melded with Taoist insight and Confucian practicality. In Tibet the central authority of the entire political realm was centered in a head figure who was selected in early childhood and spent his life with monks who trained him for this job.

Nothing like this took place in India, where Buddhism remained a solitary practice alongside various forms of Hinduism and other religious practices. In Sub-Asia, *Uniting with the Infinite Silence* prevailed as the basic mode of Buddhist practice. Indian Hinduism was influenced by Buddhism, but Hinduism remained a separate spectrum of practices. The overall culture simply accepted Buddhism as one more practice within this loose mixture of religious possibilities. Though village life is deeply communal in every culture, in Sub-Asian religious practice, the solitary person and his or her personal journey remained the emphasis.

But in China, Taoist and Confucian practices melded with Buddhist practices and gave Buddhism a more communal cast. Before the advent of modern communism, the typical Chinese person practiced all three religions. We can assume that Buddhism became a sort of "Yang" to the "Yin" of Taoist and Confusion practices that preceded Buddhism's entry into China.

Similar fusions took place in other Oriental places. For example, Japanese culture melded Buddhism with its ancient Shinto heritage as well as the Taoist and Confucian qualities it had already absorbed. Zen Buddhism might be described as a Shinto, Taoist Buddhism. One of the gifts of the Oriental primal metaphor,

Balance within the Inclusive Community, is its capacity to include every wisdom into the social whole in some appropriately balanced way.

The Orient and Greece

The Greek primal metaphor, *Ordering the Absolute Wonder*, shares with the Oriental metaphor an emphasis on social responsibility. For example, both Plato and Aristotle were keenly concerned with social ethics. But the Greek emphasis had to do with idealistic designs and with living from comprehended truth and principles. Balancing the inseparable parts of a whole society was not the essence of the Greek style. Aristotle's finding a middle way between extremes is something different from yin and yang. Plato's finding roles for all types of people in an overall ideal society is also something different from Oriental balance. Instead of an emphasis on complementary balancing, the ways of Greece and Rome tended to be highly conflictual—doing away with established errors and conquering less wise cultures. Quite early in the story of Greek culture, Alexander the Great took Greek truth to "all the world" through military conquest. Another example of this more conflictual style is the vigorous intellectual conflicts among Christians and between Christians, Jews and Muslims. These conflicts too often took on needlessly violent forms.

The Orient also has experienced deep social conflicts, and wages many wars, but a different style of conflict resolution flows from their primal metaphor. There is a wisdom about making a defeated opponent a workable part of the concluding whole. As we in the postmodern West have become more clear about the limits of rationally formulated truth and about the ambiguity of all decision-making, we have experienced more openness toward this ancient wisdom of the Orient.

The Orient and Arabia

The Arabian primal metaphor, *Dialogue with the Infinite Communicator*, shares with the Oriental metaphor an emphasis on social responsibility and communal life. The Arabian We-Thou dialogue with Final Reality was spelled out as a People of God living in history in dialogue with the Final Actor of history. This was a strong emphasis on community, in the sense of a peoplehood, a We-response to the Whole of history. This People of God, in their better moments, saw themselves as being true to themselves in order to lead all humanity in being true to themselves. They saw themselves as formulating a realism and justice on behalf of all. This was a calling from the Final Majesty that they encountered in the events of history.

This emphasis on time and history differs from the Oriental emphasis on balanced spatial relations among the parts of a society. It is perhaps fair to say that the descendants of the Arabian metaphor have felt more congenial with the solitary mysticism of Sub-Asia than with the strange societal face-saving and peacemaking of the Orient. The artistic delicateness, the subtle teachings, the enigmatic deliberating has seemed off-putting to those who feel called to preach the searing Word to a sleeping world in order to open them to take on a new life.

Nevertheless, as postmodern Christians, Jews, and Muslims become more clear about the ambiguities of all decision-making and the need for flexibility in the application of their inherited laws, mores, and principles, the Oriental style attracts them. Members of European and Arabian originated cultures can begin to see the relevance of the Orient's potential for flexibility within overarching commitments to the whole realities in which we all live. At the same time, the descendants of the Arabian primal metaphor also bring their gift of aggressive truth-telling to whatever stodginess may be present in the over-politeness of the Orient. We might view Mao as an example of embracing some of the best, as well as the worst, of the European and Arabian experience and introducing into China both gifts and flaws of the West.

Chapter 27
The Primal Metaphor of Sub-Saharan Africa

Africa is the birthplace of our species. The Primal Metaphor of Sub-Saharan Africa is the oldest of these six primal metaphors. It has to do with the motions of the body and the motions of the inner being. It has to with drumbeats and dances. It has to do with the primary energies of nature—with the way an antelope moves or a lion moves or an elephant moves or a human moves.

Intimacy with the Infinite Communicator and *Ordering the Absolute Wonder* are the primal metaphors that have characterized the cultures we often call the West. *Uniting with the Infinite Silence* and *Balance within the Inclusive Community* are the primal metaphors that have characterized the cultures we often call the East. The cultures of Sub-Saharan Africa are clearly something else, driven by a quite different primal metaphor. I will name this primal metaphor *Attunement with the Final Rhythm*.

The primal metaphor of Sub-Saharan Africa displays a stark contrast with the above four. A Greece-influenced Europe was preoccupied with the intelligibility of Final Reality; Arabia was preoccupied with a We-Thou dialogue with Final Reality, Sub-Asia with states of consciousness; the Orient with communal balancing. Sub-Saharan Africa was preoccupied with whole body vitality and with the Final Vitality to which our bodies can be attuned. All five of these preoccupations exist in some measure in all cultures, but the primal metaphorical material in each of these five sets of human cultures employs a different basic preoccupation.

The Christian West painted halos around the heads of its saintly exemplars. If Africa were to indicate saintliness with a halo, it would have to be painted around the entire body. The movement of limbs, the torso, the head, the blood, the breath, the sensations, the emotions, all these moving parts and the interactions between them constitute the "place" of human authenticity. In this primal African sensibility, Final Reality is raw movement, raw vitality. Rhythm, the rhythms expressed in drumbeats, are a religious method for awakening this whole body vitality and enabling a push toward an ecstatic union with the Inclusive Vitality of the cosmos. If the French philosopher Descartes could say, "I think, therefore I am," a reflective African shaman might say, "I dance, thereby I be."

Some of the oldest known paintings of humanity appear in French caves. In spite of their European location, those paintings probably reflect the ancient Prime Metaphor of Africa. On the uneven walls of one cave, expressively painted animals seem to move. Two bison fight each other. The place is almost alive with motion. This cave was not where people lived. It was a place for ritual. It breathes the Awe of a place of worship. It may give us a hint of a 30,000-year-old Africa.

We can further understand the essence of the Sub-Saharan African Primal Metaphor by comparing it with the other four primal metaphors already described.

Africa and Sub-Asia

Attunement with the Final Rhythm and *Uniting with the Infinite Silence* have an underlying compatibility with one another. Both seek ecstasy beyond the mind, beyond the body, a trans-body, trans-mind union with what is fully Real. "Ecstasy," in the sense meant here, is not a jazzing up of ordinary life. It simply means an out-of-body type of awareness and also an out-of-mind type of awareness. Africa and Sub-Asia both see the practical usefulness of the mind, but view Final Reality as more irrational than rational, more beyond comprehension than intelligible, more an inward realization than a practical result, more a here and now experience than a program for living.

The noisiness of African music and the stillness of Sub-Asian meditation allude to the contrast between these primal metaphors. Sub-Asia has a reserve that is wild underneath, while Africa has a wildness that is up front and overt. Yet if we contemplate deeply the experience of African ecstatic dancing, we can discern a stillness about it. And if Sub-Asian dance dramatizes stillness, it also dances that stillness with an intriguing vitality. If we contemplate deeply the experience of Sub-Asian meditation, we can discern a wildness, an *Emptiness Dancing* as the writer Adyashanti titles one of his books.

Africa and Europe

Attunement with the Final Rhythm and *Ordering the Absolute Wonder* are Primal metaphors that are almost opposite to each another. Hellenized Europe views the body in the context of the mind. Sub-Saharan Africa views the mind in the context of the body. Europe pushes the limits of the mind to find Final Reality. Africa pushes the limits of the body to find Final Reality. It is difficult to see that the same

Mysterious Wonderfulness is found in both cases. Africa returns from Wonder to a more realistically active dance of living. Europe returns from Wonder to a more realistic intelligence for living.

But in real life, the body and the mind are not separate; they are two parts of one wondrous being. The Africans that Americans imported as slaves were held in contempt—their culture seen as primitive, naive, and even worthless. Nevertheless, it has happened that the US slave culture integrated Protestant Christianity and African culture into a musical explosion that has restored the rhythms of the body to an arid, over-mental Western culture. Millions of European Americas have been healed in the depths of their body/spirit by the cultural gifts imported with these slaves. Similar gifts made their way into Europe.

The designs of the mind have been altered by experiences of and reflection upon the rhythms of the body. And the rhythms of Western experience have been given expression by those who were forced to feel them most deeply. These experiences have forced many descendants of the Greek-influenced primal metaphor to take the Primal Metaphor of Sub-Saharan Africa more seriously. Many Westerners now know that life is more than the life of the mind and that there are other-than-Western ways of accessing that profound "I Am" life.

Africa and Arabia

Attunement with the Final Rhythm and the Arabian primal metaphor, *Intimacy with the Infinite Communicator,* share a sense of the wildness of human life and the ultimate wildness of Final Reality. Unlike the Greek overemphasis on the mind, *Intimacy with the Infinite Communicator* is more preoccupied with will and freedom than with rationally formulated truth. This Arabian Infinite Communication is a personal address, aimed at awakening the heart with horror, repentance, love, and commitment. The voice of the human speaker can become the Communication of the Infinite when that Onrushing Reality amplifies the human voice.

In the Protestantism of Luther and even more so in the first and second Great-Awakenings of Protestantism in the Americas we can see a recovery of this Arabian voicing. If with emotionally grounded sensibilities, we read aloud the poetry of the Genesis stories, the Psalms, and the Prophets, we sense this quality of strong speech characteristic of the Arabian primal metaphor. The African slave communities of the Americas were able to resonate with the emotional qualities of this strong speech in Evangelical Protestantism. They could feel the emotional depths of their African rhythms being awakened. They were able to put their Christian teachings into rhythmic songs. A deep integration of these two quite different primal metaphors took place. Perhaps the deepest interaction has been the identification of the sufferings of slavery with the suffering servant of Hebrew culture and the cross in Christian practice.

Similar experiences have happened in other ways in other parts of the world. I have not studied the story of the spread of Arabian Islam into parts of sub-Saharan Africa, but there is surely wisdom to be learned about both primal metaphors in that story.

My point in this brief overview is that the African primal metaphor has not been extinguished by the horrific mistreatment of African peoples. Rather it has resisted death and given life to all of its conquering peoples. Africa was the home of a primal metaphor that has standing with all the others. Africa was not only the birthplace of the human species; Africa has preserved and brought to intricate sophistication the cultural childhood of us all. As the various groups of humanity migrated out of Africa, we began to specialize in various aspects of our humanity and reshape our approaches to Final Reality. In doing so, our African origins were obscured. Nevertheless, that whole-body vitality of Africa and its heartbeat of sensual and emotional rhythms is an ancient root that each of the other primal metaphors has in some measure carried along, as well as in large measure lost. It is important for our entire human authenticity that humanity recovers this African treasure.

Africa and the Orient

The Orient has had less interchange with African energies than the other cultures described above. Nevertheless, the Orient carries with it an emphasis on intimate communal life that we also find in the African cultures. The family life, the village life, the group music of the Orient carries an echo of something also African. Both primal metaphors support the emphasis that people reach Spirit maturity together, rather than as hermits.

But there is also a vast difference between the qualities of African communal life with that of the Orient. *Balance within Inclusive Community* is more practical and reserved than the wildness of African communal dancing and drumming and expressive living. *Attunement with the Final Rhythm* manifests a more open expressiveness of feelings and sensations, ecstasies, and rages. The Orient is more polite, more subtle and reserved, in the expression of its harsh and delicate feelings.

Nevertheless, both cultural groups seek a type of obedience to the way life is. African Attunement is an obedience to the Rhythm of the cosmos. Oriental balancing is an obedience to the Way Final Reality is balanced. Both of these modes of obedience are creative means of being communally workable societies. In each of these approaches to Final Realty, humans are seeking to find a personal and social peace, contentment, and happiness that heal the horrific perversions that are also found in all human societies.

Chapter 28
The Primal Metaphor of Native America

Many waves of people migrated to the Americas from the Orient. These migrations began 30,000 years ago or more. These earliest peoples were tribal nomads who lived before the practice of agriculture or the dawn of hierarchical civilizations. When Europeans arrived in the Americas many Native American groups were still living as nomadic tribes. Others were living in agricultural but tribal federations. The mode of hierarchical civilization had also been imported to the Americas. We don't know exactly when or how, but we do know that highly developed hierarchical civilizations existed during the last 2000 years. We know some of their names: Olmec, Mayan, Toltec, Aztec, and Inca.

We might ask if there was a single Primal Metaphor at the root of all these Native American societies. The differences between the nomadic tribes and the civilizations were great. Can we see a common primal metaphor beneath all this diversity? And if there is such a common primal metaphor, is it a unique metaphor or is it a variation of the Oriental metaphor? If it was something different, was that a factor that encouraged those ancient peoples to leave Oriental geography and move to the Americas?

These questions have never been entirely answered for me. Native American societies do seem to lean more toward the qualities found in the Orient than toward any of the other primal metaphors. But the American societies are also different from China and Japan—more different than China and Japan are from each other. If the Native American primal metaphor is rooted in the same soil as the Oriental metaphor, it is a very old root with quite different leaves and branches.

Let us look first at an interesting myth that was prominent in mid-American civilizations. This will give us some impressions to work with toward answering these still unanswered questions. The story of Quetzelcoatl is the story of a fictitious animal that is both bird and snake. The Quetzal bird is a very beautiful bird with a long green tail. Coatl is the snake half of this mythic creature. The human society and its heroes are identified with this creature. One of the root meanings of this myth is that authentic life is a union of sky and Earth, of air and land, of flight and earthiness. We might view this as reflection of the sort of yin/yang *"Balance"* we encounter in the Orient.

Another interesting clue is the custom present in many of these ancient Amerian societies of punctuating the calendar of their lives with wild celebrations. We have heard these celebrations called "fiestas" or "powwows." In these societies the calendar of living holds a balance between carefully designed social patterns that are punctuated by celebrations that touch the chaos out of which these designs have been built, the chaos to which designs return.

The typical drumbeat at a North American tribal powwow is another clue. Often we hear a heavy beat followed by lighter beats and this pattern is repeated monotonously. Two monotonous rhythms happen, the heavy beat rhythm and the lighter beat rhythm. This monotony eventually feels ecstatic. It reminds us of the monotony of the rise and fall of the sun, the flow of the seasons, the movement of the stars. Attention was paid in the early cultures of the Americas to all these flows of time. The social life was built upon a design of time. Here is my impression of the feel of these cultures: ric rac ric rac ric rac ric rac Fiesta ric rac ric rac ric rac ric rac Fiesta ric rac ric rac ric rac ric rac Fiesta ric rac ric rac ric rac ric rac Fiesta. The ric rac part of the calendar was where social order and its needful work got done, and then in Fiesta the entire social order was almost dismantled for an assigned time period. Classes, sexual order, various laws, were set-aside for a time. This pattern interests me as a ritualization of the nature of human society—a creation that could be different, a useful order placed over the wildness of nature, an order not to be mistaken for the full Order of existence.

Native American sand paintings also express this theme. Elaborate designs are built on the ground out of various colors of sand, then after a short period of participation in the healing intent of such a design, the sands are scattered— returned to an original chaos. When we look deeply at such details as these, we also see a strong emphasis on communal life. We see this precious insight about communal life: the design of society is to be a healing presence; it is made by human hands; it is vulnerable to return to the original wildness. And there is respect for this original, chaotic wildness; wildness needs to be designed into our communal life and participated in as part of the Grand Design that nurtures us at all times.

I am going to name the Primal Metaphor of these Native American cultures *Designing the Unstoppable Flow.*

Native America and the Orient

The Native American primal metaphor is probably a close relative of the Oriental metaphor *Balance within the Inclusive Community*, but the common ancestor of these two primal metaphors predates the mystical sophistication of Taoism, Confucian styles, and Buddhist enrichments. In Native America we are tasting something more ancient. And the Native American primal metaphor provides us with an opportunity to view the historical depths of a primal metaphor and watch it change from its pre-agricultural period, its pre-civilizational period, its early civilizational period, and its continuing dialogue with modern expressions of all the other primal metaphors. If we attend a Native American powwow, sit in a sweat lodge with a Native American teacher, view Native American art, go on a vision quest, wander through the Mexican archeological museum, admire Inca stone work, or whatever we might do, we can amplify our wonder by meditating on the antiquity of this quest for profound realization. We can imagine its origins in ancient Asia and its existence among those first migrating peoples to the unfamiliar lushness of the Americas.

Native America and Europe

Since the arrival of European people to the Americas, a deep but tragic dialogue has taken place between these two primal metaphors, *Ordering the Absolute Wonder* and *Designing the Unstoppable Flow*. The first descendants of Europe experienced a type of cultural shock when facing these residents. Some were also charmed by the natural connectedness and communal graciousness of Native American people. A few left their imported societies and chose to live with the natives.

European descendants have also been surprised at the passion with which Native American cultures have fought to preserve their culture and their communal ways of living. Native Americans can be very strong individuals—with strength rooted in and dedicated to healing ways that are communally manifest. Europeans are individualistic by comparison, quite alien to this Native American communal richness. Early Europeans misunderstood how deep was their cultural shock, how challenged they were by Native American cultures. Not all, but most of them turned their opportunity to learn something about being human into an attitude of contempt and genocide.

Both "Ordering and "Designing" imply a use of the mind, but Native American designing is about designing communal life amidst the flow of time in order to access the healing depths of a mysterious nature within which humans are living members. The European primal preoccupation is more about giving to the individual knower ways of finding intelligibility in order to live life under the guidance of such truth. This can mean a humbling before the Mystery of Life that is continually teaching us new wisdom, but it can also mean imposing current doctrine upon nature and ourselves and then developing defensive measures to protect our current state of "truth." These more defensive forms of the European culture result in contempt for those who do not share these particular "certainties." In the actual historical encounter with Native Americans, some Europeans were willing to learn from these people. But far more Europeans felt that they needed to teach Native Americans European wisdom. Europeans were surprised at the resiliency of Native American communal life, the confidence they had in the wholesomeness of their ways of life, the willingness they had to teach these strange Europeans who were obviously ignorant of the wisdom of he Americas. But few Europeans were able to see the limitations of their stubborn individualism and thereby open themselves fully to the communal treasures within Native American heritage. This was tragic, but perhaps predictable, for these primal metaphors are quite different and integrating the wisdom of these two approaches to living is still far from complete.

Native America and Arabia

The Arabian primal metaphor, *Intimacy with the Eternal Communicator*, has, like the Native American metaphor, a strong communal emphasis; seeing "We," the people of God, in a vast dialogue through history with the God who rules history. But this communal emphasis is quite different from the Native American communal emphasis. The People of God are a vanguard experiment in realism and justice on behalf of all of humankind. Native American community is not a vanguard mission, but a stable place of residence on a piece of "sacred" Earth. This community includes all the animals and plants that comprise the wider community in which these humans reside. When Native Americans speak of "all my relations," they mean more than grandmothers, uncles, and cousins. They include the animals, the plants, even the mountains. And the Native American community is designed as a healing fabric for humans and their living companions of other species. The Arabian "People of God" type of community is more interested in history and in historical progress toward a destination of deeper union with the Final Reality.

Yet these two types of communal emphasis (at their best) do see a common enemy in individualism, egoism, crass nationalism, crass humanism, crass rationalism. In our times of intense ecological challenge, many of those who are committed to being the People of God understand that a true union with Final Reality includes a union with nature and a commitment to build societies that preserve and enrich the natural habitat. Indeed, such descendants of the Arabian primal metaphor can include in their vision of "Union with Reality" a union with geographical places that includes all the plants and animals and humans who dwell there. Such local, grounded, communal living can be embraced as an aspect of the "Kingdom of God" toward which humanity needs to move. This vision opens Western Christians, Jews, and Muslims to Native American wisdom as well as to some forgotten elements in the life of ancient Israel. The ancient scriptures of Israel are filled with deep connections with nature and a love of natural place.

Also, a significant number of Native American people have disentangled the essence of Christianity from the oppressive features that most Christian adherents foisted upon them. They are willing to integrate some elements of this historical realism with the Great Spirit within nature. So, some integration of the wisdom based on these two primal metaphors has taken place.

Native America and Sub-Asia

Native American history has had little dialogue with Sub-Asia. America's original peoples left Asia before the expansion of Buddhism reached the Orient. While there can be intense, solitary, mystic feelings among Native American peoples, this is not the core emphasis of their primal metaphor. Native Americas have emphasized the communal rather than solitary singularity. Sub-Asia's *Unity with the Infinite Silence* is a solitary emphasis before it is a communal one. The communal life of Sub-Asia is patterned to enable solitary realization rather than the other way around. For Native America the communal is primary; the communal enriches the solitary. Though both communal and solitary are present in all cultures, the emphasis of these two primal metaphors is almost opposite.

Native America and Africa

Native American history has also had little dialogue with Sub-Saharan Africa. Their first encounters with the African primal metaphor began with the African slaves brought by the Europeans. *Attunement with the Final Rhythm* and *Designing the Unstoppable Flow* are primal metaphors that do not easily attract each other. Each manifests wildness, but the wildness is different. The Native American drum develops a monotony punctuated by shouts and cries of liberation from this monotony. The African drum is complex, a thousand different heartbeats, emotional feelings, all teaming together in rich textures that can hardly ever be described as monotonous. Native American wildness is part of a communal regularity and reserve and courage punctuated by explosive energies appropriately placed in the ongoing communal schedule. African wildness is an exploration of the always-present vitalities of singular persons, communities, and natural surroundings. African community is rooted in a common joining in the rhythms of these vitalities, rather than constructing a detailed, disciplined design.

Yet beneath these differences there is a common connection with nature, with sensations, with animal forms of consciousness, with the ongoing irrationality of Final Reality. Both Native American communal-nature designing and African natural vitalities can be seen as joined in a common challenge to any overemphasis on intelligibility, inflexible social order, or dogma that has lost contact with the Earth and our rich sensations, vitalities, and feelings that connect us to one another and to the Mysterious Overall that is beamed to us through the natural geography in which we are embedded.

Chapter 29
Spirit Completeness Beyond all Metaphors

So what does all this cultural analysis mean for our understanding of religion? First of all, it dramatizes that no religion or religious culture dropped down from the realm of Final Truth. No primal metaphor is the right one or the best one. All primal metaphors and all the religions they have spawned or will spawn are creations of human beings. Further creation is plausible. Further recognition of the gifts and the limits of each of these primal metaphors is possible. Further developments and elaboration within each of the primal metaphor zones of experience can happen.

Since no existing primal metaphor is the complete one, shall we invent something that includes the wisdom of all of these primal metaphors? Shall we invent a primal metaphor that works better and more inclusively that all of these? Not so fast! We need to recognize that each of these primal metaphors was developed and explored by millions of people over thousands of years. It is arrogant in the extreme to assume any of us has the personal depth even to understand the profundity of each of these metaphors much less the capacity to invent something that includes or excels them all.

But we can reflect on how the dialogue between these six zones of experience can take us where no people have gone before. We can intuit that there exists a profound humanness that underlies all of these metaphors and zones of culture. We can experience the joy of discovery as we dialogue deeply across the boundaries of these zones of religious creation and culture building.

I have heard people say that the cultural divisions on our planet are so deep that they can never be fully breached. I certainly agree that these divisions are deep. However, I have been encouraged by a number of experiences that make me more hopeful about breaching these differences than the more common view suggests. Here is one of those experiences:

I was teaching an eight-week, residential, religious program in Australia in which there were six Aborigine people from a traditional outback village. These people had learned English and other things from a Presbyterian mission, but their ancient culture was still very much in evidence. I am guessing that their primal metaphor is a form of the Sub-Saharan African metaphor that their ancestors had taken to Australia at least 12,000 years ago in a pre-civilization form, even a pre-agricultural form. This culture is very different from my own. At first I found many of their comments cryptic. Occasionally, it dawned on me what some of their strange talk meant. I was not sure that anything I was saying was getting through to them. Then one morning after I had given a talk on "The Land of Mystery," a tall, slender, very dark-skinned Aborigine man came to me and made this striking and memorable statement: "When you give a talk like that, I can hear you in my own stories." I had no idea what his stories were, but as I looked him in the eyes I knew that we had communicated.

This experiences and others similar to it have convinced me that all these truly vast cultural boundaries can be crossed, even at the most profound levels— perhaps especially at the most profound levels. We live in an interreligious and intercultural era. We are all already hybrids. And we can all become wiser about our own profound humanness, as we listen ever more deeply across these cultural boundaries.

Herein is a new vision that is happening to many of us today: there is a profound humanness that is common to all humans, whatever their culture or their religion. We now realize ever more clearly these important awarenesses: (1) All our religions are human creations that are limited, and yet reach out for the same profound humanness. (2) All our primal metaphors upon which our religions are built are limited and yet are created by humans seeking to share among one another the same profound humanness. (3) All the cultural formations and religions rooted in these primal metaphors are limited, partial, incomplete, yet each of these heritages of human invention reflects in its own way a considerable measure of the profound humanness that we all share.

Three Approaches to Truth and Six Basic Cultural Areas

In Part One of this book, we explored how there are three basic approaches to truth: the *It-approach* or scientific approach, the *I-approach* or contemplative approach, and two *We-approaches*, the intimacy approach and the commonality approach. All six of these major cultural areas use all three approaches to truth. And every primal metaphor is part of that culture's "I" approach to truth, part of the reflection upon our inner experiences of being human.

Nevertheless, another way to picture how these six primal metaphors differ is to notice how each primal metaphor leans toward one of the three approaches to truth. Here is a chart that suggests what those leanings seem to be:

Area	Primal Metaphor	Approach to Truth Lean
Sub-Asia–	**Uniting with the Infinite Silence**	—contemplative approach
Arabia–	**Intimacy with the Eternal Communicator**	—intimacy approach
Europe–	**Ordering the Absolute Wonder**	—scientific approach
The Orient–	**Balance within the Master Community**	—commonality approach
Sub-Saharan Africa–	**Attunement with the Final Rhythm**	—intimacy approach
Native America–	**Designing the Unstoppable Flow**	–commonality approach

What does this tell us about these societies? Here are some suggestions:

The complexity of the Chinese culture may be explored with such insights as these: the Confucius base of that culture emphasizes the commonality approach. Taoism provided some emphasis on the intimacy approach, which was well combined with the commonality approach. Buddhism, arriving from Sub-Asia, provided a deepening of the contemplative approach. The scientific approach was not absent in classical China, but it was profoundly strengthened by the impact of the Maoist revolution that brought significant aspects of European thought. All these enrichments have made China a very strong culture. If Chinese creativity brings all these approaches to truth together in a balanced mix, that culture will be even stronger.

Europe is a blend of the classical Greek structures of thought and Arabian influences that arrived through the spread of Christianity and Judaism and the fight with Islamic cultures. This means a strong emphasis on the scientific approach, enriched by the intimacy approach. The contemplative approach is most needed by European cultures and this approach to truth is now being added through strong encounters with the immigration of citizens, teachers, and teachings from Sub Asia. Most missing in European cultures is the commonality approach to truth emphasized in the Orient and by Native American cultures.

North America, as well as Central and South America, are now basically European cultures, but they have been enriched by the Native American emphasis on commonality. This gift can be much more fully adopted, especially in North America where it has been pushed onto reservations. In Central and South America, that Native American commonality emphasis has impacted religious, family, and neighborhood life, but it is still held in a second-place status. Further enrichment of all the American cultures from the Native American commonality emphasis is needed. Enrichments from the Oriental form of commonality would also be strengthening. American cultures, more fully than European cultures, have received the gifts of the African emotional and body movement intimacy emphasis.

These ongoing enrichments taking place among the world cultures illustrate the importance of interreligious learning, dialogue, and cooperative mission to their respective cultures.

Concluding Comments on Primal Metaphor Research.

Everything said so far on this topic could be viewed as a mere scratch on the rock of the understandings that we deeply need. A lifelong study of primal metaphor insights could be outlined for each geographical area of the planet. And such study could be fine tuned for specific places—that is, Germanic Europe is different from Mediterranean Europe. Mississippi is different from New England. And strongly Native American Bolivia is different from almost every other place.

All six primal metaphors and all three approaches to truth need to be distinguished and carefully taught across the world in secondary and university classrooms as well as religious, civic, and business associations. Culture is not simply given from the past: it is also created in the present. And the unavoidable future of intercultural mixing across the planet is challenging every cultural enclave to open up hearts and minds to the enrichments of our entire planet-wide human experience.

Part Six

The Ethics of Response-Ability

Table of Contents for
Part Six: The Ethics of Response-Ability

30. A Being Basis for Responsible Action
31. The Roots of Motivation
32. The Ethics of Radical Monotheism
33. Contextual Ethics and Responsible Action
34. The Universal League of Profound Humanness
35. The Battle with Dysfunctional Religion

Introduction to Part Six

Being alive and being conscious of being alive means making responses to our specific environments of living. These environments include our outer encounters as well as our inner feelings, rumblings, desires, emotions, thoughts, and awarenesses.

The main point to be developed in Part Six is that the action that flows from the religious ferment described in this book can no longer be based on religious beliefs or religious moralities. Nor can such action be based on secular principles, philosophies, or ideologies. Does this mean that there is no basis for action or that everyone is "right" to select their own basis and do whatever they want? No, it does not mean that. Such thoroughgoing relativism is simply one more humanly created philosophy that cannot be our basis for action if we are to begin with being our Being as profound humans.

Chapter 30
A Being Basis for Responsible Action

A viable basis for responsible action is profound humanness itself. But how can this be a basis at all? What does such a basis mean? Here are some hints:

When humans have spoken of acting from love, they have sometimes meant acting from profound humanness.

When humans have spoken of acting in freedom, they sometimes meant acting from profound humanness.

When humans have spoken of acting in hope, they have sometimes meant acting from profound humanness.

When humans have spoken of acting in trust of the goodness of Reality, they have sometimes meant acting from profound humanness.

In the following chapters I will explore what it means to act from profound humanness. Our *best* secular thinking, our best religious thinking, and all our best disciplines, rules, and principles can all have a meaningful connection with profound humanness. It is that connection that makes them *best*.

Nevertheless, all philosophy and all religion is a finite creation of the human species. Religion is a temporal social practice, not an Eternal verity. So to base our responsible action on our religion or on our secular philosophy is to base our responsible action on something less than Reality. "Less than Reality" will always mean some form of illusion or substitute for Reality, for "less than Reality" will always mean an approximation of Reality. But since Reality is Infinitely Mysterious, "approximation" means "some support from Reality" as well as "some illusion about Reality."

The development of thought in the following chapters will attempt to spell out how we can understand "responsible action" as action based on profound humanness, not human creations. I have already explored how all the religions of the planet are finite human creations, built on the foundation of some humanly created primal metaphor. Humans have not always known this. We are now living in an interreligious era that is part of an astonishing post-everything time. Humanity is undergoing a vast leap in consciousness. When we confront the bigoted craziness of so many people, political leaders, and social movements, we may jump to the conclusion that human consciousness is in a worse state than ever before. But that understanding does not go deep enough. The desperate hubbub of our times is in large measure a terrified reaction against the big changes that are happening and are required of us. These changes, if embraced, rather than fled or fought, are positive possibilities.

All religious communities, all philosophical communities, and all ideological communities are being challenged by the times in which we live to consider a fresh basis for responsible action. In the next chapter I will describe the interior roots of our motivation for responsible action. And in the chapters after that I will explore the more outward aspects of choosing specific responsible actions in real life situations.

Chapter 31
The Roots of Motivation

In this chapter I will explore how the motivation to act, either in glorious compassion or in horrific malice, is not rooted in our thoughts or sensations or emotions but in our states of consciousness.

So what are thoughts? What are sensations? What are emotions? And most of all, what are states of consciousness? The following chart holds these interrelated dynamics in an order that helps me share my experience of these dynamics, how I distinguish them, and how each relates to the topic of motivation.

	Thinking	Thinking includes the human capacity for language, for art, for mathematics, often called the symbol-using capacity. Symbols are mental entities that stand for assemblies of imaged content. Images are a more primitive aspect of thinking. They are the multi-sensory reruns of specific experiences.
States of Bodily Function	**Sensations**	Sensations include the outwardly focused dynamics of seeing, hearing, tasting, smelling, and the tactile sensations of the skin. Also included are the more inwardly focused sensations of pain, of muscular and bone movement, and of the chemical qualities in the blood and other fluid systems. We can consciously notice and distinguish all these varieties of sensation.
	Emotions	Emotions are bodily feelings, but they are energies that rise from the dialogue of the conscious self with outward experiences or with what we think are our outward experiences. Emotions come in pairs: anger and affections, fear and safeness, sadness and gladness, sorrow and contentment, anxiety and ease.
States of Consiousness	Consciousness is a deep enigma. It is the core self, the deep me, the noticer, and the doer. Consciousness is not thinking, it is the thinker. Consciousness is not the sensations; it is the sensor. Consciousness is that within the body that knows itself experiencing and using these bodily functions. Here are names for some of the deepest states of consciousness: Trust and Despair Compassion and Malice Freedom and Bondage	

Trust and Despair

Despair is not an emotion; it is the absence of trust. And trust is not an emotion; it is a state of consciousness that can exist along with any emotion. We can live in trust and still be angry. We can live in trust and still be fearful. We can live in trust and still feel affection or safeness. We can live in trust and at the same time experience all the variations of sadness and gladness, sorrow and contentment, anxiety and ease. Trust is not a feeling: it is a willingness to have whatever feelings we have. Trust is an openness to and a curiosity about what our feelings mean. Trust is a willingness to feel our feelings and use them to identify what is happening to us. Trust can also put our feelings to work for us. Anger can be useful to the trusting person. Fear can be useful to the trusting person. Trust is trustful of anger and fear as well as of affection and safeness. Trust is an effortless letting be of our emotions. And trust is an effort to manifest freely our emotional richness. Deep trust trusts what is real. Our emotions are real and therefore part of what deep trust trusts. Deep trust is also trustful that despair is a doorway back to the deep trust of the Real. Trusting persons by thought, deed, and presence invite despairing persons back to the community of trusting the Real.

Compassion and Malice

Similarly, malice is not an emotion; it is the absence of compassion. Malice has many forms including a sentimentality that replaces the true courage of self-affirmation. Malice is also a substitute for our natural enchantment with Being and for an outgoing affirmation of others and of being with others. As a deep state of essential consciousness, compassion has many forms but none of them can be understood as a state of emotion; compassion can exist alongside any emotion. We can live in compassion and still be angry. We can live in compassion and still be fearful. We can live in compassion and still feel affection or safeness. We can live in compassion and at the same time experience all the variations of sadness and gladness, sorrow and contentment, anxiety and ease. Compassion is not a feeling: it is a willingness to compassionately affirm whatever feelings we are having. Compassion is an openness to and a curiosity about what our feelings mean. Compassion is a willingness to feel our feelings and use them to identify what is happening to us. Compassion can also put our feelings to work for us in our relations with others. Anger can also be useful to the compassionate person. Fear can be useful to the compassionate person. Compassion includes compassionate toward anger and fear as well as toward affection and safeness. Compassion includes an affirmation of our entire emotional being. Compassion includes our effort to manifest freely our emotional richness and to assist others to do the same. Compassion is compassionate toward what is real. Our emotions are real and therefore part of what compassion is compassionate toward. Compassion is also compassionate toward self and others in our estrangement from the real. Compassion seeks to assist self and others to be open to experiences of the "hell" of despair over Reality, and thus open to being welcomed home to the glory of Reality.

Freedom and Bondage

Bondage is also not an emotion; it is the absence of freedom. And freedom is not an emotion; it is a state of consciousness that can exist along with any emotion. We can live in freedom and still be angry. We can live in freedom and still be fearful. We can live in freedom and still feel affection or safeness. We can live in freedom and at the same time experience all the variations of sadness and gladness, sorrow and contentment, anxiety and ease. Freedom is not a feeling: it is liberation from the compulsive quality often given to our feelings. Freedom is also a willingness to have whatever feelings we have. Freedom is openness to and curiosity about what our feelings mean. Freedom is a willingness to feel our feelings and use them to identify what is happening to us. Freedom can also put our feelings to work for us. Anger can be useful to the free person. Fear can be useful to the free person. In its free actions, freedom freely employs anger and fear as well as affection and safeness. Freedom is an effort to manifest freely our emotional richness and to assist others to do the same. Freedom is free to live what is real. Being freedom is what is real; bondage is a substitute for freedom. Our emotions are real and therefore part of what freedom freely enjoys and uses. Freedom is the absence of the compulsion to act out our feelings in some addictive or unconscious way. Freedom is also free to address estrangement from the real—to assist self and others to be open to experiences of the "hell" of despair over Reality, and thus open to being welcomed home to the glory of Reality.

Motivation and Emotions

Emotions attend our actions and enrich our actions, but they do not motivate our actions. Motivation is a deeper dynamic than our emotions. Motivation is rooted in these profound dynamics of consciousness: our trust or despair, our compassion or malice, our freedom or bondage. It may seem sometimes that we are motivated by our anger or fear, but most of us can recall times when we have not acted-out our anger or when we have acted courageously in spite of our fear. Fear probably evolved in our psyches because it aided our species in fleeing dangers. And anger probably evolved in our psyches because it aided our species in fighting challenges to our survival. But these associations can trick us into believing that we need to be angry to fight for social justice, but we do not. Injustice may anger us, and we may find that anger useful. The motivation to act and to shape the quality of our action comes from a deeper source.

We are motivated by our compassion or by our lack of it. We are motivated by our trust of Reality or by our lack of it. We are motivated by our freedom or our lack of it. This is a very important awareness. We do not have to drum up anger to act boldly. And we certainly do not need to act out our anger in some thoughtless manner every time we are angry. But also, we do not need to hold our anger in contempt or think that we have to replace it with affection. We can learn to let our feelings be our feelings, and we can learn from our feelings. At the same time we can distance ourselves from addictive obedience to what we think our feelings are urging us to do.

Living beyond our feelings is not always easy to realize in our practical living, for our feelings are very subtle and our awareness of them may still be emerging. Also, we may be unconscious of the extent of our malice and how it joins forces with our anger. We may be unconscious of the extent of our despair and how it joins forces with our fear. We may be unconscious of the many ways that our consciousness and our emotions are mingling.

The key point here is that we cannot trust our emotions to be an absolutely trustworthy guide. Our emotions are doing their job, but they can be misleading. Emotions are a valuable energy that arises in relation to both our perception of the external world as well as from the current state of our consciousness. If our state of consciousness is malice and our thinking about the world erroneous, our emotions will guide us to do malicious things in a supposed world that does not exist. On the other hand, if our current state of consciousness is compassion and our thinking about the world is relatively accurate, then our emotions will tend to be in line with the actions that our compassion envisions and motivates us to do.

Motivation and Sensations

It is also a mistake to view our sensations as an absolutely trustworthy guide. Consciousness needs to notice our chemically initiated signals such as hunger, thirst, and sexual desire, but these signals must be evaluated by consciousness in order to pursue optimal living. A worm may almost entirely obey these signals, but humans have evolved consciousness and thinking to assist us in choosing more wisely than a simple rendering of obedience to these important signals. Pain and muscle sensibilities also require thoughtful consciousness. Even our seeing, hearing, tasting, smelling, and tactile sensations require thoughtful evaluation for best-case actions. Our consciousness, not our sensations, is the source for our best-case actions. And our twisted consciousness is the source of our malice, bondage, and despair.

Motivation and Thinking

Thought can also be a misleading guide to the life of action. Thought is genuinely and positively motivating only to the extent that it awakens our trust, compassion and freedom and gives guidance for the engagement of these motivating forces in the external world. Thought can also give guidance to the motivating forces of despair, malice and bondage. A truly malicious person can still be quite thoughtful.

And our thinking can be grossly mistaken about ourselves and the external world. In the best-case scenario, our thinking is still incomplete, evolving, changing, and never arriving at any final certainty. Thinking is enormously useful, but still fragile in its hold on Truth.

A "belief" is a thought to which we are committed with our consciousness. Only because we are committed to a thought does that thought play an important role in our motivations. Without commitment, a thought can simply float through the mind like passing clouds. Commitment is a dynamic of consciousness, not a dynamic of thought. It is commitment that makes a thought a belief. Thoughts are without impact on our motivation until they become beliefs. It is when we organize a set of thoughts into the net of commitments that we create beliefs. Beliefs are always being acted upon in some way or another.

A ministry to our beliefs is actually a ministry to our commitments, even though the attention of this ministry seems to be focused on our thoughts. The key question we need to ask about our beliefs is, "Are they true?" That is, are they in accord with Reality with capital "R"? Trust, compassion, and freedom have to do with affirmations of Reality. Despair, malice, and bondage have to do with commitments to self-constructed "realities" we have substituted for Reality. Our despair results from our conscious or unconscious unwillingness to live in the real world and be our true selves. Malice and bondage also result from our conscious or unconscious rejection of realism. It is through our commitment to illusory beliefs that we keep ourselves in the pains of despair, malice, and bondage. When we question a belief, we are actually questioning a commitment of our consciousness. That is, we are questioning whether our commitment is illusory—whether our beliefs are truly believable even to ourselves. When we examine the sort of living that our beliefs lead us into and how we would be different without those beliefs, we are assembling data that may reveal to us the illusory nature of those beliefs, which includes revealing the illusory nature of the commitments of consciousness that underlie those beliefs.

Thinking is not the main root of realistic motivation. It is trust, compassion and freedom that provide the root of positive motivation. Accurate thinking is important for effectively manifesting our trust, compassion, and freedom. But thinking is a tail on the dog of conscious motivation. The tail does not wag the dog. It is the dog of consciousness that wags the tail of thinking, including the thinking of this chapter.

Chapter 32
The Ethics of Radical Monotheism

People typically think of monotheism as an idea or belief—almost never as a mode of action or ethics. "Radical monotheism," as elaborated by H. Richard Niebuhr, has to do with a basic center of value and a fundamental ethics.[23] The core question to which "radical monotheism gives answer is: What is good? What is best for the loyalty, devotion, and cause of my life, and of our lives as an organization, a region, a state, a nation, or a species of life? In his book *Radical Monotheism and Western Culture,* Niebuhr inspired me to see monotheism as a universal basis for responsible action, an ethics that is not merely Christian, Jewish, or Islamic, but an ethics that applies to any community (religious or otherwise).

"Radical monotheism," as defined by Niebuhr, is one of three prominent answers that humanity has given to the fundamental question of ethics. The other two answers he named "polytheism" and "henotheism." Curious as these three terms may seem, they point to basic alternatives for determining ethical action, and they apply to every human life and every society, past or future.

Contemporary Theism

For Niebuhr "theism" in the terms "polytheism," "henotheism," and "monotheism" does not mean belief in gods or goddesses, or in a supreme being (God) alongside other beings. The gods and goddesses of ancient polytheism were stories about processes within the human psyche or within the human interactions with the environments of human living. Polytheism does not mean taking these stories literally. The gods and goddesses do not exist as literal beings observable by scientific examination or contemplative inquiry. For example, Venus and Mars are just stories about the dynamics of love and war. Polytheism can include loyalty and

---

[23] Niebuhr, H. Richard, *Radical Monotheism in Western Culture* (New York: 1943 —1970, Harper Torchbooks)

commitment to both love and war and many other centers of value. The gods and goddesses point to real powers in our lives, but as mythic stories, they are artistic creations of the human mind.

Similarly, Niebuhr's radical monotheism is not a belief in One God that rules over all the other gods and goddesses, angels and devils, gremlins and fairies, and other visualizations and fictions about aspects of our lives. Radical monotheism has nothing to do with beliefs in beings or in a being. Radical monotheism is a devotion, a loyalty, a trust in what is Real, where Reality is always more than our thoughts about Reality. Reality is an ongoing surprise to whatever is our current sense of reality. In radical monotheism we are loyal to a Reality whose Wholeness is beyond our rational comprehension; nevertheless, with our consciousness we can experience conscious connection with this Unifying Mysterious Every-thing-ness. When radical monotheism is our core devotion, it relativizes all our other devotions. These devotions can remain as relative centers of value in our living, but in radical monotheism we have opted for the One center of value that renders our lives flexible with regard to all the other values.

For example, the "oneness" of devotion meant by radical monotheism is not of the same quality as the oneness of devotion meant by choosing our nation as our one overriding center of value. Though we are part of our nation and our nation is part of us, we are more than our nation. The reality of our lives is more than the presence and destiny of our nation. A devotion to Reality includes a devotion to all nations. Similarly, radical monotheism is more than a devotion to humanity; monotheism includes devotion to all beings, living and inanimate. The One center of value that constitutes radical monotheism is Reality as the Quintessence and Entirety of what is Real.

This Quintessence is more than a concept. It can be experienced. It can be visited. It can become a steady station of the consciousness in which we dwell. It can be experienced as our profound humanness, for that is what it is. Profound humanness is merely the inward experience of loyalty to the Final Reality to which radical monotheism is loyal. Radical monotheism can become the trust and devotion and loyalty of our lives. It can become the cause for which we live and die. And people who so live are around us at every moment.

Polytheism as Ethics

As an answer to the question of value and ethics, "polytheism" means having many centers of value, a pantheon of loyalties for my life or for our lives as a social group. Those many centers of value might include: family, work, sex, pleasure, money, self esteem, companionship, approval, power, status, variations on these, and many more centers of value. All of us tend to begin our living dedicated to this poly-loyalty arrangement of choosing our course in life. Indeed, we all have many or most of these centers of value. We bow our knee to whatever symbols or powers may reward us in relation to such values. Eventually, the tragedy of having multiple centers of value begins to be felt. We discover that these various centers of value fight with each other. Both family and job can each seem to demand our whole lives. Our one life can seem torn between the two. Our dedications to both pleasure and work may also tear us in two. These many centers of value each fight for an ultimate claim upon our time and energy. Furthermore, we begin to experience the sad truth that each of these centers of value can and will let us down. Our dearest friend or lover can leave us. Family can die or despise us. Our job can disappear or turn sour. Forms of pleasure can simply end forever. All these meaning-givers or centers of value in our polytheistic pantheon of values can enter the twilight of no longer functioning as meaning-givers that we can trust. So, here are the weaknesses of a polytheistic ethics: (1) the many meaning-givers war with each other, and (2) they each let us down.

Henotheism as Ethics

Henotheism is a partial answer to the weakness of the polytheistic scatteredness. Henotheism builds a pantheon of wholeness for the many gods. To the core question of value and ethics, henotheism provides a unifying cause or value that gives an overall unity and dependability within which all our other values can take a relative place. This typically means a human culture, an overall social arrangement that arranges the many values in relation to something more inclusive. This usually means choosing to identify with a common culture or a limited peer group as our overarching meaning of our living and action. Religious in-groups can easily manifest this henotheistic quality. Members bow their ultimate trust to the religious group rather than to the various gods or goddesses that the group may honor. In modern times, patriotism to a nation has been given henotheistic standing—"my nation right or wrong"—"my nation is the greatest on Earth"—"being a patriot of my nation is the to-live-for-and-to-die-for value that gives unity to my life." Such serious nationalism often includes believing that my view of being a patriot is true for all the other members of my nation: I view them as subversive if they disagree with me about my view of the nation I treasure.

Henotheism can also take the form of making my racial group or my sub-culture as my overarching center of value, identity and action. Finding a group membership that makes my life worthwhile is a strong draw, even if it includes contempt and perhaps violence toward other groups. Humanism is also a form of henotheism in which my center of value is the whole human species—"Whatever is good for humankind is good and whatever disadvantages humankind is bad." This center of value, taken alone, can exclude the value of other species and include an oppressive relationship with the entire natural planet. Finally, henotheism can be expanded to include all living forms, yet even this center of value is henotheistic, not radical monotheism, because it does not include the inanimate aspects of Reality. Henotheism differs from polytheism in that it attempts to find a unifying cause for my life, and it differs from radical monotheism in that it opts for a range of values that is less than the Whole of what is Real.

Radical Monotheism as Ethics

As an answer to the question of value and ethics, radical monotheism includes everything, inanimate and living, in its scope of values. Everything is good because it *Is*. The radical monotheistic center of value is a loyalty and a devotion to the Source from which all realities emerge and into which all that has emerged returns. Birthing and dying are equally valuable parts of the whole process of Reality. Coming and going, big and little, pleasant and painful, growing and rotting are all valuable because each process is a manifestation of the Overarching Process of Reality to which loyalty is being given. And "Reality" in this definition does not mean my or someone's sense of reality, but the encountered Reality that is constantly a surprise, a mystery, an enigma beyond understanding by any human mind.

It is often the case that monotheism degenerates into a set of ideas that are used to make sense of things, whereas radical monotheism means a commitment to That Grand Nonsense that never makes complete sense to our fragile minds. Monotheism has often degenerated into the belief that my group and its beliefs are the super-blessed, or perhaps the one-and-only truth holders. That sort of "belief in one God" is henotheism, not radical monotheism.

The "mono" in "monotheism" means that there is a single overriding loyalty, the Real. The core ethical question becomes, "What is Real?" Good-and-evil no longer means two aspects of what is Real. The Real is the good and the good is the Real. "Evil" within the radical monotheistic value-perspective means any denial of the Real—any hatred of the Real, any illusion that masks the Real, any escape that flees the Real, and any a fight with the Real that seeks to win against That which cannot be defeated. Such hopeless conflict with invincible Reality is appropriately called "despair." And despair, as we have seen, is joined with malice to self and others and with bondage to some moralism or license that substitutes for our deep freedom. Radical monotheism includes the release within human beings of these profound essential qualities: trust in Reality, compassion for all, and deep freedom from egoism, social conditioning, and fatalism.

Loyalty to my self-constructed self-image is a loyalty that must be drastically demoted when service of the One overarching Reality is one's life devotion. Polytheism, on the other hand, does not require a break with egoism. Polytheism is a form of egoism, for the polytheist trips from one source of ego enhancement to another, to another, to another, to still another. Each of the gods or goddesses of the polytheistic ethics is actually some aspect of human life viewed as a power for the enhancement of my ego. Henotheistic devotions are similar. My devotion to my nation is actually a devotion to my view of my nation as an aspect of "me." Even my devotion to humanity as a center of value is a devotion to me as a human. Radical monotheism also has a view of what is human, profoundly human, namely a devotion to the Whole of Reality—living that devotion is profound humanness. We see the call for this total sacrifice of egoism in the well-known line of Jesus, "Not my will, but Thy will be done." These words means that the cravings for ego promotion are given up in order to affirm Reality and radical realism as the best-case scenario for my life. This radical scenario of living is viewed as true humanness. But this affirmation of the human does not mean that radical monotheism is the same as humanism. Radical monotheism includes a thoroughgoing affirmation of humanity along with frogs and rocks, mountains and oceans. Here is an obtuse example of what that means for ethical action: a person living the monotheistic perspective could not favor destroying all the spiders on the planet to save a few human lives.

Radical Monotheism and Science

Natural science is a method of approaching what is True. In that sense, natural science is a servant of radical monotheism. The discoveries of science are discoveries of what is real and thus enrichments of our radical monotheism. But the formulations of scientific knowledge are always partial, incomplete, and open to further advances in the process of science. So any current scientific formulation is not the quintessence of Reality; it is only a humanly invented level of understanding of some part of Reality. Nevertheless, the process of science is an approach to the truth of Reality and, therefore, compatible with radical monotheism. Yet the specific results of science can be "idols" that radical monotheism opposes when they are substituted for the fullness of Reality.

A good scientist can be a radical monotheist. This may be present in the consciousness of those scientists who have come to see that "the more we know about nature, the more we know we don't know." Our scientific advances do not bring us to some promised land of absolute knowledge; rather, they open up even more unknowns to be explored. But scientific advances are still advances; each advance is more real than the formulations over which it is an advance. The "progress" of science is a journey into what we truly experience to be so. The keystone of science is the actual experience of our senses. Obviously, what we sense is conditioned, or at least shaped by, what we believe before we sense it. But our sensations, when we are fully open to them, can challenge what we believe—indeed, can challenge what our whole society has believed for a very long time. This willingness to let sensations challenge beliefs is the key to competent scientific research. This openness to being challenged by Reality illustrates how science, as a method, is compatible with the loyalty of the radical monotheist.

Many philosophers of science notice that modern scientific experiments are very complex and very distant from the everyday experience of our senses. Many of us cannot, even in our imaginations, reduplicate the complex interpretations of the light gathered by immense telescopes from galaxies billions of miles away. Nor do most of us understand the use of huge atom-smashing cyclotrons for exploring the microcosm of nature's smallest constituents. It can seem to us that we are stuck with simply trusting scientists in what they say rather than actually knowing how scientists arrived at their current formations of truth. As true as this is, it is also true that these scientists are trustworthy only to the extent that their science is referencing actual experiences of the senses. And if we were to became competent scientists in their field, we could also observe with our own senses whether these advances are indeed advances into truth or not. Any philosophy of science is bogus that does not keep in touch with the fact that a scientific advance is trustworthy only when a community of scientists can witness that this new formulation of truth is compatible with what can be seen, heard, smelled, felt, tasted, or otherwise sensed with our human senses.

Radical Monotheism and Contemplative Inquiry

The human senses are not, however, the only source of truth. The human senses cannot sense consciousness. The human senses can only sense the behaviors and the reports of conscious beings. Consciousness is assumed by scientists, but it cannot be explored by them as scientists. Consciousness, often called subjectivity, is a secret known to scientists, but rigorously excluded from the objectivity of scientific research. Science is objective in its tests for truth. As a scientific test for truth, subjectivity is purposefully and faithfully avoided in the scientific approach to truth. This is both the grandeur of science and its limitation. It cannot explore directly the nature of our consciousness. All exploration of consciousness is explored by a conscious human who is noticing consciousness within her or his own being. These inward noticings can be shared with other noticers of their own consciousness. We thereby construct a community of discussion about consciousness. All good art is a sharing of these inward noticings. Much psychology and philosophy is also a sharing of these inward noticings. Religion is good religion only if its assertions are rooted in this inward noticing. Psychology, philosophy, and religion may combine their inward noticings with the scientific type of knowing, but competent thinking must remain clear about what is known as a result of scientific research and what is known as a result of contemplative inquiry.

Radical monotheism is compatible with both scientific research and contemplative inquiry. Anyone who is looking honestly upon her or his own consciousness and reporting accurately about it is a potentially trustworthy source of truth. And all truth, from whatever source, is consistent with the devotion, loyalty, and cause of the radical monotheist.

Radical Monotheism and Social Ethics

It is of utmost importance to understand that Radical Monotheism is a context that leads to action in the social sphere. Radical Monotheism is the vocation of living one's whole life in a context of values that relativizes every limited center of value and lives from this ultimately inclusive center of value: the real is the good and the good is the real. This does not mean that our oppressive social patterns must be tolerated, it means that our social change actions must begin with the situations we have and the real possibilities contained in those situations. Realistic living is not a recipe for conservatism; it is recognition that the Real includes possibilities that can be realized with proper effort, as well as the obvious truth that the Real is our current situations that provide our unavoidable beginning points for action. Realistic living does not mean imposing our ideals upon reality. Rather, realism means being willing to make our choices within our real lives and in response to the real challenges that we confront.

Radical monotheism affirms that everything scientific work discovers to be real is good, and that everything contemplative inquiry discovers to be real is good. And, a radical monotheism loyalty includes the challenge to integrate our scientific truth and our contemplative truth into a workable program of action for our whole lives in the service of the whole Earth and the whole destiny of humans on this Earth. Judaism, Christianity, and Islam have been traditions that emphasize social justice as a consequence of their radical monotheism. The ethics of radical monotheism drives toward justice: it opens us to the need to serve all people and all values rather than the values of our narrow group and its preferences and delusions.

As finite religions in real world history, Judaism, Christianity, and Islam also carry perversions of radical monotheism—most often these perversions take the form of a henotheistic "worship" of the dogma and morality of particular religious groups. This decay of radical monotheism into an in-group self-worship is a temptation faced by every religious and secular group. Any such reduction of our vision of the Real robs social ethics of its flexibility and revolutionary power. It warps the ongoing quest for realistic social justice into an imposition of my group's ethical and moral thinking upon all humanity and upon the planet. This reductionism of the Real is the root attitude beneath all human and ecological oppression. When radical monotheism is our center of value, the ethical sphere is broken open for perpetual creativity toward ever-fresh inventions of justice.

Radical Monotheism and Religion

Every religion is a finite construction created by human beings. At its best, religion does nothing more than point beyond itself to that which is not finite, but which is the everlastingly True and Real. Good religion points beyond its ethical moralities and its dogmatic teachings to a depth of human experience that cannot be contained in any finite ideas, social shapes, or humanly practiced processes. Radical monotheism has to do with openness to the fullness of that ever-surprising Mysterious Reality; therefore radical monotheism cannot be contained within any religious forms—dogmas, moralities, or communal forms.

For example, Christianity as a historical community of religions has now entered an era of history in which its old dogmas, moralities, and communal forms have become ever more obviously obsolete in relation to the scientific truth, the contemplative truth, and the ethical challenges of our times. All hope for a continuation of what has been central and best about the Christian religious tradition rests on a recovery of radical monotheism. Moses and the prophets were radical monotheists. Jesus was a radical monotheist. Paul, Mark, Matthew, Luke, and John were radical monotheists. We bring deep confusion into Christian recovery if we do not see the thread of radical monotheism that unites all these luminaries. Though the expressions of these signal figures were limited by their times, this does not change the fact that radical monotheism is a common thread that unites them. And radical monotheism is the thread that unites these ancient witnesses with contemporary women and men who are dedicating their lives to the radical monotheistic cause in world history today.

The center of value that Niebuhr calls "radical monotheism" has been and still is a gift that is being carried by Western culture. Judaism began a sophisticated discussion of radical monotheism; Christianity and Islam, at their best, were a continuation of this loyalty, commitment, and discussion. All three of these Western religions have also spawned perversions of radical monotheism—usually in the direction of making an old witness to radical monotheism into a doctrinal possession with which to discredit and perhaps oppress other religions and cultures.

Furthermore, radical monotheism is not synonymous with practicing Christianity, Judaism, or Islam. Even though the term "radical monotheism" may not appear in nonwestern religions, radical monotheism is present almost everywhere as a lived center of value. When Hindus claim that all gods and goddesses are just expressions of one overall Beingness, that has an almost identical meaning with the Islamic saying "There are no gods save Allah." A clear Hindu knows that the gods and goddesses they employ in their devotions are not the Ultimate. Hindu practice, at its best, is a loyalty to the Oneness of Truth. And a clear Muslim knows that many centers of value exist that claim their relative loyalty, but these many centers of value are not "gods" for Islam—that is, they are not Ultimate for the living of human life. The moods of Hinduism and Islam are vastly different, but their depth realizations can be seen as profoundly overlapping.

The "Tao" of ancient China is another symbol for loyalty to that basic center of value that we are naming "radical monotheism." Elements of loyalty to the radical monotheistic center of value are present in almost every religion and in almost every region of the planet. The heritage of the Great Goddess, whose roots reach back at least 25,000 years, was viewed as a great womb that birthed all things and a great tomb that received them home. Humans were fed and nurtured at her breasts. Loyalty to the meaning of this symbol surely functioned for many as a symbol for the same basic loyalty as the "radical monotheism" that H. Richard Niebuhr clarified for us.

I will maintain that "radical monotheism," as I (with help from H. Richard Niebuhr) am defining it here, is a universally present ethical attitude that is available to all humans who have been made aware of their reduced loyalties and are willing to be open to the inclusive Reality in which we are all embedded.

Chapter 33
Contextual Ethics and Responsible Action

So what is the path from *Radical Monotheism* to *Responsible Action* in the everyday moments of personal life and within these challenging times of human social history? My two-word answer to that question is "contextual ethics." To clarify what I mean, I will begin by distinguishing "contextual ethics" from "right-and-wrong ethics" and "good-and-evil ethics."

Right-and-Wrong Ethics

The mode of ethical thinking that uses the concepts of right-and-wrong is older than Moses. It has always been a useful mode of thought, and it will remain so. It is based upon the concept of "law." A law is what defines right and wrong. Thou shalt not murder! Thou shalt not steal! (And so on) Law is a crude tool for ethical application. Law has to be interpreted for each specific instance by a law officer, a judge, or a jury. We might say that a judge or jury is assigned to apply the spirit of the law as well as the letter of the law. This conflict between spirit and letter in the application of law was a core aspect of Jesus' struggle with the religious establishment of his day. This basic tension continues in the apostle Paul, Luther, Dietrich Bonhoeffer, and in ourselves if we are honest. This tension between letter and spirit exists in our personal affairs. Our rules for daily living have to be interpreted for the spirit of their meaning as well as the letter of their statements. Laws or rules exist in our minds (or superego) as well as in our social discourse. Right-and-wrong is a useful way to think about ethical choices, but it is not the only way. Right-and-wrong thinking can be misused through questionable interpretations of our laws, rules, and mores or through establishing bad laws in the first place. And how do we know if a law or rule is bad? Obviously, a complete ethical discussion must probe deeper.

Good-and-Evil Ethics

The mode of ethical thinking that uses the concepts of good-and-evil is a goal-oriented type of ethical thinking that was strongly developed by Aristotle. We have goals, purposes, or aims in terms of which a specific action is judged good or bad. For example, the goal of having good teeth makes brushing and flossing good and failing to do so bad. The goal of having better economic equity in our society makes certain tax laws better than others. The limitation of good-and-evil ethics rests in the issue of determining which goals, purposes, or aims are good and which bad or evil. This question raises the issue of centers of value. If my family is seen as a center of value, then spending time with my family is a good goal, and providing economic, educational, and health services for my family is a good aim. If basic safety in my neighborhood or city is a center of value, then having competent police protection and clear laws against murder, theft and rape are good aims. But how are these centers of value to be chosen? We typically refer to more inclusive centers of value, such as life, liberty, and the pursuit of happiness.

Contextual Ethics

Contextual Ethics is a third mode of ethical thinking. It does not ask about right-and-wrong or good-and-evil, but about the qualities of the situation that we face and what responses are appropriate within that situation. This mode of ethical reflection has never been entirely absent when we are using the other two modes of ethical thought. The judge who interprets a law will typically analyze the situation in which he or she is applying that law. Similarly, the discernment of good over evil in relation to a specific center of value must also analyze the situation in which this center of value is applied. As a basic life method, contextual ethics is never absent. We are always in situations, and we must always know those situations in order to create "appropriate" responses within those situations. Whether an action is "appropriate" or "befitting" to a situation is the key consideration of contextual ethics. In order to know what is befitting we must first know the situation in which our responses are to fit. Moment-to-moment spontaneity is a misunderstanding of contextual ethics. We all have in our memories enduring contexts of interpretation about each sphere of life and each scope of consideration. The thoughtfulness that characterizes contextual ethics is letting the real situation improve our ongoing contexts of ethical thought and action.

Monotheistic Ethics

So, how has the monotheistic attitude toward life employed these three modes of ethical thought?

The Eternal Law

The ethics of ancient Israel was almost entirely about *performing obedience to an Eternal Law*. The good laws of social and personal life were seen to derive from a Final Authority that is law-giving and thereby blessing us with dependable guidance. For example, in the high Middle Ages, Thomas Aquinas assumed an Eternal Law unknowable to the human mind. Then "natural law," according to Thomas, meant that part of Eternal Law that humans could know, and "human law" meant those human constructions of further determinations of right and wrong consistent with natural law.

The Final End

When monotheism joined with good-and-evil ethics, the monotheistic theologians began to discuss what it means to *follow paths toward our Final End* (purpose or blessedness). Augustine's famous phrase "Our hearts are restless until they rest in Thee, Oh God" reflects a use of good-and-evil ethics. This saying means that Reality is an Ultimate End in the accessing of which we can find restful blessing for our hearts and heartfelt actions. With lesser ends we are restless and adrift unless those lesser ends rest within the Final End of this "realistic" Rest.

The Ultimate Context

Today radical monotheistic thinkers, such as H. Richard Niebuhr, speak of *befitting responses within the Ultimate Context*. He went further to say that if we are to be loyal to the Ultimate Reality we face today, contextual ethics is the most important mode of ethical thought. The other two can find their place within the context of contextual ethics and within the context of the Ultimate Context. For example, in our one-world era, radical monotheistic contextual ethics finds it *appropriate* or *befitting* for us to move beyond our racism, nationalism, and economic imperialism into a whole-Earth context of ethical consideration. Resolving the issues of the ecological crisis is also supported by contextual thought in which all reality is being affirmed, rather than humanity alone, or wealthy humanity alone.

Let us look more carefully at how contextual ethical thinking works in a monotheistic context of commitment. First of all, it does not mean a complete rejection of the other two modes of ethical thinking. Right-and-wrong and good-and-evil can be integrated into the contextual ethics mode. We can ask what laws are befitting to our world situation today. We can ask what ends are befitting for our government to pursue. Similarly, in our personal lives we can consider our talents, our opportunities, and the world's needs, and then ask, "What basic vocation is most befitting for the pursuit of our lives?"

Here is another important characteristic of contextual ethics: We begin our ethical thought with an interpretation of the situation that is being confronted. The whole situation is open for consideration. All aspects of it are considered relevant. Only when an approximately holistic view is reached, does creating the "befitting" response "appropriately" take place. The good action is the one that is befitting or appropriate for this situation. Obviously, there may be several different responses that can be viewed as appropriate, but the choice is not entirely arbitrary. The situation provides a vision of limits and possibilities that need to be obeyed for the response to be appropriate. The interpretation of the situation is a crucial element of the process. And this interpretation uses all three approaches to truth we examined in Part One of this book: the scientific approach to truth, the contemplative approach to truth, and the particularization of our scientific knowledge and our contemplative wisdom in terms of workability in our real-time-real-place choices. And these choices concern not just "me" but "we" who are involved in the choice to be made. We simply look and see what is happening, and then we boldly initiate a response. That is it. Behind all of this thoughtfulness, we know that some sort of response cannot be avoided. Inaction and thoughtless action are still responses to the situation. Contextual ethics is adding our thoughtfulness to the unstoppable flow of events.

Notice that beginning with the situation is different from beginning with a law that we apply to the situation. And beginning with the situation is also different from beginning with ends or ideals that we wish to pursue—hence impose upon the situation. When the contextual ethics mode of thought is primary, the traditions of right-and-wrong and of good-and-evil are made secondary to appropriate response to what is happening now. Current happenings qualify our appropriate responses, they do not determine that response, but they inform it. The response–able human observes, judges, weighs up, and then decides to act from freedom—not pleasing others or blaming the situation or following good principles.[24] We are choosing, choosing, choosing our interpretations of the situation, and choosing, choosing, choosing our free creations of appropriate responses to the situation. We have

---

[24] This is language lifted from Dietrich Bonhoeffer's analysis of freedom.

abandoned every form of authoritarian thinking and opted to rely on what we are experiencing as conscious human beings confronting the ongoing flow of history that is confronting us. That confrontation requires our rational understanding, intuitive awareness, and downright guesses. And in spite of all this fresh knowing, our confrontation with historically experienced Reality remains an experience of the Unknown and, therefore, our responses have the character of being a leap into the vast Mystery that we are always facing.

Thinking from Big to Small

Within this Ultimate Context of loyalty, what does contextual ethics look like as an ongoing feature of our lives? Without always realizing it, each of us has created some sort of enduring contexts for every layer of our awareness. We have a view of the dynamics of the cosmos and the planet and humanity's place on this planet. This view may be poorly thought through, basically just taken over from our parents and our schooling. It may be largely illusory or simplistic, but we have a context already operating in our lives. Similarly, we have a context for living in our region of the planet—whether that is a nation, a group of nations, an ecological region, or a continent. And we have our context for life in our community—whether that be a county, city, neighborhood or each of these. All these layers of context interact with each other, inform each other, enrich each other, and together make up our sense of the world in which we live.

Happenings happen to us as we live within these taken-for-granted contexts. Happenings challenge us to improve our contexts. Improving our contexts turns out to be a lifetime task. The point I am making is that we simply do not live without contexts. We do not live in some sort of mindless spontaneity. We live in a continuum of organized awareness, however in need of reorganization that awareness may be. We tend to be defensive of all our contexts, for it can seem painful to our sense of certainty to have to admit the full extent of our ignorance and take on the work of building smarter contexts.

The ongoing, inclusive rebuilding of our contexts logically begins with the most inclusive, for the larger contexts provide context for the smaller scopes of thought. When we retool our planetary outlook, we affect how we think about our local place and how we respond where our body does its doings. Of course, the planetary context does not entirely determine the local context. We need to retool our local context in the light of our local experience as that experience is seen within the context of our fresh planetary context. Much of this retooling goes on in a piecemeal and chaotic fashion. But a full dedication to contextual ethics in the Ultimate Context of radical monotheism will call for many instances of context improvement. Study and contextual thoughtfulness are an ongoing feature of a life that is responsive within the Ultimate Context.

Nothing about this emphasis on thoughtfulness needs to rob our living of its spontaneity, creativity, and freedom. No matter how realistic and clear our contexts are, when we face each particular decision, we experience a call for sheer freedom. We need to live from the heart, so to speak—while all our contexts hang in the sphere of our mind as guidelines that help us decide, but which we in our raw freedom must apply to this specific choice and to the next specific choice and the next and the next.

History Making

We are parts of communities of action within the Ultimate Context. We do not get to escape into an absolutely lonely existence. We confront the flow of history in companionship with others. This may be understood as our privilege to participate in making history. History is not a dustbin of old facts, but a vital drama in which humans are responsible for many of the major outcomes. In times as grim as ours, people are tempted to avoid full lucidity about their historical power to make a difference. Rather than do something, people are tempted to be aloof and just not care about the failures of their society. Any society is a failure if it pampers the rich and neglects the rest. Making progressive history today includes educating our citizens in responsible democratic processing rather than tolerating rule by a wealthy oligarchy. Any society is a failure if its practices are distressing the natural planet to a devastating degree. Making progressive history today includes dealing with the radial demands of climate challenge as well as, in all other ways, taking care of the ecosystems of the planet in which humanity could be an enriching part rather than a destructive force. These and thousands of subparts of these themes cry out for responsible responses from each community of humans whatever their religion or lack of religion, whatever their culture or race or sex or gifts or flaws. And such responses make history. We are not helpless cogs in some inevitable doom. Also, progress is not assured. The weight of the future is inescapably placed on the shoulders of each awake human. We are all Atlas with the Earth on our shoulders, whether we wish to be or not.

Contextual Ethics is an Interreligious Process

The ethics I have outlined above is not a Christian ethics or a Jewish ethics or a Buddhist ethics or any other ethics derived from a community of religious practice. I contend that a religion-based ethics is an obsolete idea that is no longer needed in the dialogue among religions or in the dialogue between religions and secular society.

When we use terms taken from a particular religious heritage, we are being contextually befitting only if we use those terms to describe the way life operates. In so doing we can communicate across religious boundaries. The various religious communities use different languages that point to the same or similar dynamics of humanness. Human cultures are more similar on the level of experience than on the level of beliefs or moralities. Therefore, the practitioners of the various world religions can do ethics together, providing that we recognize that we can each root our ethical thinking in the same profound humanness that each religion attempts to access. We need not start from the "authority" of our religions tradition—its dogma, morality, or religious practices. I mean no diminution of the value of these unique practices; rather I am pointing to a huge revolution in ethics. Social ethics has jumped the boundaries of every religious community and landed in a general or secular context in which all communities, religious and otherwise, share.

This secular context is not secular in an antireligious sense, but in the sense that it is not sectarian, but inclusive. Furthermore, our ordinary so-called "secular world" can now be seen as transparent to the Awesomeness of profound humanness. The ordinary is transparent to the profoundness that all truly functional religious practices seek to access. So living in the secular world no longer means leaving the profound realms of existence, but finding the profound in a manner that will seem surprising to our old patterns of two-realm thinking. We find the sacred within the profane. The sacred is revealed as the depth dimension of the profane. Indeed, the very terms "sacred" and "profane" are profoundly transformed, for they have ceased to mean separate realms.

Finally, though I have used some Christian illustrations, I am speaking on behalf of all good religion and celebrating its contributions to wholesome and inclusive social change. I will not elaborate here the specifics of this generally secular and interreligious style of ethics. With four of my friends, I have written a whole book on ethics for our moment of history. We entitled it, *The Road from Empire to Eco-Democracy*. This book employs the contextual ethics methods summarized above, and it does not reference any religious heritage for its "authority." It sticks with the relative certainties that we can derive from our common experience as human beings. All humanity can experience the same profound humanness and the same overarching Wholeness. We are all Earthlings before we are Christians or Buddhists or whatever religious practice we have or lack. I find it interesting that both the Buddha and Jesus referred to themselves as "the human." The Buddha made no pretensions about being anything other than "the awake one." And when Jesus associated himself with "the son of Adam," this means the restored and coming true human. We can demote Siddhartha, Jesus, Mohammed, and any other luminary, including ourselves, to the wondrous but ordinary status of "the human," a potential that is open to every human being. In finite qualities humans differ so vastly it boggles the mind, but before the Final Realty we are all just "the profound human," or else far less—"the inhuman."

Chapter 34
The Universal League of Profound Humanness

So, who in our actual 21st Century history are the people who will build ethical guidelines for our times based on profound humanness, on the recovery of being truly human, on an ongoing accessing of the "I Am" qualities that comprise our essential Being? The answer to this question cannot be limited to one particular religious group. Clearly, some Christians and some Buddhists are accessing profound humanness. Some Jews and some Muslims are accessing profound humanness. Some Hindus and some who practice no classical religion are accessing profound humanness. Profound humanness is our true nature that happens to us when it happens to us. No religious group has control of that. There exists in real time a league of profound humanness that cuts across every religious practice or lack of religious practice.

The boundaries of this league are not visible to any human eye. No one has all the data to even make a good guess as to who is and who is not loyally maintaining their membership in this universal league. Yet we league members do meet one another and recognize one another from time to time. We know that our league exists even though we do not know and never will know the actual extent of its presence. But we can be certain of this: Final Reality has her league members, and because being a league member means being in tune with Final Reality, this league is supported by an Invincible Power. This league is on the winning side of history. Lies and false living will ultimately lose, even though these forces can powerfully prevail for a time. Even when the league is being scorned and killed by the forces of falseness, it is falseness that is on trial, not truth, not freedom, not trust in Reality, not love of self and neighbor, not love of Reality, not unspeakable joy, not incomprehensible peace, not rest for our deep beings, not life and life abundant. These qualities are who we are as league members, and they are supported by the All-powerful support. Losing simply does not happen for this side of the core conflict within human history. When losing appears to be happening from some humanly constructed perspective, it is not losing from the perspective of Eternity. The Truth is always winning despite its many setbacks that humans are persistently creating. By "winning" I do not mean military impositions. The winners of the wars or political conflicts are quite often seeking to escape the Truth. It is a deeper insight to notice that Reality is the final Power, and Reality prevails in the end at whatever cost to human efforts.

It is in our awareness of this invincible Truth that we have an explanation for the boundless hopefulness of a Buddha, or a Jesus, or a Gandhi, or a Martin Luther King Jr. or any other courageous luminary in our human story. The courage unto death of such exemplars of profound humanness challenges us to decide whether these figures are stark raving insane or whether the rest of us are. Either most of us are lacking in accessing our humanity, or else these signal figures have gone off a deep end that we "ordinary" persons need to avoid. I believe that the evidence is on the side of viewing none of us as ordinary. We are all extraordinary luminaries just waiting to happen. Indeed "ordinary" and "extraordinary" have lost all meaning. The ordinary human is extraordinary, and the extraordinary human is just an ordinary human coming into his or her own.

So, the universal league of profound humanness is potentially everyone. Yet it is also true that falling away from our profound humanness is a fact of history that has gone on since, let us say, the second day of our human quality of consciousness. This falling away still takes place in ever-new ways. The human species is extensively resourceful in inventing escapes from our profound humanness. Each of us will spend our lives, or can spend our lives, sorting out our various escapes and allowing our beings to return to their normality of profound humanness. Herein is the valid role of religion: it helps us return to our profound humanness. Religion is a practice that we do, day in and day out, year in and year out, because doing such a practice assists us to recover our league membership in profound humanness.

The nine personality types of the Enneagram analysis are nine types of escape from our profound humanness. This window into our human journey is quite interesting because it shows us so clearly how and when we have all fallen away from our profound humanness. Operating within the absolute necessity of building a personality, we each tend to build an escape from our profoundness. Each of us has already built for ourselves a powerful substitute for the "real me." It is not that our personality is a bad thing: we need a personality and could not live without one. But our personality is not who we are. Yet we almost inevitably make this tragic mistake: we take our self-created personality to be "who we are," and thereby miss the extraordinary ordinariness of our profound humanness. In order to exit from our personality cocoons and learn to live beyond personality (which includes using our personality as one of our servants), we will need to practice a religion. The religion we practice may be very different from what we have in the past called "religion"—so different that we may be reluctant to call our practice "religion." But any practice, however secular or unreligious it may seem to us, is indeed "religion" in the truest sense of the word, if that practice assists us to access our profound humanness.

These clarifications bring our minds back to the need to renew religion as a vital and needed function in the societies of humankind. There is such a thing as a good Christian religion, even though the probability of it may seem obscure. There is such a thing as a good Muslim religion, even though the probability of it may seem obscure. And such statements are true of all the classical religions. And there may be new religions invented. All religions are invented. Any renewed religion has been reinvented. I personally see great value in the entire religious treasury of the planet. I find useful the thousands of years of religious practice by humans, many of whom were more profoundly realized humans than I. I find myself an arrogant fool when I suggest to myself that I could just start over without benefit of this long past. Criticism of the past is necessary, but in religion, as in any other social function, we need not throw out the "baby" of human experience with the bath water of obsolescence and decay.

In spite of my love of the past, I also know that I am challenged to be a bold inventor of religion for my time. I feel called to find my place among the other religious revolutionaries that I admire. If I choose to be a new sort of Christian, this need not mean that I condemn others for choosing to be a new sort of Buddhist, or something else. The league of profound humanness works simultaneously on all the religions and invents whatever newness in religion that we may need. We do not need one religion for all of us. We do not need to force our religious inventions on others. We need to assist whoever we can to find for themselves whatever practice they need to practice in order to journey ever deeper into the profound humanness we share.

We need to call upon all league members to do their utmost to assure the survival and the thriving of the human on planet Earth. This is our responsible action. Responsible action remains an enigma that each of us has to work out for ourselves, and yet we are together becoming more lucid about how we can participate in that everlasting enigma.

Chapter 35
The Battle with Dysfunctional Religion

We often speak of dysfunctional families. We need an equally strong word to characterize the deep malady that is taking place in a majority of steepled buildings on the street corners of US neighborhoods and in other such buildings across the world. If accessing profound humanness is the valid function of a vital religion, then much of what is taking place in these expensive religious buildings is fostering dysfunctional people. We need something better from our current religious organizations. If profound humanness is our deepest functionality as human beings, then none of us are fully functional; we are all recovering from some deep form of dysfunctionality. We need help—better help than most of us are getting.

We can recognize in ourselves and others the controlling rationalism that takes the place of a trusting relation with Reality that I have described as states of transparent attention, universal forgiveness, and effortless letting be. Dysfunctional religion with its promotion of authoritarian doctrines is not helping us.

We can recognize in ourselves and others the binding moralism that takes the place of the deep freedom that I have described as states of primal merging, inherent purity, and attuned working. Dysfunctional religion with its promotion of moral rigidities is not helping us.

We can recognize in ourselves and others the self-serving malice that takes the place of the essential love that I have described as states of autonomous strength, enchantment with Being, and out-flowing compassion. Dysfunctional religion with its promotion of distracting sentimentalities and half-conscious bigotries is not helping us.

About Rationalism

Rationalism has to do with withdrawing into our minds, and also with imposing the patterns of our minds upon Reality, thereby hiding from the Mystery of Reality in so doing. In religious discussions "dogmatism" is a commonly used word for rationalism. No Scripture or Bishop or ecclesiastical office can claim final authority on what is so about Final Things. Each of us has to discover profound humanness for ourselves. Unless we have the personal authority of being able to speak of what we deeply know in our own being, any religious teaching is useless. It is worse than useless; it is a pretense of wisdom that will eventually carry us into some pit of despair. Authoritative religion swallowed by gullible sheep is killing people in the most sensitive dimension of their existence. Such religious practices turn open and willing learners into fully stupid people.

About Moralism

Moralism has to do with behavior patterns rigidly followed and imposed on others. What are we to make of people who hate everyone who does not cotton to their moral teachings? What are we to make of those who burn Korans; shame Jews; insist that women use no contraceptives and never opt for an abortion; and a thousand other sectarian, moralistically rigid ravings? What are we to make of the justification of inordinate wealth while pouring contempt on the poverty-stricken and disadvantaged portion of our human family? What are we to make of angry proposals of economic and social practices that mistreat and demean large swaths of the population? Yes, and what are we most lucid people to make of our own selves when we apply our "enlightened" teachings without regard to the situations to which they are being applied? All this is moralism.

About Sentimentality

There is something very shallow in the too often heard saying, "If you can't say anything nice, don't say anything at all." Nice is a shallow and malicious standard that is both self-critical and critical of others. It is not kind to be nice. Nice is closer to hate than love. Nice is hatred toward our own feelings of anger and resentment. Nice is fearful and guilt-ridden toward speaking and acting realistically toward and among others. Nice is very far from *love* in the profound humanness sense of inclusive affirmation. Profound love is not a feeling of affection or some rules on how to be nice. To view love as pleasant feelings is a sentimental attitude. Such "love" is more concerned with my own good feelings than with any value outside myself.

Profound love includes a generousness toward my own self and toward the power and glory of being my true being, but profound love is also an abandonment of the strictly self-interested contexts and a movement toward values beyond myself. Profound love is a calling that challenges my "feel-good" interests as well as my current ideas. And profound love honors my real feelings of fear, resentment, anger, sadness, grief, and any other feeling that I may cringe to feel. Any one of these grim feelings may be present at the same time that profound love is present. We can be dreadfully afraid of what needs to be done, and still do it. We can be disturbingly angry over an injustice or foolishness we have to deal with. To deny or suppress my fear or anger is a form of malice toward myself and a withdrawal from the realism that is being signaled by these feelings.

With courage we can act compassionately in spite of our fear. Fear is just a useful signal from our bodies that danger is at hand. In realism we can respect fear without using it as an excuse for inaction. Profound love is a courageous dynamic in that it overcomes fear in the sense of acting in spite of fear. Sentimentality kills courage and leads us into superficiality and into inaction with regard to the responses that are befitting for profound love.

And anger is likewise a useful signal that our body produces. Anger often means that our perspective is out of whack with reality, but anger can also tell us something about reality. Anger is a natural energy, useful for our most challenging actions. Of course, it is also true that acting-out our anger in thoughtless self-indulgent ways is not love; nevertheless, anger, like fear, sadness, grief, or any other feeling can be honored for the creative role it can play in authentic human living.

* * * * * * * *

Rationalism, moralism, and sentimentality are three structures of escape from profound humanness that catch all of us in their subtle nets. To the extent that we notice how we ourselves have been caught in these patterns, we begin to understand what is going on in the lives of the dysfunctionally religious across the globe. Humanity is being called by Reality to sober up—to give up the rational-security opiates, the moralistic-certitude stimulants, and the sentimentality potions that drown us in their sticky goo. Love of self and others is not a web of syrupy feelings. Love of self and others is a willingness to "let be" the full spectrum of life that characterizes each human being. When our profound humanity is restored, we experience a type of relief and joy, because such healing means taking leave of the despair-producing effort it takes to not be who we deeply are. Rest in being the Being that we are posited to be by the Power that posits us is a peace that is beyond understanding and the joy unspeakable.

We the universal league of profound humanness are called by the reality of our own integrity to fight dysfunctional religion. Whatever our heritage of religious practice or lack of a religious practice, we who are the universal league of profound humanness are called to a life-and-death battle with dysfunctional religion, every dysfunctional religion, not just expressions of the religion we happen to practice. We need to say this imperative loudly to ourselves because our culture does not fully understand that dysfunctional religion must be corrected. The social process called "religion" is just as important (perhaps even more important) than processes of education or economics or politics. If our religious processes are dysfunctional, the entire society suffers dysfunctionality.

The universal league is precisely that part of a human society that knows the power of religious practices for good or for ill. The universal league consists of those who know the ruin that can be wrought by the sick religions that so many of us have already abandoned. This league of profound humanness is called by their own deep integrity to awaken the masses to the horror of dysfunctional religion. Here is the prophet Amos showing us an attitude that we can take: Speaking for the Final Reality, Amos said: "I hate, I spurn your pilgrim feasts; I will not delight in your sacred ceremonies. When you present your sacrifices and offerings I will not accept them, nor look on the buffaloes of your shared offerings. Spare me the sound of your songs; I cannot endure the music of your lutes. Let justice roll on like a river and righteousness like an ever-flowing stream."[25]

Such a stern demand for change delivered to our religious institutions is surely as needed today as it was in Amos' day. And religion deserves stern demands for correction, like any other social process of our societies. We make a mistake when we dismiss our dysfunctional religious bodies as irrelevant and not worth our time and concern. They are a pattern of living that cries out to be healed, defeated, or sidelined. Their members need to be called upon to repent and be healed of their sicknesses. And we need to take pity on the somewhat innocent sheep who are being gathered into these evil kitchens and cooked.

I have sometimes used Christian heritage illustrations for this critique of religion, but it is not only Christian organizations that are crazy making. There are Muslim movements and Jewish movements that are also crazy making, as our news reports indicate. Not all Muslims, not all Jews are paranoid fools prone to ineffective and stupid violence, but many are. Such paranoid defensiveness in religious practice is self-defeating and criminal. Many of the Hindus and Muslims of Sub-Asia have slaughtered each other in incredible fits of defensive stupidity and in astonishing examples of inappropriate rage. Of equal foolishness have been the misunderstandings and wars among Protestants and Catholics. Religion can be a mean and dangerous thing. Even when overt violence is not the obvious manifestation, people are too often being twisted out of shape by doctrines and

---

[25] Amos 5:21-24; The New English Bible 1970

moralities and communal bonds that discourage rather than assist people to open to their profound humanness.

What is going on in religions today? And what is its cure? The basic story goes something like this: The cultures of the world have changed and are changing in ways that challenge deeply the formulations of religion that millions of people have taken on as their systems of security. Rather than change the religious practices in order to live fully in this era of history, many people have revolted against the onward march of time in order to protect some false security of a religious form. They have insisted on turning back the clock. In addition to not opening to real life themselves and not reforming their own religious practices, they have engaged in the futile attempt to force their obsolete religious sensibilities upon everyone, often incorporating political means of doing so, or allowing themselves to be used by scheming politicians who prey upon their bigotry to get votes for still other tragedies. Clearly, dysfunctional religion is a permanent issue on the social-action list of any time and place.

Having now finished the reading of this book, I invite you to turn again to chapters 14, 15, and 16 and take in once more the qualities of that profound humanness we want our religious formations to help us access. Then read again Chapter 19 and see if you can discern the religious practices that you and others you know most need to practice in order to get on with our journey into the full enigma of the deep consciousness and wonder that is our profound life.

A Short Reading List

for further study of these topics

Richard Feynman: *The Character of Physical Law*

Adyashanti: *Emptiness Dancing*

Chögyam Trungpa: *Cutting Through Spiritual Materialism*

Pema Chödrön: *Taking the Leap: Freeing Ourselves from Old Habits and Fears*

Wendell Berry: *Life is a Mystery: An Essay Against Modern Superstition*

Susanne K. Langer: *Philosophy in a New Key: A Study in the Symbolism of Reason, Rite, and Art*

Søren Kierkegaard: *The Sickness Unto Death*

A. H. Almaas: *Brilliancy: The Essence of Intelligence*

Sandra Maitri: *The Spiritual Dimension of the Enneagram: Nine Faces of the Soul*

Charlene Spretnak: *Relational Reality: New Discoveries of Interrelatedness that are Transforming the Modern World* and *States of Grace: The Recovery of Meaning in the Postmodern Age*

H. Richard Niebuhr: *Radical Monotheism and Western Culture* and *The Responsible Self: An Essay in Christian Moral Philosophy*

Paul Tillich: *The Courage to Be*

Rudolf Bultmann: *Jesus Christ and Mythology*

Joseph W. Mathews: *Bending History: Selected Talks of Joseph W. Mathews* and *Bending History: Vol II Societal Reformulation-toward a New Social Vehicle*

About the Author

Gene Wesley Marshall began his education as a mathematician and physicist. In 1953 he decided to leave a mathematics career and attend seminary at Perkins School of Theology in Dallas, Texas. He has served as a local church pastor, a chaplain in the army, and in 1962 joined a religious order of families (the Order:Ecumenical), and traveled the United States, Canada, Latin America, Europe, India, Hong Kong, and Australia as a teacher and lecturer of religious and social ethics topics. These trips included an in-depth study of world cultures and a vivid sense of the social conditions of the world's peoples. He was an active participant in the civil rights revolution, serving for one year as the Protestant executive of The National Conference on Religion and Race. For six years he served as dean of an eight-week residential academy that trained leadership for religious and social engagement work throughout the world. In 1984 Gene and Joyce Marshall organized a nonprofit educational organization, Realistic Living, and began publishing journals, books, and essays. The couple were also organizers of bioregionalism, a geographically sensitive form of ecological realism, radical feminism, and interreligious sensibilities. This book is Gene's eighth book-length project. Gene and Joyce live in Bonham, Texas in a straw-bale house.

Printed in the United States
By Bookmasters